BOSNIAN WAR POSTERS
BOSANSKI RATNI POSTERI

DAOUD SARHANDI

With Forewords by Carol A. Wells,
Bojan Hadžihalilović & Vehid Šehić

Interlink Books

An imprint of Interlink Publishing Group, Inc.
Northampton, Massachusetts

FOR BROTHERHOOD AND UNITY; *Branka Hegedušić; Croatia, 1945*
Six women represent the republics that formed Tito's Yugoslavia—a country that lasted less than 50 years. Its violent breakup into seven countries ended an intricate sociopolitical dream that began in the Balkans in the late 17th century. Thanks to the Croatian History Museum, Zagreb, for sharing this poster.

PAPER COPIES OF POSTERS ACQUIRED DURING RESEARCH WERE DONATED TO THE ARCHIVE OF BOSNIA-HERZEGOVINA IN SARAJEVO. THE POSTERS AND OTHER GRAPHICS IN THIS BOOK HAVE BEEN ARCHIVED IN DIGITAL AND 35 MM SLIDE FORMATS AT THE CENTER FOR THE STUDY OF POLITICAL GRAPHICS IN LOS ANGELES.

ŠTAMPANI PRIMJERCI POSTERA PRIBAVLJENI TOKOM ISTRAŽIVANJA DONIRANI SU ARHIVU BOSNE I HERCEGOVINE U SARAJEVU. SVI POSTERI I DRUGI GRAFIČKI RADOVI U OVOJ KNJIZI ARHIVIRANI SU U DIGITALNOM FORMATU ILI KAO 35-MILIMETARSKI SLAJDOVI U CENTER FOR THE STUDY OF POLITICAL GRAPHICS U LOS ANGELESU.

SADRŽAJ

CONTENTS

WAKE UP, EUROPE!; *Trio; Sarajevo, 1994*
One of Trio design studio's famous redesigns reproduced as a poster for the Sarajevo Winter Festival. It
was inspired by *Wake Up America! Civilization Calls Every Man Woman and Child!,* a celebrated World War I
propaganda poster designed by James Montgomery Flagg.

FOREWORD
MESSAGE FROM SARAJEVO
Bojan Hadžihalilović

Bosnian War Posters is, without a doubt, one of the most significant books about the war in Bosnia, especially regarding Sarajevo. It reflects all the horrors of the siege of my city.

The book captivates with unusual and hectic energy—just as Daoud did with his personality and the mission he had for Bosnia and Sarajevo.

Also, this book is probably the last document on war propaganda from the last century: a time when there was no Internet, no TikTok, no Fake News.

A frantic rhythm of madness and emotion permeates the book, like the relationship between propaganda, art, war, life, and Bosnian civilians' fight for survival.

During the war, designers, illustrators and artists used posters, leaflets, magazines, and newspapers to express themselves—to fight for truth and to join the struggle between good and evil.

Our work at Trio, dedicated to Sarajevo, was at first done as hand-painted posters. Later, we printed the designs in a smaller postcard format, intending to send them around the world to publicise the disaster and siege of Sarajevo, the longest in modern history. Postcards became a unique part of our resistance.

We tried to portray the soul of Sarajevo in a palette of dark humour, anger and hope. There was a message on the back of the postcards:

This document has been created in war circumstances. (No paper, no inks, no electricity, no water. Just good will.)

Bosnian War Posters is not a romanticised visual biography of the Bosnian War, but an almost punky book about good and bad, love and death, the role of the media, and the truth.

Ultimately it is also about the evil that still lives here, there, and everywhere.

Bojan Hadžihalilović co-founded Trio design studio in Sarajevo in 1985 with his wife, Dada. Along with Lejla Mulabegović, they ran Trio throughout the siege of Sarajevo, where Bojan and Dada still live and work. Between them, these three artists produced countless design classics.

THINK; *Forum of Tuzla Citizens; Tuzla, 1995*
The subtitle reads, "Because there is little time and there will be no more time". The symbol of Tuzla as a goat is often used in Forum of Tuzla Citizens' posters. It relates to a legend about Tuzla being a resilient city (see page 134). The original idea to use the goat was graphic designer Jasminko Arnautović's. The spider here represents the evil of nationalism in Bosnia-Herzegovina.

FOREWORD
THE CITIZEN'S WAY
Vehid Šehić

The first thing I must say is that Tuzla is the only city in Bosnia-Herzegovina that has not elected a nationalist party since 1990, when the first multi-party elections were held. We are a free people and have never followed the call of nationalism. Tuzla's tradition is togetherness, not differentiating people by their opinion or religion.

Tuzla is an old salt mining city and our miners have always stood up to tyranny and demonstrated a sense of solidarity between people. We have a rich history of rebellion, independence, but also culture —the first theatre in Bosnia-Herzegovina was established here. Tuzla's working-class dates back to the Austro-Hungarian period when many people came to work here from Austria, Hungary, the Czech lands, Italy, and Germany. Many nationalities lived in Tuzla at the beginning of the twentieth century and each one of them brought a piece of their culture. This created an interesting way of life here.

During 1992, just after the start of the war, a group of Muslim intellectuals in Tuzla set up an organisation and held public meetings every Sunday. Their messages, including the benefits of Sharia law, were unacceptable as they went against our philosophy and way of life; they prioritise Muslims over other groups and this is a form of extreme nationalism.

A friend and I realised that we had to confront these ideas and so, on the 28th of February 1993, seven of us established the Forum of Tuzla Citizens at a public event in Hotel Tuzla. Over 900 local people turned up to show their support. The hotel was completely packed.

The Forum's founding declaration addresses everyone interested in the democratic future of Bosnia-Herzegovina, and warns that religious or ethnic "solutions" for our country are very dangerous. Up to this very day we show by personal example that a life of freedom is possible—if there is respect for each citizen's rights, regardless of nationality or religion.

About 13,400 people supported this idea by joining the Forum and, after we started to work, those groups of Muslim intellectuals stopped their activities. They didn't have enough local support and even today the Islamist party doesn't have any power in Tuzla.

The Forum became known all over Bosnia-Herzegovina. During the war we would get messages from all sides saying that our example was their only hope. We also got international recognition; the Helsinki Citizens Assembly, for example, set up a branch in our office in Tuzla and the Verona Forum and some members of the European Parliament helped us organise two big international conferences during the war. The second of these conferences, held in October 1994, was attended by anti-war activists from Serbia, Croatia,

Montenegro, Slovenia, and Macedonia. The guests had to come through the front lines and over small mountain roads, escorted by the armed vehicles of UNPROFOR [United Nations Protection Force]. All the major international TV stations were here and it was the only conference of this nature held on former-Yugoslav territory during the war. It's hard to say what impact these events had on the final peace conference.

For us the most important thing was to end the war, although we aren't satisfied with the system we now have for organising Bosnia-Herzegovina. The biggest mistake that was made at Dayton [the 1995 Peace Agreement that ended the war] was that they didn't set up a protectorate for Bosnia. Protectorates date back to the Roman Empire when a territory's foreign policy and defence were taken care of by the empire. The most relevant example for us is Germany after the Second World War, when the Allies formed a five-year protectorate, during which time all political parties were banned and no elections were held. If there had been an election in Germany in 1946 a reconfigured Nazi Party would have won.

In London, in 1995, I met Robin Cooke, Britain's shadow foreign secretary, and I recommended a five-year protectorate be imposed on Bosnia-Herzegovina. During this time, I suggested, political parties and elections should be banned. After that five-year period a less powerful type of protectorate could be applied—like the one we now have under the OHR [Office of the High Representative]—and only then would free elections be permitted. Why? Because it's not natural that the nationalist political parties that were active during the war—SDA, HDZ, SDS—were then made responsible for implementing the peace; that's completely irrational. This is why we are still living in the wartime period of 1992 to 1995. Robin Cooke told me that

a protectorate would indeed be the best solution but, in his view, the great powers would not be willing to take on such a responsibility.

During the war we didn't have a lot of media. Two newspapers, *Oslobodjenje* and *Tuzla List,* would sometimes be available, and we had intermittent access to *Radio Sarajevo.* There were two local radio stations in Tuzla *(RTV Tuzla* and *Radio Kameleon)* but there was so little electricity available that people could only rarely turn on their radio sets. One of the most efficient systems of communication during the war was *Radio Free Europe*, which signed contracts with local radio stations all over the former Yugoslavia. Each of these stations would rebroadcast their Bosnian-language content. They broadcast several programmes about the Forum of Tuzla Citizens and in this way we became known all over the former Yugoslavia.

It was really hard to communicate with citizens in Tuzla during the war and this problem resulted in our solution: poster campaigns. It was the only way we could talk to the public as well as the politicians, and we got really good at it. Creating these posters was always a team effort. As well as myself and our graphic designer—Jasminko Arnautović designed most of the posters—there was an illustrator and three other people involved. When a new idea was suggested, I would gather the team and we would get to work producing a new poster.

What's interesting about a poster is that it's a way a person can express something complex quickly—a message or an idea. But above all a poster has to be clear. And the simpler it is the more it can make people think.

We would print at least 300 copies of our posters, and the most we printed of any one poster was 3,000 [see page 256]. They were distributed around town by our volunteers, and always at night. In some cases posters were ripped off the walls, but most of them stayed up for ages. We also managed to find a particularly strong glue, which made it really difficult to tear posters off the wall. All people with opposing ideas could do was deface them or cut them into little pieces.

During the war an officer from Bosnia-Herzegovina's national security agency came into the Forum. He asked for a copy of a particular poster and told us he had tried to rip one off a wall but had been unable to. I was happy to give him a copy of the poster he wanted. Another time during the war, when it was raining heavily, I bumped into an old teacher on the street. He thanked me profoundly for refreshing his day. I asked what he meant, considering the heavy rain falling all around us. He said that he always felt refreshed when seeing our posters. For sure, our posters awaken people's optimism, giving them hope that something is going to change.

When I walk the streets today I still get approached by people who express their support for the Forum's work. I get this positive feedback all over Bosnia-Herzegovina where I'm now recognised because of the TV interviews I do. Bosnians are a very good people, but they are often afraid to show this goodness. However, with me, they open up and share their fears, hopes, and appreciation. This is what has given me the power to get through the war and up to the present. I'm 69 years old now and I could have quit a long time ago; I could have made a lot of money, but the ordinary people have always made me feel it's worth it.

Vehic Šehić was born in Tuzla in 1952. He graduated in Law from Sarajevo University, before going on to work as a prosecutor, lawyer, and judge. Since 1994 he has been the full-time president of the Forum of Tuzla Citizens. This text was edited by Rupert Wolfe Murray, from an interview he conducted with Vehic Šehić in Tuzla in August 2021.

ABOVE
FOUNDING ASSEMBLY
Forum of Tuzla Citizens
Tuzla, 1993
This is the first poster produced by the Forum, to announce it's founding. More than 900 people attended the event. Indeed, it was such a success that it eradicated support for other groups dedicated to nationalist, and specifically Islamist, causes. Slobodan Stuhli—graphic designer Jasminko Arnautović's colleague at the Forum—had the idea of using Tuzla's Atlas statue on their posters.

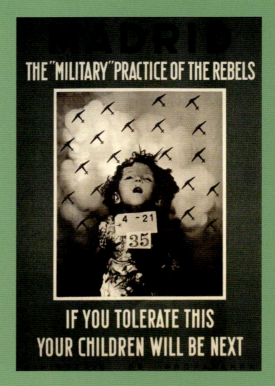

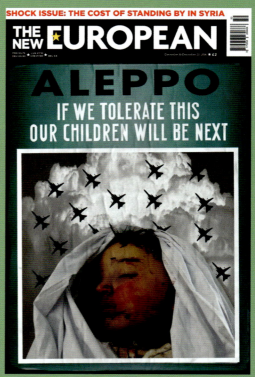

IMPOSSIBLE! ENOUGH! (top left) was produced in 1992 by FIA, a Belgrade-based art group. A young girl idealistically looks forward to a future where she can live and thrive, unlike the baby's fate in the 1937 Spanish Civil War poster (top right) that inspired FIA: the aeroplane background in the FIA poster was appropriated from the famous Republican poster from Madrid. When the Serbian poster was designed, the Bosnian War was just beginning and there was hope among many that it would end soon, limiting casualties. That did not happen, of course—but the artists couldn't have known that at the time. The 1937 poster (complete with its slogan that was even appropriated by Manic Street Preachers for a song of the same name) has been used in various ways, at different times, to highlight a whole range of social causes: for example, the destruction of Aleppo by Syrian and Russian forces (The New European, December 2016). The recycling of political imagery—and even non-political visual iconography, as Trio and Art Publishing did wholesale in Bosnia—is common in the design world and among protest groups. (See page 86 for another poster also linked to the Spanish Civil War.) Indeed, in the Internet meme age, this process is even rifer and happening with greater speed and fluidity.

FOREWORD
BOSNIAN WAR POSTERS: A CAUTIONARY TALE

Carol A. Wells

When the Bosnian War (1992–95) was being waged it felt distant and confusing to many North Americans who could not understand how family, friends, and neighbors could suddenly turn on each other. Reading this book now, in light of the attack on the U.S. Capitol in early 2021, the Bosnian War has new meaning and relevance. It has become a most cautionary tale.

At the present time, throughout the U.S. and much of the world, nationalism is growing, religious fundamentalism is spreading, and hate crimes are becoming more common. As societal splits continue to intensify in the United States, the disintegration of Yugoslavia is no longer so hard to comprehend. These posters help to clarify the past while offering warnings for the future.

It is not surprising that so many artists made posters during the Bosnian War, as they are one of the most accessible, easily disseminated, and popular art forms for expressing conflict and resistance. What may surprise those who are seeing these posters for the first time is their variety, abundance, and often extraordinary design.

Although few of these posters are well known, many of them may look familiar because they incorporate images from advertising, fine art, film posters, album covers, and popular culture. Even Mickey Mouse, Superman, Santa Claus, and the Flintstones make an appearance. Trio,

from Sarajevo—one of the best-known of the artists' groups represented in this book—frequently appropriated images, calling their work "redesigns." Worldwide, image appropriation has long been a popular technique. It enables artists to grab viewers' attention by showing something both comfortably familiar and provocatively unfamiliar.

Most of the appropriations are blatant and brilliant—such as Trio's now-iconic Enjoy Sarajevo slogan using Coca-Cola's trademark script (see page 101), and This is Not a Pipe of Peace by Art Publishing (see page 179), playing off Rene Magritte's *Ceci n'est pas une pipe* (This is not a pipe). While the majority of the appropriations are obvious, some are so subtle that they require familiarity with the history of the region, as well as the history of art and the history of political poster design.

The Bosnian posters in this book incorporate art from prehistoric to Renaissance, from Pop to Punk. The referenced art includes work by Masaccio, Dürer, Leonardo, Munch, Picasso, Warhol, Lichtenstein, and Fukuda. Posters that were originally made for World Wars I and II, as well as the Spanish Civil War, were redesigned for the Bosnian War. The familiarity of these shared cultural references draws us in.

The United States, European Union, United Nations, and NATO are addressed in many posters—primarily criticizing their unsuccessful, even pathetic, attempts to resolve the conflict. It is still argued whether the involvement of many countries, as well as intergovernmental agencies like the UN, prolonged or shortened the war that destroyed Yugoslavia.

The frequent visual references to Hitler and Nazism remind viewers that during World War II Croatia was allied with Nazi Germany and many fascist groups proliferated throughout the region. These references simultaneously warn that fascist groups continue to thrive. For example, a poster titled HEEELP by Began Turbić (see page 92) uses photomontage to transform an Orthodox Christian-style cross into a swastika by attaching traditional peasant-made brushes to the ends of the cross. Sixty years earlier, the German artist John Heartfield used this technique to create a swastika out of four bloody axes.[1]

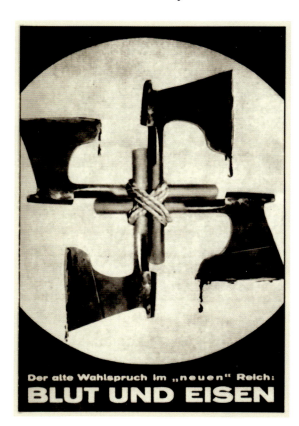

Der alte Wahlspruch im „neuen" Reich:
BLUT UND EISEN

Heartfield was one of the originators of photomontage and made many anti-fascist magazine covers and posters using this technique. Turbić's use of photomontage thus connects the past with the present. The average viewer may not have known this reference, but it would have been recognized by other political poster-makers, as Heartfield is often considered one of the earliest designers of mass-produced protest posters.

Many images refer directly to Bosnian history, both ancient and contemporary, and the captions are critical for understanding the posters. A red and white checkerboard design is the ancient heraldic emblem of Croatia, and appears in numerous posters, as does the Bosnian *fleur-de-lis.* Sometimes they appear together, but more often they are separate, representing opposing sides in the war.

A 1992 poster by Adin Šadić (see page 87)—an artist who was also a Bosnian Muslim fighter—presents a striking merging of the two nationalist symbols.[2] The caption explains that in the early days of the war there was optimism, albeit short-lived, that the combined efforts of Bosnia's Croats and Muslims could stop Serb expansionism in Bosnia. This poster is particularly important because it documents the brief attempt for unity in order to defeat a common enemy. The Croat/Muslim split soon resulted in a tripartite war between Serbs, Croats, and Bosniaks (Bosnian Muslims).

That same year, Trio produced two versions of Aggression Against Bosnia-Herzegovina (see page 76). Both have the same title and layout, visually emphasizing that they are intended as a pair, thus evoking a diptych (a religious altarpiece). One shows a war-damaged minaret; the other a statue of St. Joseph holding a young Jesus, which stands in front of an artillery shell-damaged wall. Posters from this war rarely show simultaneous compassion for Christian and Muslim victims.

One of the most visually powerful posters in the book illustrates the effort to rewrite the history of the region by erasing the impact that 500 years of Ottoman Islamic culture had on Serbia.

Began Turbić's The Core is Istanbul—The Rest is Myth features a book with a gaping hole in the center (see page 69). The book is titled *Serbian History, Culture and Traditions,* and the absent section is labeled "Turkish cultural heritage." The oversized corkscrew used to remove this history remains upright, stabbed into an embossed star and crescent, a symbol of the Ottoman Empire.

The next spread features another stunning but wrenching poster, titled Brotherhood and Unity, by Čedomir Kostović (see page 71). In the former Yugoslavia, "Brotherhood and Unity" was a government slogan used to encourage cooperation between the republics and diverse nationalities. Kostović uses it with chilling irony, as the poster features a bloody saw labeled "Bosnia."[3]

These two posters focus on the primary features of ethnic cleansing: mass murder and historical erasure. Historical erasure has been used throughout history to rewrite history. The term "ethnic cleansing" was coined during the Bosnian War, giving painful insight into the events documented by these posters. That the term has gained broad use says a lot about the state of our world today.

Posters have been essential for promoting and opposing wars at least since World War I, and continue to be used all over the world. They are inexpensive to produce, and when pasted onto a wall or carried in a demonstration are easily and widely seen, especially when TV and Internet transmit the images. Posters continue to be used in today's high-tech world because they are effective.

And because they are effective, they are frequently destroyed by those opposing their messages. Add this intentional destruction to the damages of war and natural destruction by the elements, and it is remarkable that Daoud Sarhandi and Alina Wolfe Murray were able to find so many posters from the Bosnian War. It is also remarkable that these posters continue to have existential lessons for us today. We need to pay attention.

NOTES

1. Heartfield's 1934 work was ironically titled Blood and Iron *(Blut und Eisen),* which was the motto of the Third Reich. Heartfield anglicized his name, from Helmut Herzfeld, as a protest gesture.

2. For this poster, Šadić reworked a 1937 Spanish Civil War poster by Emeterio Melendreras. In Melendreras' celebrated poster, a helmeted soldier's head is covered with eight flags and insignia of supporters of the Spanish Republican cause, including Anarchists, Communists, Basques, and Catalans. It translates: All These Militias Merge into the People's Army (see page 86). Decades later, and for another war, Šadić covered the same helmeted soldier's head with Bosnian and Croatian heraldry.

3. Similar to John Heartfield's use of the Third Reich motto as a poster title (see footnote #1), Čedomir Kostović's Brotherhood and Unity poster re-used a Yugoslav government slogan to show disunity.

Carol A. Wells is the executive director of the Center for the Study of Political Graphics, which she founded in 1988 in Los Angeles. An activist, curator, art historian, lecturer, and writer, she was trained as a medievalist at the University of California, Los Angeles, and taught the history of art and architecture for 13 years.

GUIDE TO ABBREVIATIONS

ABiH
Sometimes also ARBiH, where R stands for Republic. *Armija Bosne i Hercegovine* (Army of Bosnia and Herzegovina, or Bosnian Army): 1992–95. The only armed force recognised as legal during the Bosnian War. After Dayton, the ABiH became the Army of the Federation of Bosnia and Herzegovina. Later, in 2004, the AFBiH was transformed into the Armed Forces of Bosnia and Herzegovina (OSBiH: *Oružane snage Bosne i Hercegovine*).

AFBiH (see above).

BiH
Sometimes also B&H or B-H. *Bosna i Hercegovina* (Bosnia and Herzegovina, or Bosnia-Herzegovina): 1945–92. Bosnia-Herzegovina came into being as an independent state at the United Nations on 21 May 1992. Before this, it was one of the six Yugoslav republics. It was first recognised as a republic in 1943 and this was reaffirmed in 1945 and 1946, as Yugoslavia slowly defined its constitution.

BOSS
Bosanska Stranka (Bosnian Party): 1994–. A multi-ethnic, populist, left-leaning political party.

EC
European Council: 1961–. Consisting of the heads of the EU member states, the European Council defines the EU's overall political direction and is considered the EU's "supreme political authority".

EU
European Union: 1993–. A political and economic union comprised of 27 member states. Replaced the European Economic Community.

EUFOR
European Union Force Bosnia and Herzegovina: 2004–. Also called Operation Althea. EUFOR replaced NATO's SFOR in 2004. As of March 2019, the total EUFOR force in Bosnia was 600 troops from 19 countries.

FRY
Federal Republic of Yugoslavia: 1992–2006. Comprised of Serbia and Montenegro, sometimes called Rump Yugoslavia. FRY no longer exists since Montenegro voted for independence in 2006—a process that completed peacefully.

FY
Former Yugoslavia: 1946–92. Yugoslavia was established by Marshal Josip Broz Tito after World War II. The precise date of its founding is unclear. However, the Federal People's Republic of Yugoslavia (with six republics and two autonomous territories) came into being on 31 January 1946.

HDZ
Hrvatska demokratska zajednica (Croatian Democratic Union): 1989–. Founded by Franjo Tuđman in 1989. A Croatian nationalist party that continues to dominate the country's political scene. (Tuđman died in 1999.)

HOS
Hrvatske obrambene snage (Croatian Defence Forces): 1991–93. A paramilitary army that took orders from the HSP. Operated in Croatia as well as Bosnia. In Bosnia, HOS was composed of Croats and Bosniaks. At its peak, it had 8,000 men under arms.

HSP
Hrvatska stranka prava (Croatian Party of Rights): 1861–. A right-wing Croatian party with a profoundly racist platform. It originated in 1861 and was reborn in 1990. The HSP still exits but wields little parliamentary power.

HVO
Hrvatsko vijeće obrane (Croatian Defence Council): 1992–96. A Bosnian Croat army, funded by Croatia, that committed many brutal crimes—such as the massacre of civilians at Stupni Do in central Bosnia, for which commanding officer Ivica Rajić was convicted at the ICTY. In 1995 the HVO had 50,000 men under arms, It was disbanded after the war.

ICTY
International Criminal Tribunal for the Former Yugoslavia: 1993–2017. A United Nations court of law that dealt with war crimes that took place during the conflicts in the Balkans in the 1990s. Judged to have completed its work, the Tribunal was dissolved in 2017.

IFOR
Implementation Force: 1995–96. A large military force with a one-year mandate. Established by NATO—but also incorporating non-NATO members, including Russia—to implement the Dayton Agreement. IFOR replaced UNPROFOR in 1995 and was replaced by SFOR in 1996.

JNA
Jugoslovenska narodna armija (Yugoslav People's Army): 1941–92. In its heyday, the JNA was a large, well-equipped European army. It no longer exists since each former republic now has its own national armed forces.

NATO
North Atlantic Treaty Organization: 1949–. NATO is a military alliance comprising 30 European nations plus the United States and Canada.

OHR
Office of the High Representative: 1995–. Oversees the civilian implementation of the Dayton Agreement.

OSBiH (see ABiH).

OSCE

Organization for Security and Co-operation in Europe: 1975–. The OSCE comprises 57 member states and carries out political, military, economic, environmental, and human missions around Europe. It oversaw elections in Bosnia and the implementation of civil aspects of the Dayton Agreement.

RS

Republika Srpska (Serb Republic): 1995–. RS was legally recognised at Dayton, Ohio, and comprises 49 per cent of Bosnia-Herzegovina. During the war, the name was illegally used by breakaway Bosnian Serbs to refer to the parts of Bosnia they seized by force.

SDA

Stranka demokratske akcije (Party of Democratic Action): 1990–. Founded by Alija Izetbegović and other Bosniaks in 1990. At its founding, the party had an openly Muslim character that has been retained to this day.

SDG

Srpska dobrovoljačka garda (Serb Volunteer Guard): 1990–96. A Serbian death squad, also known as the Tigers, run by Željko "Arkan" Ražnatović.

SDS

Srpska demokratska stranka (Serbian Democratic Party): 1990–. A militaristic Bosnian Serb political party. Founded by convicted war criminal Radovan Karadžić. Although he was gaoled for life, the SDS is still active in Bosnian politics today.

SFOR

Stabilization Force: 1996–2004. Following a UN Security Council Resolution in 1996, this NATO-led peacekeeping force took over from IFOR in 1996. Replaced by EUFOR (Operation Althea) in 2004.

SNSD

Savez nezavisnih socijaldemokrata (Alliance of Independent Social Democrats): 1996–. Led by Milorad Dodik—who was initially considered a "moderate"—the SNSD has become an ultra-nationalist Bosnian Serb political force that, at the time of writing, is threatening the unity of Bosnia by relentlessly promoting the idea that Republika Srpska should secede from Bosnia-Herzegovina.

SPO

Srpski pokret obnove (Serbian Renewal Movement): 1990–. Ultranationalist political party founded by Vuk Drašković and Vojislav Šešelj. The SPO remains active in Serbian politics today, as are the party's founders.

SRS

Srpska radikalna stranka (Serbian Radical Party): 1991–. Ultranationalist political party founded by Vojislav Šešelj. The SRS remains active in Serbian politics today.

SSJ
Stranka srpskog jedinstva (Party of Serbian Unity): 1993–2007. Ultranationalist political party founded by the war criminal and death squad leader Željko "Arkan" Ražnatović. In 2007 Arkan was assassinated, and the party was dissolved.

TO
Teritorijalna odbrana (Territorial Army): 1990–92. Each republic of the former Yugoslavia had its local TO to provide defence in the event of a foreign invasion. In Bosnia, TO was an essential part of countering JNA, VRS and Serb paramilitary aggression. In May 1992 TO officially became the Bosnian army.

UN
United Nations: 1945–. This powerful organisation allowed itself to be repeatedly humiliated during the breakup of the former Yugoslavia. It largely failed to protect the civilian population from the worst consequences of nationalism in the Western Balkans.

UNHCR
United Nations High Commission for Refugees: 1950–. The UNHCR was a key player in wartime Bosnia in the provision of essential food and other humanitarian supplies.

UNICEF
United Nations Children's Fund: 1950–. UNICEF addresses the long-term needs of children and women in developing countries all over the world.

UNPROFOR
United Nations Protection Force: 1992–95. Established to keep various territories of the former Yugoslavia safe during its violent dissolution. Local people often joked, however, that UNPROFOR's principal task often seemed to be protecting itself.

VRS
Vojska Republike Srpske (Army of Republika Srpska, or Bosnian Serb Army): 1992–2006. VRS committed numerous crimes during the Bosnian War, including the four-year siege of Sarajevo and the ethnic cleansing of Srebrenica and Žepa. Led by General Ratko Mladić, currently serving a life sentence for genocide, it advanced the political interests of Radovan Karadžić's SDS. At its peak, the Bosnian Serb Army had 80,000 men under arms. It was assimilated into the Armed Forces of Bosnia and Herzegovina (OSBiH).

GUIDE TO BOSNIAN PRONUNCIATION

Ć/ć: as in itch; *Č/č:* as in chess; *Đ/đ:* as in fudge (this letter is often written as *dj*); *Š/š:* as in sheep; *Ž/ž:* as in leisure. Some common letter combinations are: *dz*: ridge; *lj*: billion; *nj*: nuclear; *tj*: tune; *ij*: tree. The letter *j* is always pronounced as *y* in English (i.e. Jugoslavija).

All the former republics of Yugoslavia, plus Kosovo, are now independent states. As this book goes to press, however, Kosovo has been legally recognised by only 115 other countries around the world. Serbia still considers Kosovo as a region of her Republic, on a par with Vojvodina in northern Serbia.

AUSTRIA

HUNGARY

ROMANIA

SLOVENIA

● ZAGREB

CROATIA

VOJVODINA

● BELGRADE

BOSNIA AND HERZERGOVINA

SARAJEVO ●

REPUBLIC OF SERBIA

ITALY

ADRIATIC SEA

MONTENEGRO

KOSOVO

BULGA

REPUBLIC OF NORTH MACEDONIA

ALBANIA

GREECE

2021 POPULATIONS
Bosnia and Herzegovina: 3.3 million
Croatia: 4 million
Kosovo: 1.8 million
Montenegro: 620,000
Republic of North Macedonia: 2 million
Republic of Serbia: 7 million
Slovenia: 2 million

TOTAL 2021 POPULATION: 20,720,000
PRE-WAR YUGOSLAV POPULATION (1991): 23,528,230

The Bosnian diaspora of all ethnicities (Bosniaks, Croats and Serbs) is now estimated at seven million displaced persons and their descendants—more than double the current population within Bosnia. Mass-displacements occurred in the late 19th century, during two world wars, and again during the Bosnian War in the 1990s when around 1.2 million became refugees.

INTRODUCTION
DEATH, DESTRUCTION, BETRAYAL ... AND POSTERS
Daoud Sarhandi

I made my first trip to Bosnia in October 1995, three months after the civilian massacres in Srebrenica. I wanted to do something, anything, to express my revulsion at what had happened there, to provide what little assistance I could, and to demonstrate that I was not part of a world that had tacitly condoned such atrocities. So I joined an aid organisation called Workers' Aid, which was based in Manchester, and ended up driving to Tuzla, a town in northeast Bosnia within the Muslim-Croat federation.[1]

The idea for this book came in Tuzla just over two years later. On my fourth trip to the town in the autumn of 1997, this time alone, I visited Jasminko Arnautović, the main designer of posters for the Forum of Tuzla Citizens, and a friend. While looking at Jasminko's anti-nationalist work, I talked with him about the information battle that had been waged for the hearts and minds of the Bosnian people. It was then that I realised that a collection of posters would produce a fascinating insight into how the Bosnian people were addressed, by whom, and to what ends during the conflict. I felt certain that it would also show us how they responded, intellectually and emotionally, to the conflict that eclipsed their lives. *Bosnian War Posters* focuses on posters that were produced between the start of the Bosnian War in April 1992 and its end in 1995, after a peace agreement was reached at Wright-Patterson Air Force Base in Dayton, Ohio, between the presidents of Bosnia, Serbia, and Croatia.

Collecting the posters wasn't easy; it took me and my research assistant, Alina Wolfe Murray, one year between late 1997 and the end of 1998. The research required countless trips across the war-torn country. Artists often worked alone, and many emigrated during the war, taking their work with them; most of these artists we managed to trace, some we could not. Very few printers kept copies of posters they had produced, although they often remembered them and pointed us in the right direction. Posters were generally printed in limited numbers due to the shortage of materials, making them even harder to track down.[2]

After the war ended, posters still played a vital role in the dissemination of information in Bosnia, particularly regarding such important issues as refugees, freedom of movement, land mines, reconstruction, and politics. The United Nations, the OHR (Office of the High Representative, which holds responsibility for the civil implementation of the Dayton Agreement), SFOR (the NATO-led Stabilization Force in Bosnia), the OSCE (Organization for Security and Co-operation in Europe), and various non-governmental organisations all produced large amounts of public information. This material vied for the attention of the Bosnian people alongside posters produced by a dizzying number of political parties. Given these realities,

we also included key posters produced after the Dayton Agreement, as well as several from before the outbreak of war in Bosnia. This last category includes a selection of posters that Alina unearthed in Croatia. These powerful images, created in 1991 during the Serb-Croat War, express sentiments and themes similar to those that later surfaced in Bosnia.

During the Bosnian War, posters became tremendously important. With normal communications damaged, most news came by word of mouth. In such an environment, posters were a cheap and effective way of disseminating information. Not surprisingly, poster "battles" took place in Bosnia. Rival ideological groups tore down each other's work and tried to dominate the best sites. A town might wake up to see an entire area emblazoned with multiple copies of one poster, only to find them gone the next day, replaced by another creation. Posters were also pasted onto the sides of trucks and driven around. In Sarajevo, bill-posters were paid danger

money to put up posters on the most lethal streets, such as the infamous Sniper Alley.

Poster designers came from all sectors of the artistic community and sometimes from outside it: professional graphic designers who had been working in artistic, cultural, and commercial fields before the war; fine artists who adapted their talents to the new reality; and amateur designers who were propelled toward design as a way of expressing themselves or serving their cause.

In extreme situations, posters were painted by hand. Mostly, however, they were printed by lithography or silkscreen—the latter being more common. Beyond the artistic merits of silkscreening, lithographic plates were in short supply during the war and there was often no electricity to run the presses. Silkscreens also had the advantage of being reusable—once the embedded image was washed away, screens could be used for other work. For these reasons, original plates of the posters that were produced during the war were hard to find.

Since the end of World War II, poster art has played a significant role in Central and Eastern European politics, due to the nature of socialism and the influence of Soviet-style propaganda techniques. Posters were originally used by socialist states to mark anniversaries and deliver simple political statements. With the death of Stalin, poster art began to mature. Although posters were still commissioned for ideological purposes, states were becoming more interested in the power of television. New designers were coming out of art schools and posters started to develop along different lines. But as long as they were not openly confrontational, the designers were left pretty much alone.

Many of the works in this volume owe something to post-war Polish poster design—in particular its visual playfulness and stark simplicity. Also like Polish posters, many of those from the Bosnian War use strong symbolism and minimalist typography.[3]

The mood in many of the Bosnian posters is one of desperation: bullet holes, blood, and Serbian slogans juxtaposed with the Nazi swastika. Bosnians are notorious for their sharp, irreverent sense of humour, and these posters are often characterised by black comedy as well. When looking through this collection, one is struck by the diversity of the work. The artists' sheer eclecticism, combined with their emotional commitment, impresses most of all.

Balkan politics have a reputation for being impenetrably complex. In some ways this is true, and it stems from the fact that for centuries foreign interests competed in the region. Tragically, this complexity was used to obscure the basic facts about the fracture of the former Yugoslavia. Issues were deliberately clouded. A campaign of misinformation was orchestrated in Yugoslavia several years before war broke out. It intensified during the military campaigns and persists, in some forms, to this day. While the principal objective of this book is to tell a visual story, a short literary account of events that took place is necessary to understand the larger context.

The Bosnian War did not erupt spontaneously because of irreconcilable differences between the ethnic and religious groups that inhabit Bosnia-Herzegovina. This fact cannot be repeated often enough, especially since for most of the war large swaths of the foreign media, especially those who never visited the region, simply missed the conflict's real causes.

Even though many fine journalists worked on the ground in Bosnia, this version of events—put forward by ill-informed (or duplicitous) Western politicians—was repeated so frequently that over time it achieved the status of truth. The causes of the war were widely misunderstood, and this played straight into the hands of the aggressors by masking

КАКО СУ НАСТАЛЕ РЕПУБЛИЧКЕ ГРАНИЦЕ?

ОД ВЕЛИКЕ ДО МАЛЕ СРБИЈЕ

their intentions and the precise nature of their involvement. The effect was that all groups were portrayed as barbaric, and this robbed the story of its legitimate political context.

Although ethnic hatreds in Bosnia were inflamed during the war, the conflict simply would not have happened without the instigation of Serbian and Croatian leaders. Presidents Slobodan Milošević in Serbia and Franjo Tuđman in Croatia—along with a supporting cast of nationalists in both countries—deserve the blame for what happened to the people of Bosnia-Herzegovina and the rest of the former Yugoslavia.[4]

National identity was always a topic of currency in Yugoslavia. Polls were regularly taken about real and perceived nationality. To pretend that any of the republics was ever an entirely happy melting-pot of its constituent peoples is fanciful. Tensions did exist. But it was not until the mid-1980s when Yugoslavia began to lose its

RIGHT: TOP TO BOTTOM

KOSOVO'S GOLGOTHA
Intervyu magazine
Serbia, October 1988
This magazine uses an emotive World War II image to illustrate a contemporary news story. The image relates to the idea that Serbs are defending their homeland and fighting for their lives (a narrative that fed into the national Serb myth that they were the victim, rather than the initiator, of the war).

SAVE SERBIA
Politika reproduction poster
Serbia, May 1992
As the war in Bosnia was gaining pace, *Politika* (Politics)—a Serbian daily newspaper—printed three posters that were originally published in France during World War I, when Serbia and France were allies.

EXODUS–300 YEARS
NIN magazine
Serbia, September 1990
The technique of linking past and present conflicts was used repeatedly in Serbia to propagate the myth of Serb persecution. This powerful cover, from Serb magazine *NIN*—published by the newsgroup Politika Novine i Magazini (Politics Newspapers and Magazines)—combines an old painting depicting the exodus of Serbs from Kosovo in 1689 with a contemporary protest march by Serbs from Kosovo to Belgrade. The march, organised by the Milošević regime, was itself a work of stage-managed propaganda.

OPPOSITE: LEFT TO RIGHT
WE ARE BUILDING OUR SOCIETY TOGETHER
OSCE, 1996
The word tolerance in this poster—produced by the Organization for Security and Co-operation in Europe—is spelt with a combination of Latin and Cyrillic letters to emphasise unity.

WHO IS WHO?
Local Democracy Embassy
Tuzla, 1997
One of the few posters of the time that refers to Bosnia's other ethnic minorities: Roma and Jews.

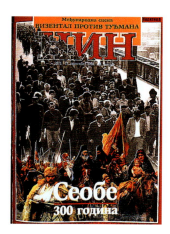

strategic Cold War importance and its economy started to crumble that dangerous nationalist sentiments were revived by leading academics in Serbia.[5]

At first, Milošević—who was still a loyal Communist—condemned this Serb nationalism. Later, however, when he realised he could harness its forces to his advantage he began to promote this ideology, playing on and exacerbating the existing tensions, spreading first mistrust, then fear, and finally hatred. Enemies (as well as Serb victims) were needed in the pursuit of a Greater Serbia, and Milošević found them everywhere.

Kosovo was an early and important focus for the radicalisation of Serbs as Milošević rose to power. Most Serbs consider Kosovo the ancient seat of their church and culture. As early as 1987 Milošević incited the Serb minority there. At a rally in Kosovo in April 1987, he told the crowd: "It was never part of the Serbian and Montenegrin character to give up in the face of obstacles, to demobilise when it's time to fight." And again in Kosovo in 1989—celebrating the martyred defeat of Serbs at the hands of the Turks in 1389—he warned: "Six centuries later, we are again in battles and quarrels. They are not armed battles, though such things should not be excluded yet."[6] According to The Hague Tribunal's indictment of Milošević, in making statements such as these he "broke with the party and government policy which had restricted nationalist sentiment in [Yugoslavia] since the time of its founding by Josip Broz Tito".[7]

In 1989 Milošević rammed constitutional amendments through parliament which stripped Kosovo of its autonomy. Under the 1974 constitution, Kosovo and Vojvodina enjoyed one vote each at the federal parliament, on an equal footing with the six republics of Yugoslavia.[8] Serbs had long grumbled that in this way the two provinces, which were part of Serbia, could outvote Serbia. The constitutional changes

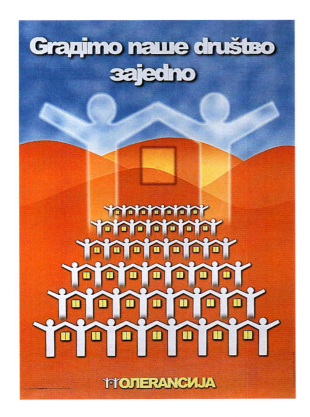

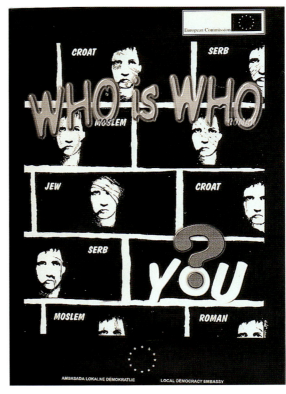

enacted in 1989 imposed Milošević's control over Kosovo. Protests erupted in the province and Kosovo unilaterally declared independence, but this was ignored internationally. Serbia then dissolved the Kosovo government and imposed direct rule from Belgrade. Against this background of Serbian muscle-flexing, Slovenia and Croatia began to fear for their status within Yugoslavia. These two republics then held referenda (in December 1990 and May 1991 respectively) and voted to secede from Yugoslavia. Bosnia and Macedonia followed suit in early 1992.

Milošević then attempted to grab by force as much of crumbling Yugoslavia as he could using the Yugoslav People's Army (*Jugoslovenska narodna armija* or JNA)—one of Europe's largest standing armies.[9] The JNA had been a pan-Yugoslav army, but by the end of the 1980s it had been purged to the extent that it was effectively a Serb

force, loyal only to Milošević and the idea of a dominant Serbia. When Milošević ordered the JNA to move against Croatia in 1991, he precipitated a protracted, bloody conflict. As ugly as the war in Croatia was, however, its horrors were eclipsed in 1992 by the carnage and destruction that overwhelmed Bosnia-Herzegovina.

The wars in Croatia and Bosnia were fought on the shallow pretext that the Serbs who lived there were in mortal danger from Croats and Muslims. The obsession and the mythology that surrounds the idea of a Greater Serbia had been exploited by a succession of Serbian politicians down through the ages, and the outcome has always been fatal.

In the late 1980s, nationalism in Serbia encouraged nationalism in the other Yugoslav republics. This created the right political climate for other nationalist leaders to get elected, such as Franjo

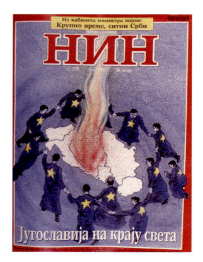

NIN magazines
Serbia, 1991–92
The international community was often caricatured in Serbia as a demonic cabal of greedy capitalists, wantonly carving up Yugoslavia. While it is true that inaction, competing interests, and a gross lack of understanding did real damage, these caricatures inflamed a sense of victimhood, even paranoia, among Serbs.

FOR SERBIA
Photograph by Daoud Sarhandi
Belgrade, 1998
Two of Serbia's leading nationalist politicians: Vuk Drašković with Slobodan Milošević's head pasted over him. Serb nationalists such as these presented themselves as strongmen at home and victims abroad. Their images were all over Serbia in the late 1980s and 1990s.

S J E Ć A N J E NA SREBRENICU I ŽEPU

UNPROFOR

11. JULI 1995 - 11. JULI 1996.

Tuđman in Croatia—and to a lesser extent, presidents Milan Kučan in Slovenia and Alija Izetbegović in Bosnia—to step into the limelight and seize power. Once nationalists were elected by the republics' dominant ethnic groups, fear spread among the minorities. These fears were then exploited. It was a downward spiral of fear and political opportunism that started in Serbia and spread like wildfire across Yugoslavia.

Milošević's nationalistic appeal to Serbs was greatly aided by Tuđman's own nationalistic behaviour, even though he was in no position to start a war. Bosnia's situation was always slightly different and potentially more explosive than those of the other republics because of its ethnic composition. Although Bosniaks (Bosnian Muslims) were the largest single group in the country—constituting 44 per cent of the population—Orthodox Serbs accounted for 33 per cent and Catholic Croats for 17 per cent. Jews, Turks, Roma and other minorities made up the rest.

Bosnian President Izetbegović, voted into power in 1990, was aware of the devastating consequences that war in Bosnia would have and initially did everything in his power to prevent it. By early 1992 there was a small contingency of UN peacekeepers in Sarajevo, but Izetbegović implored the UN to deploy a larger, more robust force in the country. War was already raging in Croatia, and the political division of the population in Bosnia along ethnic lines had already taken place. Izetbegović's pleas to the international community, however, fell on deaf ears.[10]

Dismembering a country with a population as ethnically entwined as Bosnia's was not easy. But the more inter-ethnic brutality that occurred, the more it reinforced the notion that the three groups could not live together. This had the effect of making ethnic partition a seemingly unavoidable solution.

The JNA was a professional army and couldn't be relied on to perform the kind of brutality needed to accomplish ethnic cleansing. So, covertly financed by Milošević, paramilitary forces from Serbia were used: Šešelj's *Četniks,* Drašković's Serbian Guard, Arkan's infamous Tigers (or Serb Volunteer Guard), and many other death squads harassed, raped, and killed civilians—implementing ethnic cleansing in Bosnia-Herzegovina.[11] This technique

dr. Franjo Tuđman Sigurna budućnost Hrvatske

HDZ

ABOVE
COMMEMORATION OF SREBRENICA & ŽEPA
Fuad Kasumović
Tuzla, 1996
This poster marks the first anniversary of the fall of Srebrenica and Žepa. UNPROFOR has been crossed out and replaced with the word Treason.

LEFT
A SECURE FUTURE FOR CROATIA
HDZ
Croatia, date unknown
As president of Croatia between 1990–99, Franjo Tuđman's jingoistic brand of nationalism caused real suffering in the region.

АКО ЈЕ ОВО НЕЧИЈА ИДЕЈА ЗА МИР У
БОСНИ И ХЕРЦЕГОВИНИ,

МОЖДА БИ ТРЕБАЛИ ПОСЛУШАТИ НЕКОГА ДРУГОГА... osce

ABOVE

**IF THIS IS SOMEONE'S IDEA FOR
PEACE IN BOSNIA-HERZEGOVINA,
THEN MAYBE YOU SHOULD
LISTEN TO SOMEONE ELSE ...**
NATO
Sarajevo, 1996

This poster contained one of the
strongest messages produced by
the international community: a
photograph showing fresh graves
in a Sarajevan cemetery. The
poster was commissioned by the
NATO-led IFOR (Implementation
Force) in support of the September
1996 elections. It was withdrawn
after officials in Republika Srpska
complained that it was biased
against Serbs.

RIGHT

TANKS? NO THANKS!
Anonymous
Croatia, 1991

A poster provided by the Croatian
History Museum in Zagreb.

OPPOSITE: LEFT TO RIGHT

INVINCIBLE FRONTIER
Intervyu magazine
Serbia, February 1993

The White Eagles were a Serb death
squad that took orders from two
political parties: Serbian National
Renewal (SNO), and Vojislav Šešelj's
Serbian Radical Party (SRS). Here
they are pictured in the *Krajina*
(borderland) region of Croatia—a
criminal mini-state run by local
dentist-turned-politician Milan
Babić, along with Milan Martić, the
head of police. Martić oversaw a
network of Serb paramilitaries.
Both men were eventually
convicted at the ICTY.

TANKS?

NO THANKS!

FOR PEACE AND HUMANITY IN CROATIA.

ČETNIK WOODSTOCK
Vreme magazine
Serbia, May 1998

Vreme is the leading independent
news magazine in Serbia. This
photograph, taken at a Serbian
religious festival in the spring of
1998, illustrates nationalism in
Serbia. The *Četniks* were a royalist
armed group that, at various times
in the region's history, attempted
to carve out a Greater Serbian
kingdom. Their ideas were revived
during the wars in the former
Yugoslavia, most notably by Vojislav
Šešelj.

THE TIGERS ARE COMING
NIN magazine
Serbia, December 1991

NIN is another leading Serbian
magazine. This edition features the
gangster and death-squad leader,
Arkan—who did extensive damage
in Croatia, Bosnia, and Kosovo.
These three mainstream magazines
show how normalised political
violence had become in Serbia.

was perfected in Croatia and then used
to devastating effect in Bosnia as well as
Kosovo. Also, local Serb civilians were fed
a 24-hour diet of nationalist propaganda
from Belgrade. When the time came, they
were armed and incited to violence against
their long-time neighbours. In Bosnia,
Radovan Karadžić metamorphosed into a
warlord under Serbia's patronage, and the
Bosnian Serb Army (officially the VRS, which
stands for *Vojska Republike Srpske*: Army
of Republika Srpska) was created out of
civilians and units of the JNA to carry out his
and Milošević's bidding.

The expression "ethnic cleansing" was
initially used by the media in Serbia to
describe acts committed against Croats
in areas of Croatia taken over during the
Serb offensive. It has since entered the
vocabularies of languages around the world.
Although no side in the Bosnian War was
entirely innocent of practising such crimes,
the elimination of minorities was never an
official policy of the elected government
in Bosnia, nor was it routinely practised by
the Bosnian Army (ABiH).[12] Ethnic cleansing,
however, very quickly became the raison
d'être of Serb and Croat forces and their
death squads. Territorial domination
of Bosnia was the goal of Milošević and
Tuđman, who saw ethnic purity as their
only means of achieving it. Ethnic purging of
the areas they had seized was their central
strategy, not a by-product, of the wars they
waged.[13]

Although Western powers were not the
cause of the war, there was an element of
collusion with the instigators of the Bosnian
War. In their efforts to find the most
expedient solution to the region's problems,
some Western statesmen legitimised
the worst nationalists. This situation
degenerated from passive complicity to
tragically active involvement when the
UN Security Council, at the behest of its
permanent members, insisted on enforcing
an arms embargo against a legitimate UN
member-state—Bosnia-Herzegovina—that

patently needed to defend itself against Serbia and to a lesser extent Croatia.[14] Under the guidance of Secretary-General Boutros Boutros-Ghali and his special envoy Yasushi Akashi, the UN stood by and watched a massive displacement of civilians and the commission of war crimes on a scale not seen in Europe since the 1940s.[15] For more than three years, European Union observers, UN soldiers, and designated Safe Areas coexisted with internment and rape camps, as well as snipers who openly bragged that nimble Sarajevan children were a better test of their marksmanship than the elderly. The lowest point came in July 1995 when Bosnian Serb forces, under the command of General Ratko Mladić, overran Srebrenica, a Safe Area under the protection of the UN's Dutch Battalion (Dutchbat). The entire population was expelled and more than 8,000 men and boys were murdered. The UN ordered Dutchbat to stand by and do nothing.

Largely as a result of what took place in Srebrenica, the United States took charge of events. Led by the US, NATO forces started bombing the Bosnian Serb Army on 30 August 1995, while simultaneously the Bosnian Army began to make gains right across its territory. This had the effect of forcing the Serbs, represented by Milošević,

to the negotiating table. Peace talks were held in late 1995 at Wright-Patterson Air Force Base, in Dayton, Ohio. With great difficulty, an agreement that ended the fighting was hammered out and signed by Milošević, Tuđman and Izetbegović on 21 November that year. The central problem with the Dayton Agreement is that it awarded the Serb aggressors with 49 per cent of the country—effectively making Bosnia ungovernable.

There were no winners in Bosnia. Some 100,000 people died, more than two million were left homeless or displaced, a beautiful country was littered with landmines, much of it was reduced to rubble, and just about everyone was emotionally or physically scarred. Those deluded enough to claim some kind of victory gained nothing more than the right to live in ethnically pure but morally bankrupt ghettos. Between 1999–2020 unemployment has never dropped below 18 per cent and has risen as high as 31 per cent. At the time of writing, it is estimated that 640,000 of its 3.8 million people live in absolute poverty.

The peace that still holds in Bosnia is a fragile and artificial one. Dangerous divisions exist between its two entities: the Muslim-Croat federation and Republika Srpska (Serb Republic).[16] Refugees of all

ETKE

nationalities are still unable to return to their homes, and those who committed crimes during the war remain at large. Although the situation is improving in places, nationalism on all sides, but especially in Croat- and Serb-controlled areas, seems dug in for the foreseeable future.

Immediately after the Dayton Agreement was ratified, the British historian Noel Malcolm wrote:

The new Bosnia, presaged by yesterday's peace accord signing in Paris, will be the geopolitical equivalent of an artwork by Damien Hirst. Hirst takes a cow, saws it in half, and pickles each half in formaldehyde. It may be an ingenious work of art, but is it still a cow? Similarly with the new Bosnia. It may have the cleverest of constitutions, but is it still a country?[17]

Although it took the convoy I was with more than two weeks to reach Tuzla from Britain on my first trip to Bosnia in October 1995, we could stay for only three days. I was keen to return to Bosnia: to see people I had met, and to ensure donated television equipment I was responsible for reached its final destination—TV Tuzla. My next trip to Bosnia was in late December 1995, when the Dayton Agreement was coming into effect. Although the weather and the roads were punishing, it was easier to drive through Bosnia than it had been for years. Roadblocks that had been a feature of the Bosnian War had disappeared. Gone too were the red and green UNPROFOR (United Nations Protection Force) flags used to indicate the threat of sniper activity.

Although the transition to the more robust NATO-led Implementation Force (IFOR) was in full swing, we did not entirely trust the route through still-disputed Serb-held territory around Sarajevo and decided to enter Tuzla the way we knew, across snowy mountains and muddy tracks. This time I stayed on in Bosnia for several weeks,

PREVIOUS SPREAD
THE RED BERETS OF BRČKO
Anonymous
Brčko, 1995
From a calendar produced in 1995 by the Serb army in Brčko. The detail at the top right shows Serb soldiers seated on the remains of a mosque. We found this calendar in the possession of a disabled Serbian boy who had lost his entire family in the fighting. In a musty apartment devoid of furniture, the boy showed us his military archive and shook his head; his face was grave as he told us that the war was simply a *"katastrofa".* (Other posters from the boy's collection appears later in the book.)

ABOVE: TOP TO BOTTOM
PRE-WAR MOSTAR
Anonymous
Mostar, date unknown
A jigsaw puzzle of the Stari Most (Old Bridge) in Mostar.

POST-WAR MOSTAR
Photograph by
Daoud Sarhandi
Mostar, January 1996
The destroyed Stari Most (Old Bridge). A temporary suspension bridge was strung up in an attempt to unify predominantly Bosniak (Muslim) east Mostar and predominantly Croat (Catholic) west Mostar. A replica bridge has since been built (see page 43), but strong divisions persist in Mostar.

CLOCKWISE FROM TOP LEFT
CONTINUITY
Anonymous, 1992
This poster shows Bosnian coats of arms through the ages. It points out that on 21 May 1992 Bosnia-Herzegovina was recognised by the United Nations as member state number 177. Combined Cyrillic and Latin scripts indicate unity between Bosnia's three ethnoreligious groups: Serbs, Bosniaks, and Croats.

®BiH
Forum of Tuzla Citizens
Tuzla, 1997
The 25th of November (Statehood Day, which is distinct from Independence Day) was the day in 1943 that Bosnia-Herzegovina was recognised as a republic within Yugoslavia. On that day, the Anti-Fascist Council for the National Liberation of Bosnia and Herzegovina affirmed the country's statehood within its medieval borders, and stressed equality for all Bosnia's ethnic groups.

Radovan Karadžić and other nationalists later rejected this date, and Statehood Day is still not celebrated in Republika Srpska. The ® symbol stands for "Registered" as well as "Republic" of BiH. This poster was designed by Jasminko Arnautović.

SDA—MUSLIM PARTY
SDA
Sarajevo, 1991
In the year before the war broke out, all of Bosnia's political parties played the ethnicity card in the elections. Alija Izetbegović's Party of Democratic Action (SDA) appealed to the country's predominant Bosniak (Muslim) electorate with a message that differentiated between the Muslims from the other ethnic groups. This created division rather than encouraging unity. The text reads: "They will come to negotiate about the future of our life together: Milošević, Tuđman, Kučan ... But who will represent us? SDA—our destiny in our hands."

On 21 November 1995, an agreement was reached in Dayton, Ohio, that ended the war in Bosnia-Herzegovina. The Dayton Agreement was ratified in Paris on 14 December 1995. As a result of the treaty, Bosnia was formally split in two: the [Muslim-Croat] Federation of Bosnia-Herzegovina and the Serb Republic. Brčko was claimed by both entities due to its strategic position, and so was given a special status that pleased neither side. More than two decades on, deep divisions still exist.

ZAGREB

OSIJEK

VUKOVAR

CROATIA

SLAVONSKI BROD

BOSANSKI ŠAMAC

BEJELJINA

BRČKO

BELGRADE

PRIJEDOR

ZVORNIK

BIHAĆ

OMARSKA

REPUBLIC
OF SERBIA

BANJA LUKA

TUZLA

ZENICA

TRAVNIK

SREBRENICA

VITEZ

ŽEPA

SARAJEVO

PALE

VIŠEGRAD

KUPRES

GORAŽDE

KONJIC

KNIN

FOČA

SPLIT

MOSTAR

ADRIATIC SEA

MEĐUGORJE

MONTENEGRO

TREBINJE

DUBROVNIK

BOSNIA AND HERZEGOVINA

Muslim-Croat
Federation:
51% of B-H.

Serb Republic
(Republika Srpska):
49% of B-H.

Brčko Self-governing Free
District (international
supervision is currently
suspended).

Between April–May 1993,
the United Nations
designated towns and
cities marked "Safe
Areas". Two of them,
Srebrenica and Žepa,
were ethnically cleansed
in the summer of 1995.

Bosnia-Herzegovina's external borders were
agreed at the United Nations on 21 May 1992.

eager to see more of the country than I had in the autumn. I spent a couple of weeks in Tuzla and then visited Sarajevo and Mostar.

Sarajevo—still under siege even though the fighting was over—was dotted with scores of fresh graves with simple markers bearing dates between 1992–95. Sniper barricades constructed of wrecked cars sat in front of buildings and across bridges. The warning *PAZI SNAJPER* (BEWARE SNIPER) was still scrawled on walls and nailed to trees. Mounds of rubbish lay uncollected everywhere. But amid the devastation, Sarajevans were getting used to the idea that they could once again walk the streets of their city without fear of being shot. Whatever the terms of Dayton's divisive peace—and democratic Bosnians everywhere felt those terms were essentially unjust—Sarajevans were rejoicing.

If there is one place in Bosnia-Herzegovina that illustrates what has rightly been termed "urbicide", it is Mostar. In 1993 the Tuđman-sponsored HVO (Croatian Council of Defence) tried to destroy the entire eastern (Muslim) side of the city.[18] The fate of the Stari Most (Old Bridge) is emblematic. This delicate, gracious bridge over the Neretva River was designed by the celebrated Turkish architect Mimar Hayruddin in 1566; it gave the city its name and underpinned its identity. In 1992 the bridge was damaged by Serb forces, and late in the following year it was deliberately destroyed with one shell fired from a Croat tank. In a country once full of bridges, the Old Bridge symbolised the relationship between Bosnia's eastern and western traditions, its various nationalities and faiths. The unnecessary destruction of the bridge had a negative psychological effect on the city and the country as a whole.

I left Mostar through the relatively unscathed west (Croat) side of the city and drove up to Zagreb. My route took me through the town of Knin, and then on through a series of eery, burnt-out ghost villages. This was the region that, in 1989, the media in Serbia began referring to as the Serb *Krajina (*Serb borderland).[19] This poor part of Croatia was populated mainly by Serbs and had been taken over by Serb paramilitaries in 1991 and purged of all Croats on the pretext that the Serbs who lived there—many for centuries—were in mortal danger in Tuđman's nationalist Croatian state. When it was no longer politically expedient for Milošević to prop up this criminal para-state—and he was looking for a way out of the quagmire of the wars he had started—the Krajina Serbs were abandoned to their fate. In July 1995 the area was liberated by Croatian forces in a US-backed military operation that lasted just two days. It was appropriately code-named Storm and resulted in the ethnic cleansing of the entire Serb population of nearly 200,000. They formed a desperately sad convoy that snaked its way to Serbia.

After returning to Britain in January 1996 I went to stay at a friend's cottage in the Lake District. It was a bitterly cold winter and the region was frequently snowed in. One afternoon, while hiding from the cold in a local junk shop in Kendal, I came across a box containing a jigsaw puzzle with a scenic view on the lid. The image and its identity took a few seconds to coalesce, but then it hit me. I was looking at a picture of Mostar: an inhabited, tranquil Mostar; a sunny Mostar with a bridge, bathers, and picturesque, ivy-clad houses with washing fluttering outside the windows. In short, a vanished Mostar. There is something strikingly apt about an image of Mostar as a jigsaw puzzle. Mostar remains divided. Croats govern its Catholic west side, and Muslims its east side. Children go to separate schools, where they use different vocabulary (although in essence, they speak the same language) and study different curricula.

Indeed, this puzzle metaphor can be extended to all of Bosnia. Glance at any map produced after the war, and you will see a multi-coloured patchwork with population densities highlighted by ethnic identification and religion. The various factions have all generated maps indicating overlapping nationalistic ambitions, with proposals for ethnic divisions and internal borders. On the ground, during the war, borders in the form of front lines cut through cities, towns and villages. Driving around Bosnia during the fighting—and even long afterwards—felt like driving across a huge puzzle. The international community also drew its preferred separation lines across the country. As the journalist Anthony Borden wrote:

> How many wasted hours must have been spent in the UN's Palais des Nations in Geneva, bent over diagrams of Bosnia's triangle shape, trying to envisage peace through coloured pens? Some gave more to "the Muslims", some gave more to "the Serbs", some gave dedicated territory to "the Croats", while others joined them with the Sarajevo government. What they all had in common is the link between ethnicity and territory.[20]

I am struck by how the process of defining Balkan borders by external players continues to this day—albeit with different political protagonists in the driving seat. In April 2021 a so-called "non-paper" began circulating the halls of European power, proposing afresh the division of the Western Balkans along ethnic lines.[21]

In the winter of 1995, Tuzla was cold, wet, and smoggy from wood fires and the burning of household rubbish. On New Year's Eve we danced in the streets amid the echo of hand grenades and automatic gunfire, celebrating the first peacetime new year's since 1992. A poster with a penetrating black and white eye glared over the dirty town. It advertised the play *Iza sna* (Behind the Dream). When I tried to

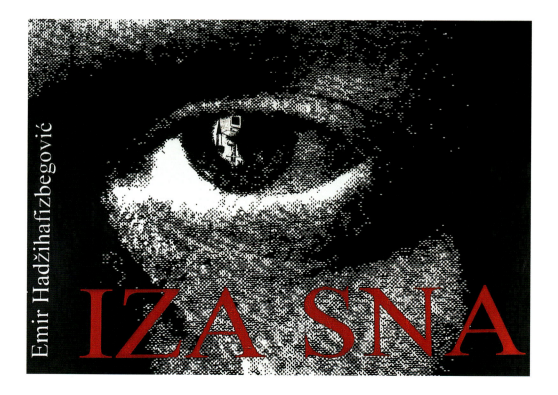

RIGHT
BEHIND THE DREAM
Adin Šadić
Tuzla, 1995
A poster for a play at the National Theatre of Tuzla, expressing Bosnia's complex relationship with Yugoslavia.

acquire the poster, I found that the theatre company had run out of copies. Three years later, when I started this book, finding a copy became something of a mission. One day I met a designer called Adin Šadić. When mentioned this striking if somewhat inscrutable poster, his face lit up: he had designed it! When I asked him to explain its meaning, Šadić told me that the eye referred to the central theme of the play— the premise that Bosnia was so blinded by its love for Yugoslavia that it remained tragically unaware of the dark, nationalistic forces that were gathering within it.

The Bosnian War matters. Not just for Bosnians, but also for the citizens of the United States, Britain, and other European nations whose governments played such a muddled role in the conflict. The breakup of Yugoslavia—and particularly the conflict in Bosnia—forced these nations to realise the limits of their foreign policy. The Bosnian War, and the world reaction to it, should also matter to the citizens of all nations that are conflicted by internal fault lines between their peoples. Just like in Bosnia, moreover, these fault lines are often exacerbated by cynical politicians whose primary responsibility is to keep their citizens safe but knowingly do the opposite.

NOTES

1. The name of the country in Bosnian is Bosna i Hercegovina. Herzegovina, in English, is the southern region. I use Bosnia and Herzegovina, Bosnia-Herzegovina and Bosnia interchangeably in this book. For simplicity, I also use Yugoslavia, rather than "the former Yugoslavia", to refer to the country as it existed before the breakup.

2. For this reason, I have chosen to include several images that were designed as posters but never printed.

3. Although the information is scant, there are cases of a direct relationship between Bosnian designs and famous Polish posters, such as those on pages 169 and 189. Thanks to design professor Jan Nuckowski, in Kraków, for pointing this out to me. Carol Wells also spotted striking similarities between two Bosnian War posters and propaganda produced by the Republicans during the Spanish Civil War (see pages 14 and 86).

4. Milošević became head of the Praesidium of the Central Committee of the League of Communists in 1986. He was elected president of the Presidency of Serbia in 1989. In 1990, after constitutional changes that led to elections in all the republics, Milošević became president of the newly formed Socialist Party of Serbia (SPS), and then president of Serbia. The SPS was little more than a renamed Communist Party. Milošević was re-elected in 1992 and then elected president of the Federal Republic of Yugoslavia (Serbia and Montenegro) in 1997. On 24 September 2000, in an election he thought he could win, Milošević was beaten by Vojislav Koštunica. After attempting to fix the result, he was deposed on 5 October. From April 1992 until 2006, Serbia was one of the two remaining republics of the Federal Republic of Yugoslavia (FRY)—the second being Montenegro. In this text I often use Serbia when technically I should use FRY. Montenegro exited the federation in 2006 and is now a separate country; Serbia, encompassing the semi-autonomous Vojvodina region, is now called the Republic of Serbia. President Tuđman died of cancer in December 1999. He was replaced by the relative moderate, Stjepan Mešić. Croatia and Slovenia are currently the only two former Yugoslav republics to have been admitted into the European Union.

5. The earliest and most influential nationalistic statement was a "Memorandum" penned in 1986 by 16 leading intellectuals

from the Serbian Academy of Sciences in Belgrade. The document was a tirade against non-Serbs, warning prophetically of the imminent destruction of Serbs in Yugoslavia unless steps were taken to remedy their plight.

6. Laura Silber and Alan Little, *The Death of Yugoslavia* (London: Penguin Books/BBC Books, 1995), p. 37–38. This book cannot be recommended highly enough for background, detail, and analysis of the dissolution of Yugoslavia.

7, Miloševič and four of his closest aides were indicted by the International Criminal Tribunal for the former Yugoslavia (ICTY) in The Hague for crimes against humanity and war crimes in connection with the conflicts in Croatia, Bosnia and Kosovo. The indictment was signed on 22 May 1999, while the last of these wars was still raging. After the end of the war in Kosovo, Miloševič's power and influence rapidly ebbed away, and in early October 2000 he was finally removed from power. Suspected of corruption, abuse of power, and embezzlement, Yugoslav federal authorities arrested the former president on 31 March 2001. At the end of June, he was extradited to The Hague to stand trial. Unfortunately for his countless victims, that trial never concluded: Miloševič suffered a heart attack and was found dead in his cell on 11 March 2006.

8. These autonomies were granted under Marshal Tito's rule in 1974. The act was seen by disgruntled Serbs as a betrayal of their interests by Tito, who was half-Croat/half-Slovene. Although Kosovo and Vojvodina did not achieve the status of full republics, remaining constitutionally part of Serbia, they enjoyed important political, judicial, educational, and cultural rights of self-determination. Vojvodina remains part of Serbia. Serbia still officially considers Kosovo as part of her territory, although Kosovo has so far been recognised as an independent state by around 115 countries.

9. After the breakup of the former Yugoslavia, the Yugoslav People's Army changed its name to the Yugoslav Army, or Vojska Jugoslavije (VJ). Today, the Serbian Armed Forces.

10. Radovan Karadžić was head of the Democratic Party of Serbs (SDS) and the so-called "leader of the Bosnian Serbs". In 1995, shortly after the ethnic cleansing of Srebrenica, Karadžić was indicted for war crimes by The Hague tribunal. He evaded capture for over a decade, moving between Republika Srpska (Serb Republic) and Serbia. Finally captured in Belgrade in 2008, he was extradited, tried, and convicted of genocide, crimes against humanity and war crimes. At the time of writing, he is still in prison and will probably remain there for the rest of his life.

LEFT
ON WE GO!
SDS
Republika Srpska, 1996
Although initially an anti-nationalist, it is said, after receiving support from the Serb academic and arch-nationalist Dorbica Ćosić, in 1989 Karadžić founded the Serbian Democratic Party with the aim of unifying Bosnia's Serb communities—together with Serbs in Croatia—in case Yugoslavia fell apart. His actions, along with those of other regional actors, ensured that Yugoslavia did indeed swiftly descend into bloody chaos.

11. Warlord, gangster and businessman, Željko "Arkan" Ražnatović was shot dead in the lobby of Belgrade's Intercontinental Hotel in January 2000. Vojislav Šešelj is currently still active in Serbian politics; he is president of the ultra-nationalist Serbian Radical Party (SRS), which he founded in 1991. Between 1998–2000, Šešelj was a Deputy Prime Minister of Serbia. The International Criminal Tribunal for the former Yugoslavia accused Šešelj of

war crimes, and he turned himself in. His court case in The Hague led to an acquittal in 2016. This was partially overturned two years later when he was found guilty of incitement of crimes against humanity committed in Croatia, but—-strangely, many people commented—not in Bosnia. He was given a ten-year sentence, but was not returned to jail since he had already served 11 years in pre-trial detention. In elections held in June 2020, Šešelj and his party failed to enter the Serbian Parliament, winning fewer votes than the required three per cent threshold. Vuk Drašković remains a political figure in Serbia, even if he has been somewhat marginalised. He is reportedly still involved with the pro-monarchist parliamentary party, the Serbian Renewal Movement (SPO)—founded by him and Vojislav Šešelj in 1990. Drašković is also a writer, specialising in historical novels with a macabre nationalistic tone. Drašković was one of the earliest and most virulent exponents of a Greater Serbia. However, for his views and writings, he was never indicted by the ICTY.

12. ABiH stands for *Armija Bosne i Hercegovine* (Army of Bosnia-Herzegovina) and is also known simply as the Bosnian Army. During the war, the ABiH was the legitimate armed force representing the elected Bosnian government, comprising mainly, but not exclusively, of Muslims. For example, the second-in-command, Gen. Jovan Divjak, was a Serb, and many Serbs, as well as Croats, fought with ABiH to preserve a multi-ethnic Bosnia. This information was played down during the war by Serb nationalists as well as by many international journalists, who thought it might confuse the public.

13. In 2021, the Serbian government's role in aiding and abetting death squads responsible for war crimes committed during the Croatian and Bosnian wars was finally proven in court. Jovica Stanišić (head of the formidable SDB, the Serbian State Security Service, between 1991–98) and Franko Simatović (who ran SDB's Special Operations Unit during the same period) were convicted at the UN war crimes tribunal in The Hague. The trials of these immensely powerful apparatchiks, who worked directly for President Slobodan Milošević, lasted from 2003 until their convictions on 30 June 2021—making it the longest-running international war crimes trial in history; during the court proceedings, a massive amount of evidence from various intelligence agencies was presented to the tribunal. Although Stanišić and Simatović's convictions were based only on "providing support" to death squads operating in 1992 in Bosanski Šamac, a small northern Bosnian town straddling the Croatian border, in reality ethnic cleansing by Serbian death squads was carried out all over Bosnia and Croatia for the duration of the wars. This trial, however—as limited in its scope as it was—marked the first time anyone from President Milošević's chain of command had been held accountable for their role in the slaughter—proving how difficult it is to get high-value war criminals into court. Nataša Kandić, the founder of the Humanitarian Law Center in Belgrade, believes, however, that this historic conviction shows that "no one can now clear Serbia and say that it did not participate in these crimes". Stanišić and Simatović were sentenced to 18 years apiece, reduced to 12 years for time already served.

14. Bosnia was recognised as a member of the United Nations on 21 May 1992. During the war, great efforts were made by the government in Sarajevo to have the arms embargo lifted, and indignation about the failure of this to happen mounted around the world. Bosnia did receive small arms during the war, however, and rumours abound as to their source; these arms, however, were not enough to turn the war in Bosnia's favour.

15. Boutros Boutros-Ghali, the sixth Secretary-General of the UN, and Yasushi Akashi, Boutros-Ghali's Special Envoy to the conflicts in Yugoslavia, failed to protect Srebrenica or Žepa, and stop the massacres

and ethnic cleansing that took place there in the summer of 1995. Both these officials seemed entirely in awe of Serbia's strongman president, Slobodan Milošević, endlessly willing to trust him and give him one more chance. On the international stage, however, Boutros-Ghali and Akashi were far from alone in their apparent preference for division and bloodshed over unity and humanity. In order not to forget the troupe of mostly British, US and UN career politicians and diplomats who endlessly shuttled between the world's capitals and what was left of Yugoslavia, allow me to name them. On one side of the Atlantic, there was President Bill Clinton—who eventually redeemed himself far too late and by far too little—accompanied over the years by various secretaries of state (James Baker, Cyrus Vance, and Warren Christopher) and defence ministers (Leslie Aspin and William Perry). On the other side of the Atlantic, there were Prime Minister John Major, foreign secretaries Lord (Peter) Carrington, Douglas Hurd, and Malcolm Rifkind (who was also Secretary of State for Defence between 1992–95). There was also the British ex-politician Lord (Dr David) Owen, working as a UN Peace Negotiator. Owen expended considerable effort selling plans to the warring parties that meant the division of Bosnia into homogeneously ethnoreligious cantons. These plans, as opposed to making peace, actually worsened the conflict by rewarding the aggressors. (Indeed, so overjoyed were Bosnian-Croat separatists with what one plan offered them—more of Herzegovina than they dreamt they could get away with—they reportedly joked that "HVO" should in future stand for *"Hvala Vance-Owen"*: "Thank you Vance-Owen.") Looking back on those dark years in Europe's history, one cannot help feeling that Bosnia was truly cursed to be in such a dire situation at the same time as such appeasers dominated the international stage. It is no underestimation to say, I believe, that each of the men I have named here (plus others too numerous to mention) in his way was to Milošević (and to

Tuđman, too, to a lesser extent) what British Prime Minister Neville Chamberlain was to Adolf Hitler in the 1930s. Combined, this cast represented a catastrophe for Bosnia's citizens, and especially—but not exclusively— for her Bosniak Muslim citizens.

16. Republika Srpska (Serb Republic) was officially recognised at Dayton, Ohio, in 1995. It constitutes 49% of Bosnian territory. An "inter-ethnic boundary line" separates it from the Muslim-Croat federation, forged in separate peace talks between Croatia and Bosnia in 1994. This federation constitutes the other 51% of the country.

17. Noel Malcolm, "Why the Peace of Paris Will Mean More War in Bosnia", *London Daily Telegraph* (15 December 1995).

18. The Croatian Defence Council (HVO, which stands for Hrvatsko vijeće odbrane) was a Herzegovinian, Croat army that, under Tuđman, was financially and militarily backed by the state of Croatia. Some members of the HVO—particularly in Sarajevo and around Tuzla—continued to fight alongside the Bosnian Army (ABiH), and there was often widespread distaste among Croats outside

Herzegovina for what was being done there to Muslims. The HVO is now an official part of Bosnia's military structure, as is the now-defunct Army of Republika Srpska.

19. There are many *krajinas* in the territories of the former Yugoslavia. During the Hapsburg Empire they served as a defence against the Ottomans. The majority of these outlying fortified regions were populated by Serb settlers who were encouraged to defend Europe's dominant Christian values and culture.

20. Anthony Borden, "The Lesson Unlearned", *War Report 58* (London: The Institute of War and Peace Reporting, 1998).

21. This explosive, anonymously written "non-paper" is said to have originated in Slovenian Prime Minister Janez Janša's office. Rumours suggest that Slovenia's President, Borut Pahor, is supportive and that they are perhaps working in cahoots with other nationalist leaders in the region. Innocently titled "Western Balkans: A Way Forward", this document is so provocative that, at the time of writing, the EU still hasn't commented on its contents, despite it reportedly having been presented by Prime Minister Janša to Charles Michel, the current President of the European Council. The paper argues that the former Yugoslavia has not yet finished its dissolution (seen by President Pahor as essential if EU integration of the region can proceed) and that this process should conclude with a series of land swaps between Serbia, Bosnia and Croatia on the one hand and Kosovo, Albania, North Macedonia and Serbia on the other. Šefik Džaferović, the Bosniak member of Bosnian's complex tripartite Presidency, believes that the paper is a blatant attempt to destabilise the country: "The document [...] showed that secessionist powers are eager for signals from the EU to launch a bloodbath. I don't think this came from Brussels officials, but rather from radical circles who are trying to present their retrograde ideas as being

European." But let's be clear, he said, "Any redrawing of borders along ethnic lines would destabilise not just Bosnia and the region but also affect the stability of the entire continent." (Quotes are taken from *EuroNews*, 20 April 2021. The source of this story was the Slovenian investigative news outlet *Necenzurirano,* to which the non-paper was leaked in mid-April.) We will have to wait and see what the effects of this kind of thinking-out-loud are. But the fact that thoughts such as these can be publicly voiced at all does not bode well for Bosnia's future.

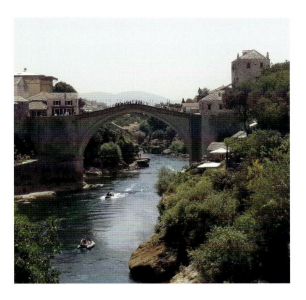

OPPOSITE
WELCOME TO REPUBLIKA SRPSKA
Photograph by Rupert Wolfe Murray
Slavonski Brod, 2021
Crossing over the Sava river between Croatia and Bosnia. Slavonski Brod is on the Croatian side of the river, and Brod—now in Republika Srpska—is on the Bosnian side.

ABOVE
MOSTAR'S NEW STARI MOST
Photograph by Rupert Wolfe Murray
Mostar, 2021
Mimicking the ancient construction techniques Mimar Hayruddin used in the 16th century, Mostar's emblematic Old Bridge was eventually reconstructed. Rebuilding the delicate bonds between Bosnia's distinct faiths and ethnicities, however, has proven much more difficult.

LEFT TO RIGHT

PRESIDENT SLOBODAN MILOŠEVIĆ; *Photograph by Daoud Sarhandi; Belgrade, 1998*

Serbian president Slobodan Milošević looks out from an election-period wall, saturated with Serbian nationalist imagery and party political slogans. Responsibility for the tsunami of nationalism that overwhelmed Yugoslavia largely belongs to Milošević.

REVOLUTION; *BOSS; Tuzla, 1998*

An election poster by the Bosnian Party (BOSS) featuring a portrait of Josip Broz Tito, who, alongside his Partisans, created Yugoslavia in the mid-1940s from the ruins of post-war Europe. As the map superimposed over his face suggests, Tito embodied Yugoslavia—so much so that it rapidly disintegrated without his strength of character and convictions—torn apart by competing nationalisms.

PLATES

TITO'S STATE FUNERAL PROCESSION
Anonymous (Public Domain)
Yugoslavia, May 1980
On Sunday 4 May 1980, Yugoslavian television programmes were interrupted with the following message, read by the well-known Slovene presenter, Tomaž Terček (below):

> *The Central Committee of the League of Communists of Yugoslavia and the Presidency of Yugoslavia, announces to all the working people and citizens of all nations and nationalities of the Socialist Federal Republic of Yugoslavia: Comrade Tito has died.*

Tito's coffin travelled along the Brother and Unity highway from Ljubljana in Slovenia to the capital, Belgrade, in Serbia. This photo was taken passing Zagreb, Croatia.

CIAo!
Asim Đelilović
Travnik, 1997
At the end of World War II Josip Broz Tito managed to create Yugoslavia, a new federal state formed of six republics: Bosnia-Herzegovina, Croatia, Macedonia, Montenegro, Serbia, and Slovenia. Although Tito was essentially a dictator he was adored by most Yugoslavs and ruled for more than 30 years. Yugoslavia under Tito was at the centre of the Non-Aligned Movement of countries that were neither committed to the US or the Soviet Union. Tito died at the age of 88 in May 1980. Asim Đelilović, the creator of this poster, is the author of 27 pieces of graphic art which are collectively titled *After Paradise* and tell the story of the Bosnian War. The large-format (100 x 70 cm) silkscreened designs were conceptualised between 1992–96, although some of them, like this example, were produced in 1997. This image of Tito saying *Ciao!* (an Italian greeting) is the first in the *After Paradise* series. The typographic play on words refers to the rumours as to whether or not foreign powers played a role in Yugoslavia's breakup.

Poring over news magazines in the National Library of Serbia—where the staff were extremely helpful—we discovered a fascinating and powerful way of seeing how history, political interests and prejudices played out in Serbia. Years of this kind of (dis)information, as well as wall-to-wall nationalistic television programmes, primed the Serbian population for the conflicts to come.

RIGHT
KOSOVO 1389: THE SERBS DEFEATED THE TURKS
Pogledi magazine
Serbia, June 1988
The history of Serbia's relationship with Kosovo was used as a powerful means of indoctrinating the Serb population. This popular tale of heroism, martyrdom and inconsolable loss in defence of a Christian Europe against the Muslim hordes has historically been disastrous for Serbia. *Pogledi* (Viewpoints), an ultranationalist Serb magazine, ceased publication in 2005.

OPPOSITE
KOSOVO POLJE—SIX CENTURIES LATER
Ilustrovana Politika magazine
Serbia, July 1989
Soon after being elected President of Serbia, in May 1989, Slobodan Milošević began creating the myth that the Serb minority in Kosovo was being persecuted. In June 1989, he attended the 600th anniversary of the Battle of Kosovo when, in 1389, the Serbs were defeated by the Ottoman Turks. His speech inflamed the Serb minority in Kosovo, which claimed it was persecuted by the Albanian majority in the region. This rattled the Kosovars as well as the other non-Serbs in Yugoslavia. *Ilustrovana Politika* (Illustrated Politics)—one of many magazines and newspapers published by the powerful Serbian newsgroup Politika Novine i Magazini (Politics Newspapers and Magazines)—celebrated Milošević's speech. President Milošević harnessed this newsgroup for his nationalist ends as soon as he came to power.

ИЛУСТРОВАНА
ПОЛИТИКА

КОСОВО ПОЉЕ –
ШЕСТ ВЕКОВА ПОСЛЕ
ИМАМО СА ЧИМ
ПРЕД МИЛОША

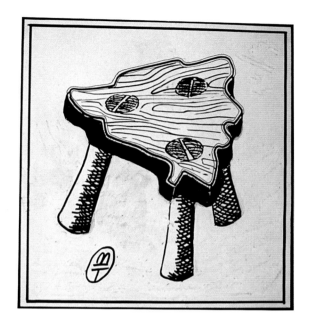

BOSNIA
Began Turbić
Tuzla, 1992

Bosnia-Herzegovina's heart-shaped form is a recurring motif in Bosnian posters. Here the artist portrays the country as a wooden stool, supported by three legs representing the country's dominant faiths: Islam, Catholicism, and the Eastern Orthodox Church. Of all the republics within the federal state of Yugoslavia, Bosnia, with its delicate ethnoreligeous mix combined with its geographic location—sandwiched between Catholic Croatia and Orthodox Serbia—was the most vulnerable to destabilisation.

OPPOSITE
1981–1988
NIN magazine
Caricature by Dušan Petričić
Serbia, January 1988

The political temperature in Yugoslavia started to rise almost as soon as its lifelong leader, Josip Broz Tito, died in 1980. After the 1986 publication of a nationalistic Memorandum by 16 intellectuals from the Serbian Academy of Sciences and Arts in Belgrade, Yugoslavia got hotter still. These intellectuals were led by Dobrica Ćosić, who called Tito "the greatest enemy of my people in the last century". By "my people" he meant Serbs. When this caricature was published on the cover of the widely read Serbian government news magazine, *NIN (НИН* in the Cyrillic alphabet), Milošević had yet to become President of Serbia (a role he took on in 1989). In April 1987, however, he addressed crowds in Kosovo, rallying Serbs for the battles ahead. As the 1980s came to an end, the political temperature in Yugoslavia would keep on rising, until it boiled over in 1991 in Croatia, followed by Bosnia in 1992. Thanks to Vesna Manojlović for pointing out the identity of the leading Serbian caricaturist who drew this eerily predictive illustration.

FOLLOWING SPREAD
SERBIAN RULERS
Anonymous, place and date unknown

Nationalism surged back into Serbia following Tito's death. Memorabilia with historic figures from Serbia's past—including the *Četniks*, a royalist Serbian guerrilla group that fought Tito's Partisans in World War II—were sold everywhere. This poster of Serbian rulers was purchased by the author, Daoud Sarhandi, on the street in Belgrade in 1998.

НИН

ПОЛИТИК

1931 3. јануар 1988.

Italija 2000 Lit Francuska 6,30 Ff Švedska 9,00 Škr Švajcarska 3,00 Šfrs Austrija 20,00 Asch Nemačka 3,50 DM Belgija 40,00 Bfrs

СРПСКИ

1820

ВЛАДАРИ

ABOVE: LEFT TO RIGHT
REFERENDUM FOR CROATIA
Anonymous
Croatia, 1991
A poster for the Croatian referendum for independence from Yugoslavia, held on 19 May 1991.

SOS CROATIA
Ranko Novak
Croatia, 1991
Croatia and Slovenia both declared independence from Yugoslavia on 25 June 1991. Three days later the Yugoslav People's Army (JNA) invaded Slovenia, but Serbia withdrew these forces after ten days and used them to attack Croatia. The ensuing war lasted four years, although the first year was the bloodiest—as represented in this poster, which is essentially a Croatian cry for help. In Croatian, the word *šah* means chess and the red and white checkerboard, called *šahovnica,* is the ancient heraldic emblem of Croatia.

OPPOSITE
KRVATSKA
Borislav Ljubičić
Croatia, 1991
In Croatian, the word *krv* means blood and the country's name is *Hrvatska*. The first syllables of these words rhyme, and this poster amalgamates them into a new word: "Blood-Croatia". All the images relating to Croatia on the next few pages were found at the Croatian History Museum in Zagreb.

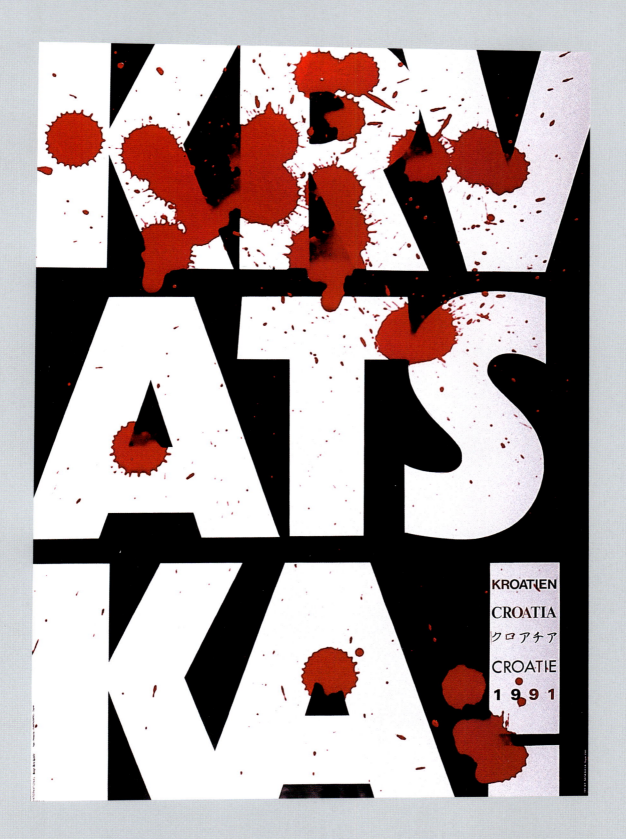

KROATIEN
CROATIA
クロアチア
CROATIE
1991

STOP THE WAR IN CROATIA
Ante Verzzoti
Croatia, 1991
Yugoslav People's Army: boots on the ground in Croatia.

MY FATHER IS A CROATIAN SOLDIER
Ivo Vrtarić
Croatia, 1992
A call-up poster for the newly formed Croatian army.

JNA
Anonymous
Croatia, 1991
JNA was the acronym for the Yugoslav People's Army, a relatively large European force that after Tito's death was taken over by Serbia and used to terrorise the former republics of Yugoslavia. The text at the bottom of the poster reads:

> *Trademark*
> *for aggression,*
> *crime,*
> *murder*

NO YU
Anonymous,
Croatia, 1991
YU was the official abbreviation for Yugoslavia. The symbol of the tank was especially poignant, as Serbia had seized Yugoslav People's Army tanks and other war material, leaving the other five republics effectively defenceless. This poster was faxed anonymously to the Croatian History Museum in Zagreb.

STOP THE WAR
IN CROATIA

I MOJ JE
TATA
HRVATSKI
VOJNIK

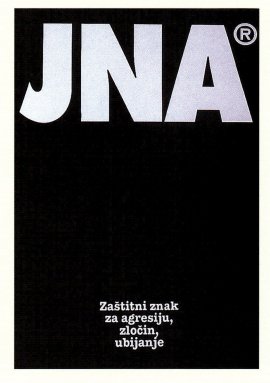

JNA®

Zaštitni znak
za agresiju,
zločin,
ubijanje

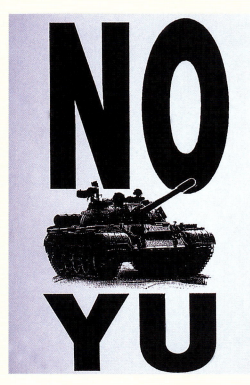

NO
YU

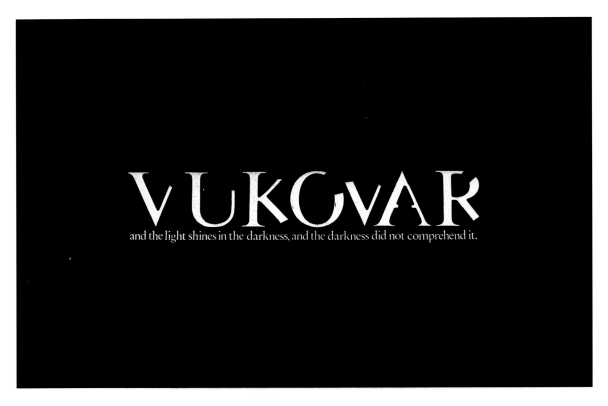

VUKOVAR

and the light shines in the darkness, and the darkness did not comprehend it.

VUKOVAR
Anonymous
Croatia, 1991

Vukovar was a baroque, multi-ethnic Croatian town located on the Danube. It was the first European town to be entirely destroyed since World War II—a wanton act carried out in 1991 by the Serb-controlled Yugoslav People's Army. Against all the odds, a small Croatian defence force used the sewage network to stage a heroic resistance. They managed to hold out for nearly three months against heavy artillery and tanks. After 87 days, however, the city fell. Those inhabitants who had not fled or been killed were expelled by the Serb forces. Vukovar's ruins were handed back to Croatia after the Dayton Agreement.

OPPOSITE
DO YOU REMEMBER DUBROVNIK?
Minute
Croatia, 1991

Dubrovnik, on Croatia's Dalmatian coast, is one of the most beautiful cities on the Adriatic. The old town is a Venetian medieval fortress jutting out into the sea. Before the war, Dubrovnik had been one of the most popular tourist attractions in Yugoslavia. After Croatia seceded from Yugoslavia, Dubrovnik was attacked by Montenegrin troops of the Yugoslav People's Army from the hills above the city and then by Serbian naval forces. At the time, it seemed as if the international community was more concerned about the damage caused to Dubrovnik's famous old Venetian buildings than about the fate of Croatian civilians in cities that were being hit much harder, such as Vukovar.

In the following four images we travel from Biblical times to the Austro-Hungarian empire, from present-day destruction to historic Croatian nationalism, from second world war fascism to more recent *Četnik*-style Serb terror.

RIGHT: TOP TO BOTTOM
SLAVONSKI BROD—WAR 1992
Mario Kudera
Croatia, 1992
This poster symbolises the destruction in Slavonski Brod, a town in eastern Croatia on the river Danube.

DERELICT HOUSE
Photograph by Modzzak
Slavonski Brod, 2007
A house in Slavonski Brod, ethnically cleansed of its Croatian inhabitants in 1991and still standing vacant many years after it was destroyed. Among the nationalistic slogans daubed on walls, can be read:

Usraše se Ustaše

This frightening rhyming slang translates as "The *Ustaše* are shit-scared"—using a derogatory word for Croats, linking them to the Croatian *Ustaše* fascists who ran the Nazi Independent State of Croatia between 1941–45.

OPPOSITE: LEFT TO RIGHT
OUR DAILY BREAD—VUKOVAR
Anonymous
Croatia, 1991
A reference to a biblical phrase from the Lord's Prayer. Croatia is an overwhelmingly Catholic country, unlike Serbia which is predominantly Orthodox. Before the war, Bosnia-Herzegovina was split 44 per cent Muslim, 33 per cent Orthodox, and 17 per cent Catholic (six per cent identified with other faiths/ethnicities, or none).

CROATIA AFTER VUKOVAR
NIN magazine
Serbia, November 1991
Two Serb fighters pose on a pedestal in an utterly destroyed Vukovar. The subtitle asks, "Tuđman or Paraga?" Franjo Tuđman was President of Croatia between 1990–99; Dobroslav Paraga was the first president of the Croatian Party of Rights (HSP) after this ultra-right-wing nationalist party was re-established in 1990. HSP was not only a party, but had an armed wing, as did many other political parties.

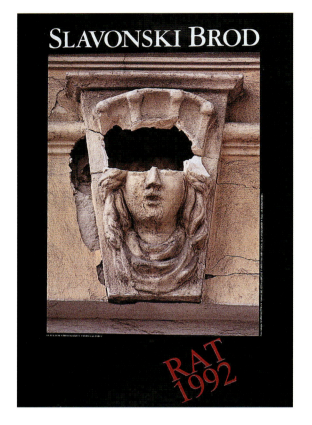

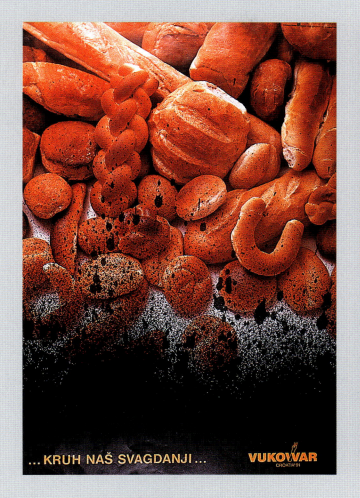

... KRUH NAŠ SVAGDANJI ...

VUKOWAR
CROATIA'91

Александар Петровић:
Три одговора на прљави рат

ПОЛИТИКА

НИН

2134 23. новембар 1991.   50 динара

Хрватска после Вуковара

Туђман или Парага?

BOSNIA: GAMES WITHOUT BORDERS
Intervyu magazine
Serbia, January 1993

The infamous Radovan Karadžić—a Montenegro-born Serb psychiatrist turned war criminal—dressed in a tie showing Serbia's national colours and a shirt embossed with CCCC, a Cyrillic acronym for Only Unity Saves the Serbs. After forming the Serbian Democratic Party in 1990, Karadžić became known as "the leader of the Bosnian Serbs" after unilaterally naming part of Bosnia's territory "Republika Srpska" (Serb Republic). He led his people into three-and-a-half years of hellish war. Karadžić is currently spending his life in prison, after being convicted in The Hague of genocide and other high crimes. Thanks to Vesna Manojlović for pointing out that the title of this caricature is taken from a popular former Yugoslav TV games show. Teams from the different Yugoslav republics would compete against one another in water fights and suchlike. Here Karadžić is depicted stitching together a Frankenstein's monster of a country from the social fabric of Bosnia-Herzegovina. *Intervyu* (Interview) is a leading Serbian news magazine.

OPPOSITE
STOP MILOŠEVIĆ
Began Turbić
Tuzla, 1992

In this poster, an inverted hand in the position of a three-fingered Serb salute is transformed into a hooded executioner. The eye and mouth holes of the hood form the letters SDS in Cyrillic, which stands for *Srpska demokratska stranka,* the Bosnian Serb political party that was led by Radovan Karadžić and supported by Slobodan Milošević. The positioning of the fingers signifies the trinity in the Serb Orthodox church. It is also commonly used by Serb soldiers as a victory sign, much as British and American troops use the two-fingered "V" sign. In Bosnia, three raised fingers became a hated symbol of Serb military aggression.

FOLLOWING SPREAD: LEFT TO RIGHT
NOW ART
Asim Đelilović
Travnik, 1997

From a series of posters titled *After Paradise,* conceptualised between 1992–96. Most of these large-format silkscreened works fuse linguistic and visual elements.

BOSNA
Asim Đelilović
Travnik, 1997

In the Bosnian language, "Bosnia" is spelt without an "i".

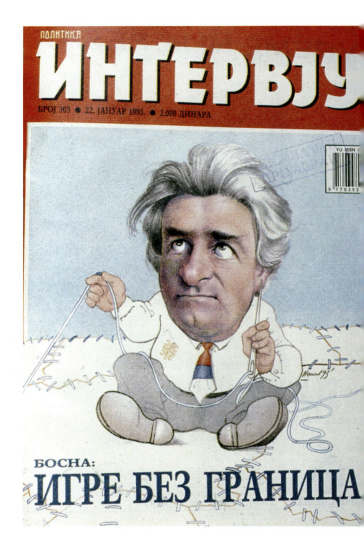

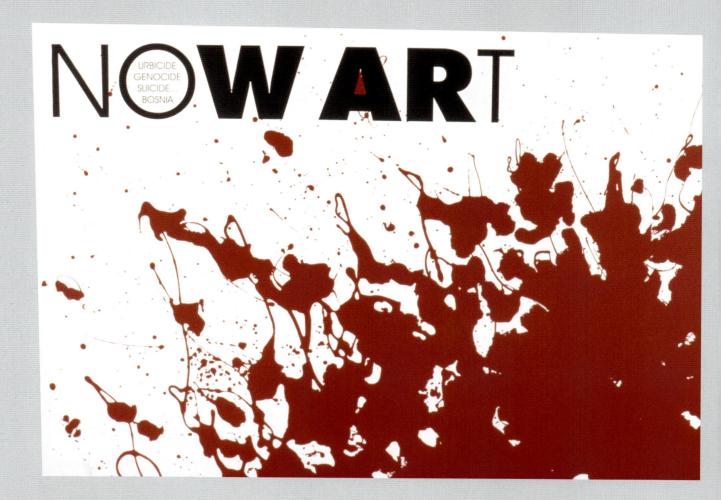

MEIN KAMPF—DOBRICA ĆOSIĆ
Began Turbić
Tuzla, 1992
The bubble in the poster reads:

> THIS EDITION OF THE MASTERPIECE IS BOUND IN MUSLIMS' SKIN

Dobrica Ćosić was the head of the Serbian Academy of Sciences and Arts in Belgrade. In 1986 the Academy published an ultranationalist document known as the Memorandum. It is widely believed that Ćosić was responsible for writing it. The Memorandum states that Serbs had been in a subservient position within the Yugoslav Federation ever since constitutional changes were made under Tito in 1974. In that year, Muslims were recognised as a "nationality" in Bosnia, and Kosovo and Vojvodina were given the status of autonomous provinces. The Memorandum claims that Serbs became the victims of genocide in Kosovo and an endangered nationality within Yugoslavia generally. This document shocked the whole of the former Yugoslavia as it presented Tito as anti-Serb; in many ways, it was a call to arms for the Serb nation. Initially, the Memorandum was attacked by many politicians in Serbia, including Slobodan Milošević, who was a Communist politician before he decided to ride the tiger of nationalism. Later, at the height of the war in Bosnia, Milošević made Dobrica Ćosić president of the new Yugoslav Federation.

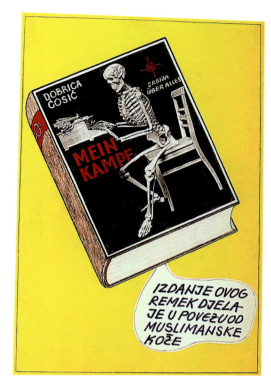

FROM CONCERN TO HOPE
Intervyu magazine
Serbia, November 1990
This edition of the popular news magazine *Intervju* (Interview) features the thoughts and opinions of the Serbian intellectual, and obsessive nationalist, Dobrica Ćosić. One imagines he felt hopeful about the imminent liberation—as he undoubtedly saw it—of the persecuted Serbs throughout Yugoslavia. Hope, however, would soon turn to despair for millions of Yugoslavs, no matter what their ethnoreligious identity.

OPPOSITE
THE CORE IS ISTANBUL—THE REST IS MYTH
Began Turbić
Tuzla, 1992
The book in this poster is titled *Serbian History, Culture and Traditions.* The heading suggests that if Turkish cultural heritage is removed from Bosnia's history, all that will remain is a gaping hole.

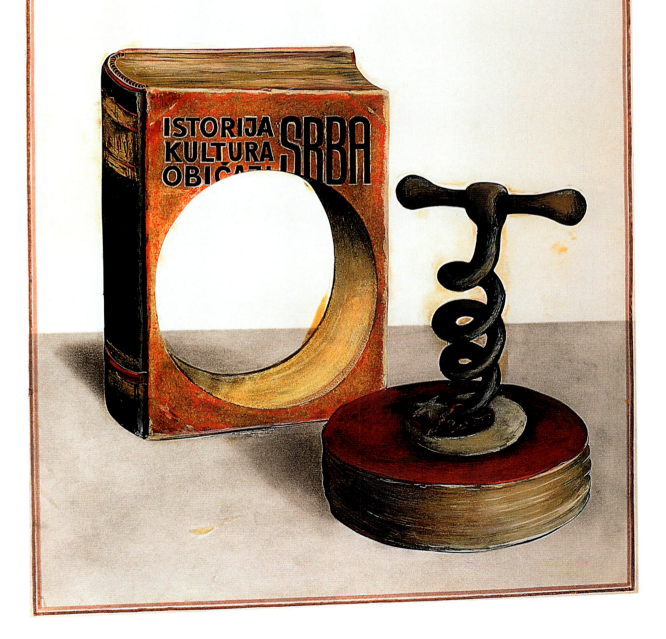

ABOVE
BOSNIA
Čedomir Kostović
USA, 1995
Čedomir Kostović was a leading graphic designer
in Bosnia before the war. He was part of the team
responsible for the graphic design of the XIV Winter
Olympics in Sarajevo in 1984, and in 1991 he moved to
the United States. All his posters included in this book
were produced with the assistance of Ken Daley at Old
Dominion University in Norfolk, Virginia.

RIGHT
SAW
Began Turbić
Tuzla, 1992
A similar sentiment to that in the poster opposite is
expressed in this three-dimensional graphic, made from
cardboard and clothes pegs.

OPPOSITE
BROTHERHOOD AND UNITY
Čedomir Kostović
USA, 1994
Brotherhood and Unity was a government slogan in
the former Yugoslavia, used to reinforce cooperation
between the republics and the various nationalities.
Several of the republics had fought each other during
World War II, with a huge loss of life. In the years following
the victory by Tito's Communist Partisans, this slogan
became the unifying doctrine of the Yugoslav state.
Kostović's poster speaks of the abandonment of this
concept and the brutality that was used to cut up multi-
ethnic Bosnia.

Brotherhood and Unity

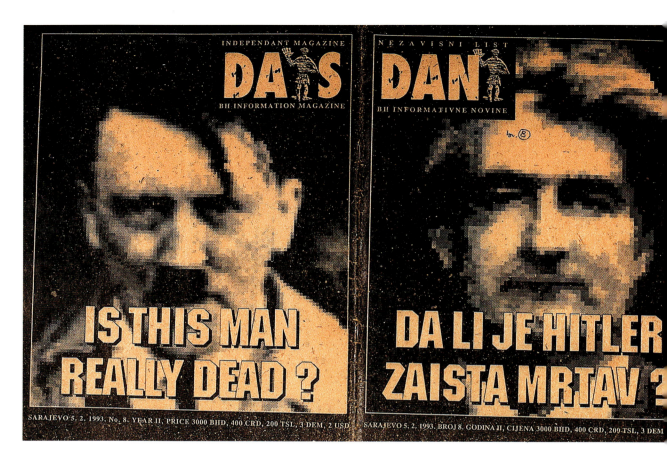

INDEPENDANT MAGAZINE

DAYS

BH INFORMATION MAGAZINE

NEZAVISNI LIST

DANI

BH INFORMATIVNE NOVINE

IS THIS MAN REALLY DEAD?

DA LI JE HITLER ZAISTA MRTAV ?

SARAJEVO 5. 2. 1993. No. 8. YEAR II. PRICE 3000 BHD, 400 CRD, 200 TSL, 3 DEM, 2 USD   SARAJEVO 5. 2. 1993. BROJ 8. GODINA II. CIJENA 3000 BHD, 400 CRD, 200 TSL, 3 DEM

BH Dani—or more simply *Dani* (Days) magazine—was launched in Sarajevo in August 1992. It was founded by one of Bosnia's now leading writers, Semezdin Mehmedinović, alongside Senad Pećanin, Ivan Lovrenović, Marko Vešović, and others: a united team comprised of Bosniaks as well as Bosnian Croats and Serbs. Independently run for eight years, *Dani* was one of the most respected news publications produced in Bosnia during the war. It won a number of important awards, and was financially supported by the Swedish branch of Helsinki Committee for Human Rights (now Civil Rights Defenders), Press Now, and Open Society Foundation. *Dani* was purchased by the powerful Oslobođenwje (Liberation) newsgroup in 2010.

ABOVE
IS HITLER REALLY DEAD?
Dani magazine (front and back covers)
Sarajevo, February 1993
Dani magazine's covers were often controversial. There was a great deal of discussion among the youthful staff about their subject and style, and feelings about this could be strong. The design group Trio created many of the covers for the magazine, including this one.

Radovan Karadžić was head of the Serbian Democratic Party. He was elected to political office in the first free elections in Bosnia in November 1990, when he styled himself the "leader of the Bosnian Serbs". He became a warlord, and forces loyal to him rampaged across Bosnia for the duration of the conflict. Democratic Bosnians of all ethnicities soon realised that Karadžić's brand of nationalism was thinly disguised fascism. It took Western European politicians much longer to acknowledge this (if they ever did). Early *Dani* editions used the front and back covers to great effect. Covers were almost punky until the magazine was eventually enlarged, when they became more mainstream, although often equally satirical.

OPPOSITE
DEATH TO TERRORISTS—MESSAGE LILIES
Ismet Hrvanović
Tuzla, 1992
Lilies have been the symbol of Bosnia since medieval times. After Bosnian Serbs and Croats adopted their neighbouring republics' flags, however, lilies became exclusively associated with Bosnia's Muslims. Today, lilies no longer appear on Bosnia's national flag, which was replaced in 1998 by a yellow and blue design with stars.

ГАРДА У ПОСАВИН

БРЧАНСКИ ЗИ

93

ИЗЛОЖБА РАТНЕ
ФОТОГРАФИЈЕ
Т.ПЕТЕРНЕК

пантери

TERORISTI·AGRESORI:
PUSTOŠ·GENOCID·UŽAS
BEZUMLJE·NOŽ·KRV·SMRT

POSAVINA GUARD
Photograph by T. Peternek
Posavina, 1993
A poster for Serb special forces group possibly active in Posavina, a region that stretches along the Sava river. This poster was shown to us in the house of a young Serb collector of war memorabilia. The war, he told us, had been a catastrophe.

SDS—JNA
Ismet Hrvanović
Tuzla, 1992
The text translates as:

> TERRORISTS—AGGRESSORS—WILDERNESS—GENOCIDE—HORROR—MINDLESSNESS—KNIFE—BLOOD—DEATH

The letter "S" is "C" in the Cyrillic alphabet, and the cross with four Cs is the national Serb emblem. The abbreviation stands for *Samo Sloga Srbe Spasava,* which means Only Unity Saves the Serbs. In this poster, the emblem is transformed into four snakes within an egg.

RIGHT AND OPPOSITE
AGGRESSION AGAINST BOSNIA-HERZEGOVINA
Trio
Sarajevo, 1992
Two posters with the same title but representing different faiths: Islam and Christianity.

FOLLOWING SPREAD: LEFT TO RIGHT
I AM "TO"—AND YOU?
Zdravko Novak
Tuzla, 1992
This poster was produced in Tuzla at the end of 1992 when there was an emphasis on creating propaganda material aimed at encouraging men to enlist. Three thousand copies of the poster were printed and circulated, but few remain. We found this one in the Bosnian Army Museum in Tuzla.

WE ARE "TO"
Territorial Defence (TO)
Sarajevo, 1992
TO stands for *Teritorijalna odbrana,* meaning Territorial Defence. TO also means "it", giving the title a double meaning—i.e. "We are it." In the former Yugoslavia, each republic had its own Territorial Defence. These reserve forces were made up of civilians who could be mobilised at short notice in the event of an invasion. On 4 April 1992, following attacks by the JNA and Serb paramilitaries, Bosnian President Alija Izetbegović mobilised the Bosnian TO—thereby providing a rudimentary military defence force. Although Radovan Karadžić claimed that Izetbegović's mobilisation constituted a declaration of war against Bosnia's Serbs, the war had already been initiated by Milošević.

AGRESIJA NA BOSNU I HERCEGOVINU

REPUBLIKA BOSNA I HERCEGOVINA

JA SAM TO, A TI?

TO-BIH

DIRECTION FREEDOM
Ismet Hrvanović
Tuzla, 1992
In this poster, the acronym for Karadžić's Bosnian Serb party is crossed out, and the slogan calls for freedom.

OPPOSITE: CLOCKWISE FROM TOP LEFT
GENERAL MOBILISATION
Anonymous
Bijeljina, 1992
The words on this Bosnian Serb call-up poster read:

GENERAL MOBILISATION FOR ALL—ABSOLUTELY ALL—MEN AGED BETWEEN 18 AND 60

An urgent message in a conventional poster design. The Bosnian Serb Army was created in the first few months of the war. It was supplied by the Serb-controlled Yugoslav People's Army (JNA) as well as freelance Serbian death squads.

BOSNIAN SERB ARMY CALENDAR
Anonymous
Bijeljina, 1994
A local Rambo lookalike from Bijeljina illustrates this Serb calendar. The Bijeljina massacre by Serbian death squads, in 1992 resulted in the murder and expulsion of its entire Bosnian Muslim population. This ethnically pure town is now under the control of Republika Srpska (Serb Republic).

ARMY OF THE REPUBLIC OF BOSNIA AND HERZEGOVINA
Anonymous
Tuzla, 1992
An early lithograph poster for the Bosnian Army.

PATRIOTIC LEAGUE—FIRST ANNIVERSARY
Fuad Kasumović
Tuzla, 1992
The Patriotic League was the armed wing of the Party of Democratic Action, the Muslim-dominated ruling party in Bosnia-Herzegovina. In 1992 the Army of the Republic of Bosnia and Herzegovina was created out of the Territorial Defence and the Patriotic League.

PRAVAC SLOBODA

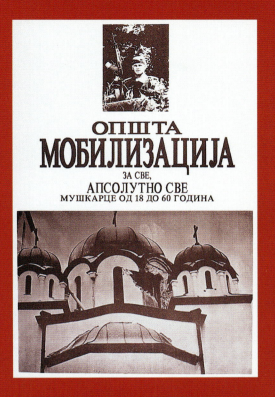

ОПШТА
МОБИЛИЗАЦИЈА
ЗА СВЕ,
АПСОЛУТНО СВЕ
МУШКАРЦЕ ОД 18 ДО 60 ГОДИНА

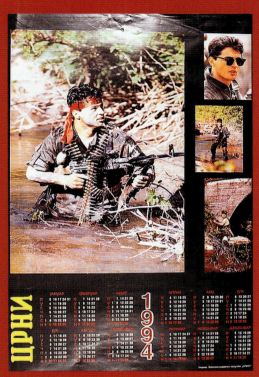

ЦРНИ 1994

PRVA GODIŠNJICA
PATRIOTSKE LIGE
TUZLA

25. 11. 1991 – 25. 11. 1992.

ARMIJA
REPUBLIKE
BOSNE I HERCEGOVINE

OPPOSITE
OUR FATHER'S IN THE HVO—AND YOURS?
Art Forces
Mostar, 1993
A call-up poster from early 1993 for the HVO in Herzegovina (southwestern Bosnia). HVO stands for *Hrvatsko vijeće odbrane* (Croatian Defence Council). It was formed in early 1992 to counter the Serb offensive in Herzegovina, but was later used to attack Muslims in Bosnia.

FOLLOWING SPREAD: LEFT
THE FATE OF BiH IS IN OUR HANDS—JOIN US!
Bato Bato
Tuzla, 1992
A recruitment poster for the Bosnian Army in Tuzla.

FOLLOWING SPREAD: RIGHT: CLOCKWISE FROM TOP LEFT
JOIN US
E. Husanović and D. Srabović
Tuzla, 1993
Another naive recruitment poster for the Bosnian Army. The girl is holding a bunch of Bosnia's symbolic lilies.

BOSNIA DEFENDS ITSELF ON THE DRINA
Nijaz Omerović
Gračanica, 1994
Historically, the Drina river formed the natural border separating Serbia and Bosnia.

WE ARE IN THE ARMY OF BiH—WHAT ABOUT YOU?
Nijaz Omerović
Gračanica, 1992
A recruitment poster for the Bosnian Army.

SECOND GLORIOUS MOUNTAIN BRIGADE
Anonymous
Place unknown, 1994
Celebrating a Bosnian regiment.

armija republike bosne i hercegovine

ARMIJA BIH
5.OG
TUZLA

SUDBINA BiH JE U NAŠIM RUKAMA
PRIDRUŽITE NAM SE !

pp FIBOS - braća Azapanić

Štampa / mina štamparija 2.korpus

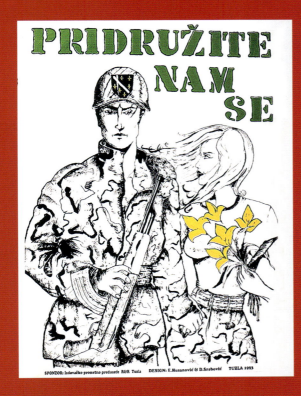

PRIDRUŽITE NAM SE

SPONZOR: Izdavačko prometno preduzeće R&R Tuzla   DESIGN: E.Husanović & D.Srabović   TUZLA 1993

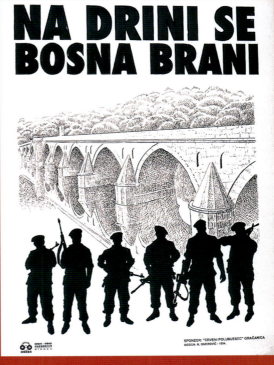

NA DRINI SE BOSNA BRANI

SPONZOR: "CRVENI POLUMJESEC" GRAČANICA
DESIGN: N. OMEROVIĆ - 1994.

DRUGA SLAVNA BRDSKA BRIGADA

22.05.1992. - 22.05.1994.

MI SMO U ARMIJI BIH A VI

Sponzor: "SPEKTRA" Gračanica
Design: N. Omerović

LILIES OF COURSE
Anonymous
Place unknown, 1992

The title of this poster refers to the ancient identity of Bosnia-Herzegovina: five golden lilies on a blue shield. After the war, these symbols were excluded from Bosnia's national flag because of Serb and Croat objections.

BOSNIA'S NEW IDENTITY
Photograph by Rupert Wolfe Murray
Gračanica, 2021

Bosnia's redesigned post-war flag perched on the top shelf of a café in Gračanica, close to Tuzla.

OPPOSITE
TOGETHER
Adin Šadić
Tuzla, 1992

Šadić, a Bosnian Muslim fighter in the Tuzla region, produced this image in 1992. He was a member of the Black Swans, an elite fighting force made up of Croats and Muslims. Šadić drew this picture before the Croat-Muslim split, which led to a tripartite war between Serbs, Croats, and Bosnian Muslims. The helmet is depicted in the red colours of the Croatian flag and Bosnia's blue and white *fleur-de-lis*—and may have been inspired by this poster (by Emeterio Melendreras) for the Republican *Ejercito Popular* from the Spanish Civil War period. The slogan here reads: All the Militias Merge in the People's Army. (Thanks to Carol Wells for pointing out this poster's connection to the Spanish Civil War, as well as another poster's links to the same war—see page 14.)

At the beginning of the Bosnian War, there was genuine optimism that Serb expansionism in could be defeated through the combined efforts of Bosnia's Croats and Muslims. In Herzegovina and central Bosnia, however, this hope was short-lived. In 1993 Franjo Tuđman, the president of Croatia, decided to annex Herzegovina; Bosnian Croat forces, the HVO, were ordered to attack their Muslim allies.

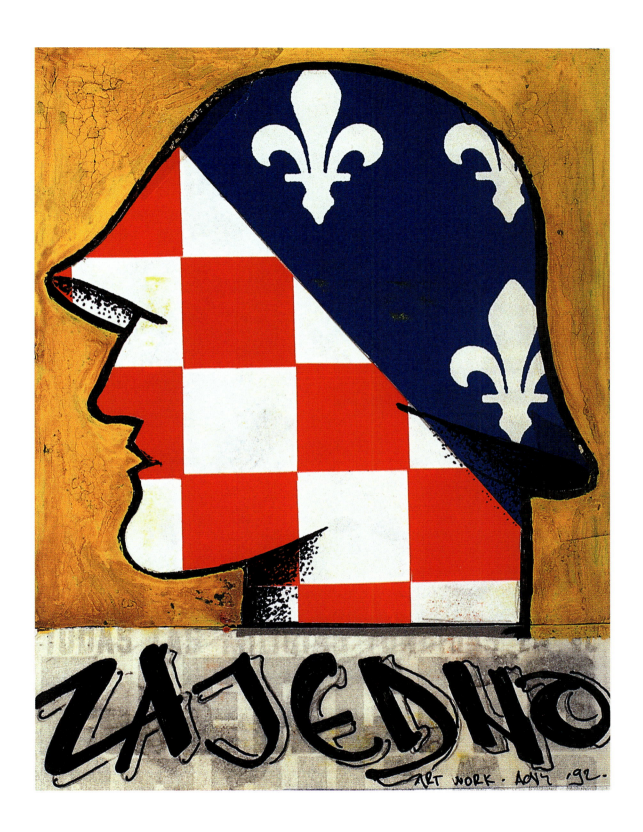

ZAJEDNO

ART WORK · AOÛT '92.

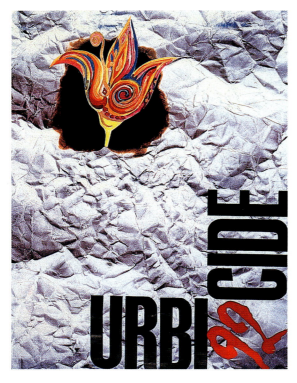

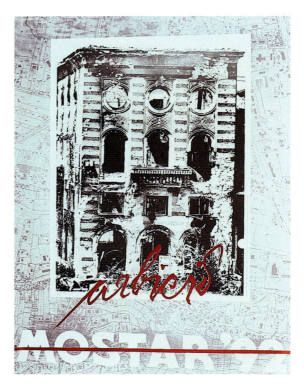

ABOVE: LEFT TO RIGHT
URBICIDE '92
Alija Hafizović Haf and Vanja Fundić Hafizović
Sarajevo, 1992
The term "urbicide" was coined during the Balkan wars as a way of describing the deliberate destruction of cities. Countless towns and cities were devastated by Serb and Croat forces in their attempts to destroy their former neighbour's history and culture, and achieve ethnic purity.

URBICIDE—MOSTAR '92
Željko Schnatinger
Photograph by Vladimir Kolapić
Mostar, 1992
Long before the Croats attacked east Mostar, the Serbs had shelled the city from the hills. This poster was one of a series of five drawing attention to the material damage done to Mostar during 1992.

OPPOSITE
SARAJEVO WINTER '93
Photograph by Kemal Hadžić
Sarajevo, 1993
On 25 August 1992, the Serb artillery targeted Sarajevo's National and University Library with incendiary shells. It took two days to burn. Most of the library's literature was destroyed, including thousands of irreplaceable Ottoman treasures and ancient land ownership records. Libraries and historical sites were targeted during the war as part of Serbia's attempt to eradicate Bosnia's Islamic heritage. The poster's title references an arts festival that was first held just after the 1984 Sarajevo Winter Olympics. The festival organisation produced many posters throughout the war and still plays an important role in Sarajevo's cultural life.

festival sarajevo
sarajevska zima '93 sarajevo winter '93

ABOVE: LEFT TO RIGHT
ONE AND ONLY ONE IS POSSIBLE: A FREE BOSNIA-HERZEGOVINA
Alija Hafizović Haf
Sarajevo, 1992
A propaganda poster advocating freedom, painted by a Bosnian Muslim artist in Sarajevo.

DEATH TO FASCISM—FREEDOM TO THE PEOPLE
Alija Hafizović Haf
Sarajevo, 1992
The title of this poster is adapted from a Communist slogan that was well known to the people of the former Yugoslavia.

RIGHT
NATIONAL AND UNIVERSITY LIBRARY
Photograph by Rupert Wolfe Murray
Sarajevo, 2021
Sarajevo's beautiful library has now been fully restored, even if the literary treasures it contained were lost.

OPPOSITE
SARAJEVO WINTER '93
Enis Selimović
Photograph by Kemal Hadžić
Sarajevo, 1993
This well-known poster for Sarajevo's important arts festival was photographed in the destroyed National and University Library, where concerts were often held before the war. The cellist, Vedran Smajlović, was a legendary figure in Sarajevo. He defied all odds by staging open-air concerts in Sarajevo at the height of the conflict.

festival sarajevo
sarajevska zima '93 ✳ sarajevo winter '93

HEEELP
Began Turbić
Tuzla, 1992
An ironic take on the Orthodox Christian style cross, here turned into a swastika by the addition of peasant-made brushes. Bosnia's *fleur-de-lis* makes a discreet appearance at the bottom of the image—like a new shoot in danger of being swept up by the contraption above.

SHOO, CHICKEN HERDERS!
Territorial Defence (TO)
Sarajevo, 1992
Led by Mirko Jović, the White Eagles (also known as The Avengers) was one of many Serbian death squads operating in Bosnia. They were linked to the Belgrade based Serbian National Renewal party and had a fierce reputation. In 1992, the White Eagles attacked Sarajevo, where they were beaten for the first time in their short but violent history. A journalist asked a member of the Bosnian special forces how they had managed to defeat this supposedly invincible unit. "What eagles?" he replied, "They're just chickens!"

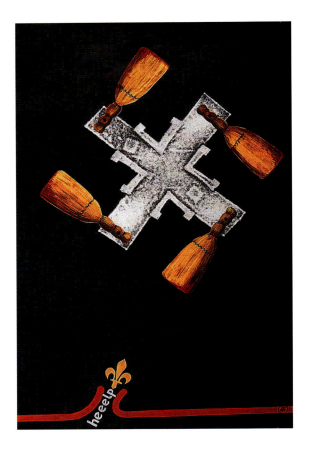

IŠ KOKOŠARI !

TO BiH

RIGHT: TOP TO BOTTOM
OATH
Began Turbić
Tuzla, 1992

Dating from the 12th–15th centuries, there are some 60,000 *stećci* tombstones in Bosnia-Herzegovina. Although these medieval tombstones can be found in other parts of the Western Balkans, there are roughly six times as many within Bosnia as outside. *Stećci* (*stećak* in the singular) are considered evidence of the country's ancient culture before it was colonised by successive foreign empires. Many of these stones show the same mysterious human figure raising its gigantic right hand. The meaning of this gesture remains unclear.

STEĆAK
Photograph by Rupert Wolfe Murray
Stolac, 2021

A *stećak* graffitied on a destroyed building in Stolac, Herzegovina. During the Bosnian War, Croat extremists ethnically cleansed the town and destroyed many monuments—including all four of the town's mosques, which dated from the 16th–18th century, and an Orthodox church.

OPPOSITE
ARMY OF BiH
Srdanović
Zenica, 1993

In this poster, a Bosnian soldier touches the hand imprint on a *stećak*. The heraldic shield on the soldier's arm is the old emblem of Bosnia, which was adopted in 1992 by the newly independent state. The emblem was, however, rejected by Serbs as well as Croats in those areas of Bosnia they controlled, as each sought to secede from Bosnia-Herzegovina. The Serbian and Croatian minorities took their emblems from the neighbouring republics, which had backed them in the war. Also, both parties were keen to suppress any symbols of ancient Bosnian existence.

FOLLOWING SPREAD: LEFT TO RIGHT
THEY CAN DESTROY OUR HOMES BUT NOT OUR HEARTS!
Territorial Defence (TO)
Sarajevo, 1992

This poster was produced by the *Teritorijalna odbrana* (Territorial Defence or TO). The Territorial Defence was a civilian fighting force that could be mobilised in the event of a foreign invasion. It existed in the former Yugoslavia long before the country started to break apart in the 1990s, and became the core of the Bosnian Army when war broke out.

WE WILL WIN
Territorial Defence (TO)
Sarajevo, 1992

A simple statement of intent—designed, printed, and distributed by Sarajevo's Territorial Defence force.

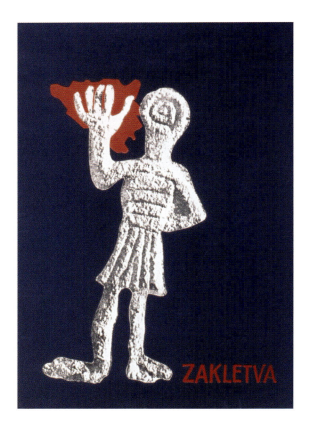

MOGU NAM KUĆU SRUŠITI, ALI SRCE NE!

(Riječi branioca Sarajeva sa Širokače)

TO BiH

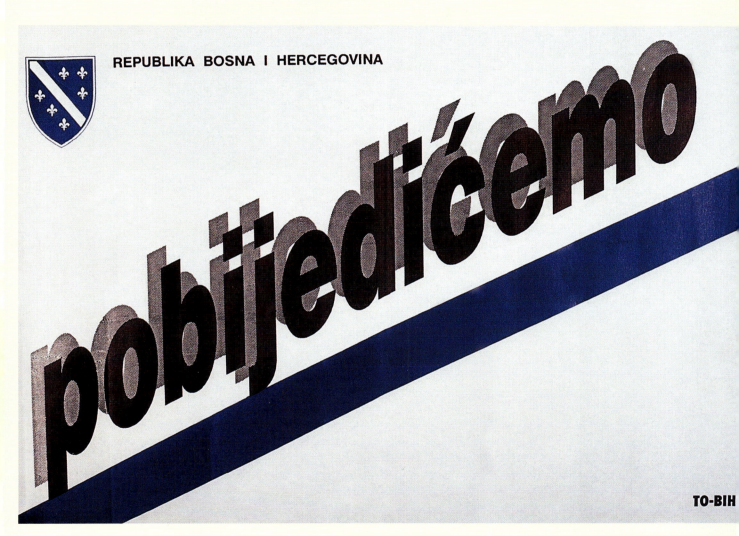

RIGHT
SUADA AND OLGA BRIDGE
Photograph by Rupert Wolfe Murray
Sarajevo, 2021
The Sarajevan bridge renamed in memory of Suada
Dilberović and Olga Sučić.

OPPOSITE
PERFECT!
Asim Đelilović
Travnik, 1992
This poster was inspired by the deaths of Suada
Dilberović and Olga Sučić in Sarajevo on 5 April 1992.
Dilberović, a 23-year-old Bosniak medical student, was
shot by a sniper during a peace demonstration. Another
young woman, Olga Sučić, was killed at the same peace
march on the same day—the day before the Bosnian War
officially began. These two young women were the first
people connected with the secession of Bosnia to die
violently in Sarajevo, and their deaths shocked those who
had not believed that full-scale war was possible. One
of Sarajevo's bridges over the Miljacka river, previously
called Vrbanja Bridge, was later renamed Suada and
Olga Bridge. The sniper in this poster wears glasses,
symbolising the involvement of Serb intellectuals in the
destruction of Bosnia-Herzegovina. The word in the
thought bubble is a play, in the Cyrillic alphabet, between
the words "perfect" (савршен) and "Sarajevo" (Сарајево).

Enjoy Sara-jevo

1993

Coca-Cola logo redesigned by "Trio" Sarajevo

ABOVE
ENJOY SARA-JEVO (POSTCARD)
Trio
Sarajevo, 1993
Trio was a Sarajevo-based design and advertising company started by Bojan and Dada Hadžihalilović. They partnered with Lejla Mulabegović in 1985. (Trio later evolved into an advertising company called Fabrika, which at the time of writing is still active.) Trio's members rarely left the city during Sarajevo's four-year siege (although Mulabegović emigrated to Switzerland) and during this time they produced many images. The most renowned of these is a series of 40 postcards known as *Greetings from Sarajevo;* all were redesigns of iconic imagery. Trio adopted the postcard format (as Bojan Hadžihalilović makes clear in his Foreword to this book on page 9) for several reasons: Sarajevo had been under siege for over a year and a half and there was a shortage of paper and ink in the city; Trio also wanted an image that could easily be sent out of the city, to reach as many people as possible in the outside world.

OPPOSITE: TOP TO BOTTOM
ENJOY SARA-JEVO (POSTER)
Trio
Sarajevo, 1993
This poster version of the Coca-Cola redesign was printed on an old Yugoslav People's Army (JNA) map. Perhaps there was also something ironic about this choice of paper, considering the Serb-controlled JNA initiated the siege of Sarajevo.

WELCOME TO SARAJEVO
Asim Đelilović
Travnik, 1992
An ironic statement by Travnik's leading wartime graphic designer. This slogan was scrawled as graffiti on bullet-riddled walls around Sarajevo during the siege. WELCOME TO HELL was another popular greeting.

FOLLOWING SPREAD
SARAJEVO CITY MAP
Anonymous
Sarajevo, 1992
This tourist map of Sarajevo was purchased by the author outside the heavily fortified TV Centre in January 1996, a few weeks after the Dayton Agreement was signed. Note the hand-drawn front lines and the dotted "Dayton Line" on the right-hand side of the map. During the conflict, vendors did a brisk trade selling these maps to aid workers and journalists. The vendors would draw the latest front lines in pencil as soon as the situation changed. In this way, they could simply rub out the lines and draw in new ones without destroying their stock of maps. These were maps that could save lives. As can be seen here, the Bosnian Serb forces occupied neighbourhoods in the city centre, enabling close-range sniping.

PAGES 104–105
FAMA MAP
Suada Kapić
Sarajevo, 1996
This map became very well-known; it was even displayed in the offices of the International Criminal Tribunal for the former Yugoslavia in The Hague. Serb forces surrounded Sarajevo on 5 April 1992 and put the city under a siege that lasted until 29 February 1996. It was the longest siege in modern times, lasting a total of 1,425 days—553 days longer than the infamous siege of Leningrad during World War II. The Serb forces had more than 250 tanks, over 100 mortars, anti-aircraft guns, and innumerable well-trained snipers ranged around the city. The red circles on the map indicate particularly dangerous crossroads that pedestrians had to sprint across in fear of the snipers. On the back of the map, it states that 10,615 people were killed in Sarajevo, including 1,601 children, with more than 50,000 wounded. More recently, the UN calculated that a total of 13,952 people were killed during the siege: 5,434 civilians, 6,137 Bosnian Army soldiers, and 2,241 besieging Serb military personnel.

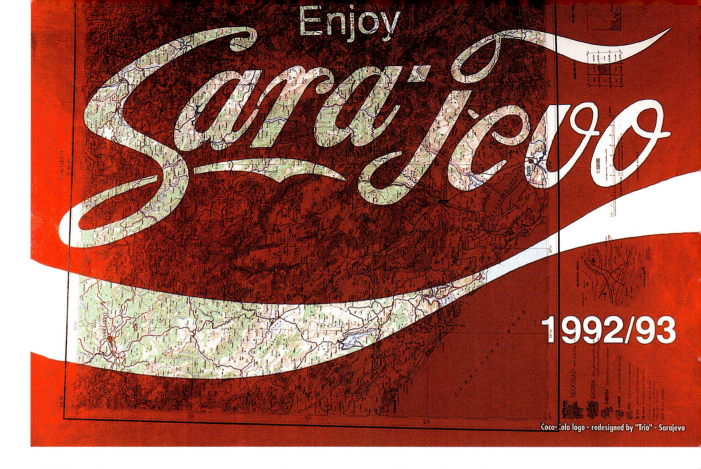

Enjoy Sarajevo

1992/93

Coca-Cola logo - redesigned by "Trio" - Sarajevo

Welcome to Sarajevo

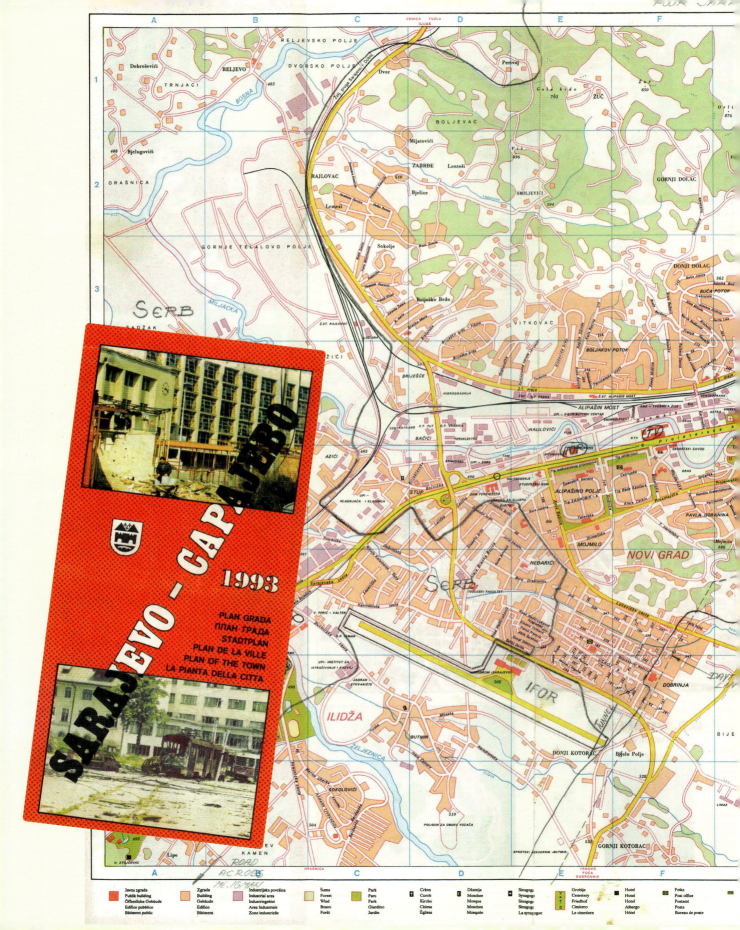

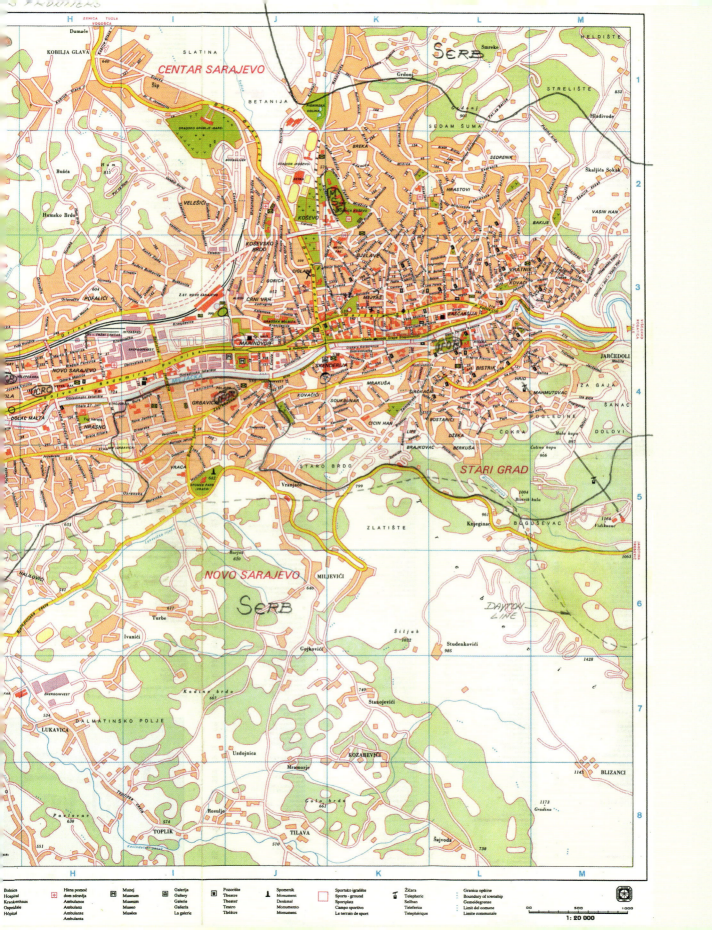

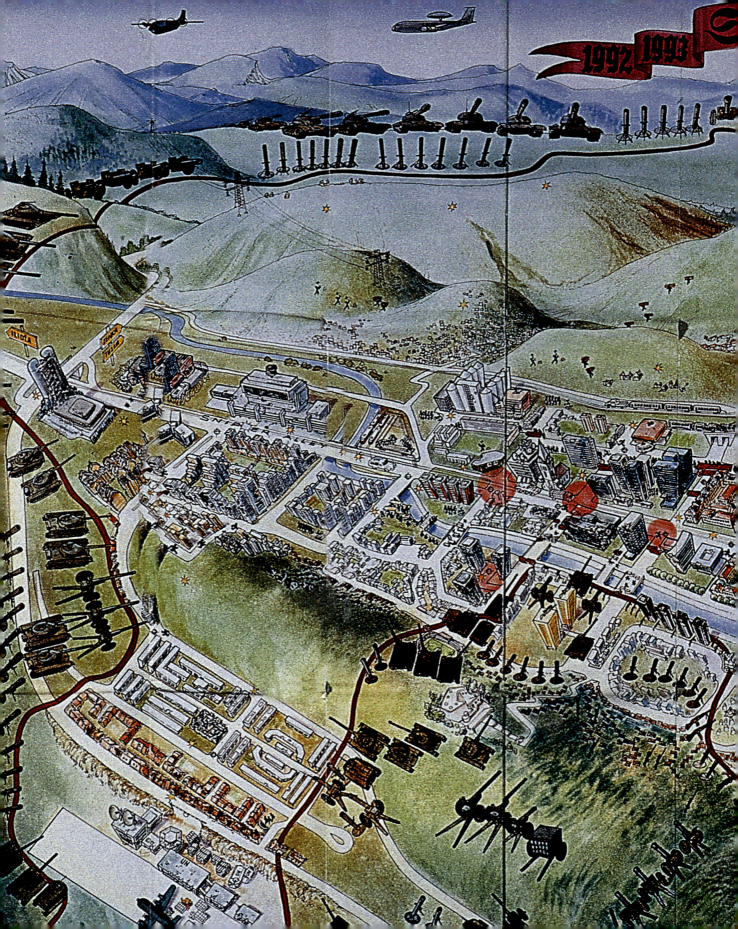

FIREWOOD; *Photograph by Christian Maréchal; Sarajevo, 1992*
Besieged Sarajevans cutting down trees for firewood in the bitter winter of 1992. Christian Maréchal, the photographer of this image—much like Steven Gordon, who took the photos of posters for this book (see his Afterword on page 291)—is a fine example of someone who gave up the comforts of a secure life in Western Europe and went to Bosnia to try to make a difference. Maréchal was working as an advertising executive in London, when he felt the need to go to Sarajevo and make portraits of people struggling to survive.

ABOVE
SARA-JE-VO
Anonymous
Sarajevo, 1996
A typographic detail from a post-war poster for an event at Obala Art Center, Sarajevo.

RIGHT: TOP TO BOTTOM
INTERNATIONAL THEATRE AND FILM FESTIVAL
Anonymous
Sarajevo, 1993
Despite the terrible circumstances, Bosnian cultural events continued to be organised and attended—especially in Sarajevo. This one uses the image of boys diving into the river, an activity that was also very popular in Mostar.

SUMMER IN OUR THEATRE
Anonymous
Sarajevo, 1993
A poster for a cultural festival in the Chamber Theatre during the height of the siege of Sarajevo. The event featured *The Memoirs of a Saint,* by René Magritte.

OPPOSITE
SARAJEVO DREAM AND REALITY
Anonymous
Sarajevo, 1994
This poster is for an exhibition of architecture, playfully subtitled *WAR*CHITECURE. The event was sponsored by Soros Open Society Foundation, Bosnia.

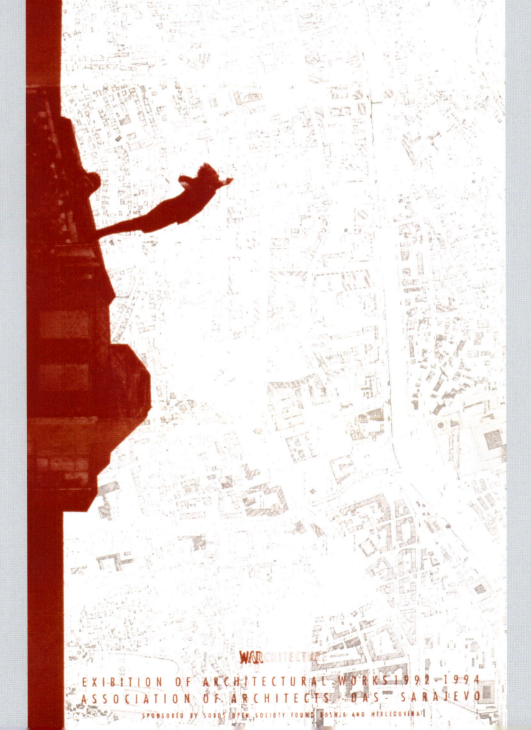

SARAJEVO
DREAM AND REALITY

WARCHITECTURE

EXIBITION OF ARCHITECTURAL WORKS 1992-1994
ASSOCIATION OF ARCHITECTS DAS- SARAJEVO
SPONSORED BY SOROS OPEN SOCIETY FOUND BOSNIA AND HERCEGOVINA

BOSNIA WILL LIVE

BOSNIA WILL LIVE

BOSNIA WILL LIVE

Selma Arnautović, Zaire
Novembra 1992.

ABOVE AND RIGHT
BOSNIA WILL LIVE
Selma Arnautović-Harrington
Zaire, 1992
Many Bosnians living outside the country also designed posters. Although we collected little of this work, these three small posters, hand printed at the beginning of the war, were sent to us by a Bosnian woman living at that time in Zaire (now Democratic Republic of the Congo).

OPPOSITE
MOTHER
Edin Dervišević
Tuzla, 1992
A poster for a theatre play in Tuzla, northeast Bosnia. The image contrasts an ancient Bosnian *stećak* tombstone with nightmarish figures that suggest ghosts, war, and death—and obliquely remind us of Pablo Picasso's 1937 Spanish Civil War painting, *Guernica*. (Picasso's anti-fascist masterpiece makes another appearance in a poster on page 137.) Because Sarajevo received most of the international attention during the war, it is often overlooked that cultural and artistic events were also organised in many other Bosnian cities and towns. These events were well-attended by the public, and often under difficult circumstances.

Generalni sponzor predstave

Design: Edin Dervišević

АМУРАДБЕГОВИК

MAJKA

РЕЖИЈА ВЛАДО КЕРОШЕВИК

IGRAJU: DRAGAN DŽANKIĆ   MILENKO ILIKTAREVIĆ   MILICA KEROŠEVIĆ
MUHAREM OSMIĆ 30 godina   ZORAN TEŠIĆ   NENAD TOMIĆ BAISA BAKI

RIGHT

HELP—NOW OR NEVER
Enis Selimović
Sarajevo, 1993

Enis Selimović, the designer of this poster, is best known for his poster of a cellist in the ruins of the National and University Library in Sarajevo (see page 91).

OPPOSITE

SARAJEVO 92 93 9?
Čedomir Kostović
USA, 1993

The unfinished date on this poster's typography seems to ask when the siege of Sarajevo will end (it would continue for another three years, until February 1996). The slogan along the bottom references the title of a film made in 1982 about political turmoil in Indonesia: *The Year of Living Dangerously*.

SARAJEVO

92 93 9?

years of dangerous living

RIGHT
KISS
Mladina magazine
Caricature by Tomaž Lavrič
Slovenia, May 1995

President Slobodan Milošević of Serbia and his Croatian counterpart, Franjo Tuđman, may have been sworn enemies—both enabling and financing the mass murder of one another's citizens—but they were cut from the same cloth when it came to Bosnia-Herzegovina; that is to say they both wanted parts of Bosnia for themselves. These two Communist-turned-nationalist strongmen had been moving closer together since they signed a UN-sponsored pact in January 1994. United Nations negotiators—including Thorvald Stoltenberg, a skilled Norwegian politician, and the Japanese diplomat Yasushi Akashi (whose name would crop up again in 1995 during the abandonment of Srebrenica and Žepa)—created a series of mechanisms that allowed Serbia and Croatia to stop fighting one another. Unfortunately, the pact had the side effect of freeing up each side's ability to attack Bosnia's Muslims with even greater efficiency. This caricature (art direction by Trio studios) was inspired by the iconic 1979 photo of President Leonid Brezhnev of the USSR kissing his East German counterpart Erich Honecker. It appeared on the cover of the left-wing Slovenian magazine, *Mladina,* based in Ljubljana. *Mladina,* founded in the 1920s, has repeatedly stood up to nationalism.

LEO NEWS
Malik "Kula" Kulenović
Sarajevo, 1993–94

Kula, as he was locally known, was a legendary figure in Sarajevo. He never left the city during the siege and produced these handmade news bulletins throughout the war, posting them in a sheltered street where Serb snipers couldn't spot him. His "paper" was called *Leo News,* and each daily edition was numbered according to the day of the siege. Because of the lack of newspapers during the war—as well as the lack of electricity for TV and radio—*Leo News* became an important source of information. *Leo News* titles were written in a combination of Cyrillic and Latin scripts to signify unity. As such, *Leo News* made a powerful political statement. Because of its colloquial use of language, we haven't offered many translations here.

OPPOSITE: CLOCKWISE FROM TOP LEFT
DAY 337
Sarajevo, 1993

DAY 425
Sarajevo, 1993

DAY 613
Sarajevo, 1993

DAY 672
Sarajevo, 1994

FOLLOWING SPREAD: LEFT TO RIGHT
DAY 531
Sarajevo, 1993

DAY 308
Sarajevo, 1993

QUESTIONNAIRE III
Sarajevo, 1993
Kula posted several questionnaires. This one asks:

WHY DID WE FIGHT?
a) FOR FREEDOM...
b) FOR AN INDEPENDENT BiH...
c) FOR A BUSINESS OFFICE...
d) FOR A COUNTRY OF THREE NATIONS...

Passers-by would contribute ironic, humorous and sometimes surreal answers.

PAGES 120–121
WE HAVE A CHANCE OF SURVIVAL
Sarajevo, 1992

"LEO NEWS" "VIJESTI" Kula93 "ВЕСТИ" "ILVJEŠĆA"

337 · SUBOTA 27/02/93.

DOBRO JUTRO SUBOTARI!

KAKO VAŠE SKIJE? ŠTA JE SA VIKENDICOM NA PALAMA, JAHORINI, RAKOVICI? TAČNO, TO SU SUVIŠNA PITANJA! JEDINO PITANJE JE ISPRAVNO, KOLIKO JE DALEK **MIR? MIR? MIR?**

NEW YORK: DELEGACIJA BiH DOBRO SASTAVLJENA! MILE A. 12 GRUDA IMA PRIGOVOR!

PREGOVORI U ZAVRŠNICI?

NA DANAŠNJI DAN 27/02/92. PRIJE 365 DANA!

LISABON

BiH: DRŽAVA TRIJU DRŽAVA

A DANAS?
A DANAS?
A DANAS?
A DANAS?
A DAHAC?
A DANASKE?

TELEFAX: BILLOVI PAKETI OD NEDJELJE! AKO TRAŽITE SVOJ PAKET, NAZOVITE IBRU S JEDNIM S. DANI br.9. PRODANI PO DRUGI PUT!!! "HAMO, HAMO, KAD ĆE XII KRUG?"

LEO NEWS "KULA VIJESTI" C MIŠ "ВЕСТИ" "IZVJEŠĆA" 5425 Kula93 PETAK 02/06/1993. 372

DOBRO JUTRO, OTPISANI!

GORAŽDE, MOSTAR, TESLIĆ, BRČKO, TOGA VIŠE NEMA NI NA CNN, RTL, RTL1-U, EUROPA SE UMORILA. VRIJEME PROLAZI, A GODIŠNJI ODMORI SE PRIBLIŽAVAJU. VI STE ZABORAVILI, ALI EUROPEJCI NISU DA OBILAZE AGENCIJE I PREURCU KATALOGE. NIHOU CILJ JE SVE, SAMO NE, PROSTORI CRNE RUPE. ONI SU ODABRALI ŽIVOT, A NAMA SU RONULI 1280. SMRT NA TISUĆU NAČINA. SVIJET JE IST NAŠE KRVI, TV JE GASI, KAD SU NAJAVLJENA IZVJEŠĆA IZ NAŠIH KRAJEVA. BRIGA NAŠIH MAJKI ZA SPAS DJECE KROZ UKIDANJE EMBARGA. SVIJET NEĆE NI POKUŠATI SHVATITI. AKO VEĆ TOLIKA UBOJSTVA PA I EVENTUALNO KOLEKTIVNO SAMOUBOJSTVO NEĆE PROBUDITI EUROPU ILI MOŽDA INTERVENCIJU. ZAZIVATI POMAŽNO SE OKRENUTI SEBI. POKUŠAVAJU GRAĐANI DEMOKRATSKE DRŽAVE IZAZVATI EUROPU. B. PERIĆ KAŽE 8. EUROPA NEMA VIŠE U NAŠE SPOSOBNOSTI DA ŽIVIMO U DEMOKRATSKOM DRUŠTVU. TO JE JEDAN RAZLOG OTPORA. TO JE PRIDRUŽIMO. AKO MI SAMI DAJEMO DO ZNANJA KAKO DEMOKRATIJOM NE UMIJEMO DA RUKUJEMO, DA SE U NJOJ NE SNALAZIMO, DA STOGA NIJE MI POTREBNA, ČAK, I DA OVA NIJE U NAŠEM NACIONALNOM INTERESU, ŠTA DO DRUGI OČEKIVATI ZA UTJEHU, NA REDU ZA OTPIS SLIJEDE...

PALE: UJEVIK SESTRA MU, PO SLIJETANJU U BOSNU ILI PRVO RADOVANA III. INALI RO DA IH UPUTI PRVO U SARAJEVO DA...

SVIJET: HARFI-CIA U SOFIJI, HERD U BUKUREŠTU, POŽURITE U BEOGRAD, PRIŠTINU, SKOPJE... MI QUIŠMO STRPLJENJE!

KAKANJ: NEMA LUGIĆA, NEMA STRUJE! GDJE SI ČENGA?

SA KRONIKA: UGLA NEMA, DRVA NEMA, A ZIMA IDE...

VRIJEME: RASPLETA NIJE DALEKO! ALI KO ĆE TO DOČEKATI?

S99 945 "VIJESTI" ВЕСТИ IZVJEŠĆA НАВЕRI LEO NEWS Kula93 642 VII DAN 06/02/94 24 ŠA BAN

DOBRO JUTRO, DAVITELJI!

KAKO STE SPAVALI? MIRNO SPAVATE! LAŽ! ČITAVU NOĆ STE SE PREVRTALI, JER VAS BRINE STANJE AKCIJA U TOKIJU. VREMENSKA RAZLIKA VAS UBI. FRANKFURTSKA BERZA I PAD CIJENE ZLATA VAS JE SKORO UDAVIO. CIJENA ALUMINIJUMA RASTE. KONZERVE ĆE BITI SKUPLJE, A UGOVOR SA HUMANITARCIMA KOJI SE UBIŠE DA POMOGNU NARODIMA, CRNE RUPE, NEĆE IMATI PLANIRANI PROFIT, NIŠTA ZATO. NAĆI ĆE KONZERVE IZ '63. BALKANCI I ONAKO, MOGU SVE POJESTI, MLIJEKO IZ ČERNOBILA, OTPAD IZ NJEMAČKE, SMEĆE FRANCUSKO. SVEZALI STE RUKE NAPAĆENOM NARODU-BOSNE, OMČU STAVILI OKO VRATA, POJAS OKO HLAČA IZGLADNJELIH-PRITEGLI, VI STE ČISTI, ČISTIH RUKU, BELIH KRAGNI, PLAVIH KOŠULJA, SVILENIH MARAMA OKO VRATA, KAD POVRAĆATE POSLIJE OBILNOG OBJEDA, DISKRETNO POVLAČITE MARAMU NA USTA. DŽELATE STE NAŠLI U FAŠIZMU, NEŽIVUĆENIM NACIONALISTIMA, PORAŽENIM SEDAĆIMA, ŽEDNIM OSVETE GRADU, POKRIVATE SE PAPIRIMA, ODLUKAMA, BEZ IZVRŠENJA. VARATE SEBE I DRUGE. I DOK OMĆE ZAMJENUJE GRANATE, UREDNO BRIŽETE U NOTESE: 296 GRANATA, 66 MRTVIH, 150 NOVIH INVALIDA. VI DAVITE-VI UBIJATE! ALI OVAJ GRAD OVI LJUDI IZDRŽAĆE! BIT ĆE NIJEMI SVJEDOCI VAŠE PROPASTI. UMRIJET ĆETE U VATRI FAŠIZMA, DAVITELJI NAŠI!

SMRT FAŠIZMU-SLOBODA NARODU!

R99 945 "VIJESTI" ВЕСТИ "IZVJEŠĆA" 613 LEO NEWS Kula93 IV DAN 09/12/93

DOBRO JUTRO, BANJA LUKA!

ČUJEMO LI SE? VRAĆA SE ČUJEMO. SAMO DO BREZE. UZ TOHOU DINA I VJETRA IZ KANJONA-NOŽDA DO ZENICE. DIJETE SA MARIJIN DVORA ZBUNJENO PITA TATU:
– A GDJE JE TA BANJA LUKA? – JEL TO TAMO, GDJE BRODOVI PRISTAJU? – NE SMIJE-TO JE NAJLJEPŠI GRAD U BOSNU.
– TO! – LJEPOTICA KOJA SE UMIVALA NA VRBASU, ČEŠLJALA UZ VJETAR, OBLAČILA U BIJELI KAPUT ZIMI, U LIPNJU MIRISALA NA LIPU, U AUGUSTU NA BOSTAN. S JESENI ZLATOM KITILA. IMALA GOSPODSKU ULICU, A SAD ULICU SUBARA. BIO JE TO CENTAR KRAJINE, DUŠA BOSNE. SAD JE TO EPICENTAR BEZUHIJA I RJANJA DUŠA. GRAD HAVERA DO HAVERA, GRAD ČEVAPA BANJALUČKIH. U SARAJEVU DESET I POLA, TAMO TRI PUTA PO ČETIRI, SA BATEROM I LUKOM. ŠEHER, BORIK, BUDŽAK, ZALUŽANI, KESTEN, BARDGEN, PREDO..., DUGA DO DUGA, MINARET DO MINARETA. SAD PITAJMO – ŠTA JE S NJOM? NE ZNAM! NE ZNA! GOSPODSKE NEHA. NEMA MINARETA. A I ŠTO ĆE!! ZMIJANJE SE SPUSTILO U GRAD. OVI NIKAD NISU GLEDALI GORE, SAMO DOLE. ANIMA MINARET NE TREBA DA SLUŽI KAO ORIJENTIR. ONI ZA KANDILOM IDU. OPIJENI NJIHOM I TAMJANOM NE VIDE DA HODE PUSTIM ULICAMA. BANJA LUKU SU NAPUSTILI SVI ONI KOJI VOLE NJENA ČETIRI GODIŠNJA DOBA. ONI ŠTO PAMET I OBRAZ SAČUVAŠE ONI ŠTO PLATIŠE (200 DEN I S HAZLOM VREĆOM STIGOŠE U TURSKU. NAPUSTILI SU JE ONI ŠTO NISU NIKAD ŽIVALI LJEPOTICU – LJUBIT. U SUSPOMENOM JE TEŠKO ŽIVJETI, A BEZ BANJA LUKE JOŠ TEŽE.

KRONIKA UŽASA: (IZ SPOMENARA)
AMERIKI: AMBASADOR U BiH ODETAŠIRAN U BEĆU TVRDI DA SU USA SPREMNE PRIMITI 3000 ZAROBLJENIKA. DO SADA PRIMILENO 1500. OSTAJE NEJASNO ŠTO SA 250.000 SARAJLIJA?
SVIJET: BiH JE JEDINSTVENA, DEMOKRATSKA PRIVATNA ČLANICA UN-A. SARAJEVO NEDJELJNO, SE PRU SDE SE NE POPUNI.
HAG: PRIJE SUĐENJA ZLOČINCIMA TREBA PRIKUPITI MIŠLJENJA RAZNIČKE PORUKA. ONIM DA DILEO NORMALAN!
SA DAKA H: BIT ĆE GASA, STRUJE, DUVA, HODE. ČUJEMO MI... – KAŽU PREGOVARAČI-VADIM VIST KAO STRPLJENJE I DODAJU PREKO U85 PAKETA AGASA? UMMER...

VRIJEME: JE ZA TVRĐAVU-HVALA MEŠA!

"LEO NEWS" Kulag3

RADIO 99 "95"

"VIJESTI" "BESTI" IZVJEŠĆA

531 SUBOTA 18/09/93

DOBRO JUTRO, EUROPO!

ŽESTOK RITAM JUTRA, RATNOG SARAJEVA. SLUŠAM RADIO.
MUZIKA SRETNOG VREMENA. MUZIKA OPTIMIZMA I DRAGA IMENA:
HAMO, RADENKO, FUDO, ZOLA, MESAR I SARMER FAZLA...
HOR, GLASOVI MLADOSTI, GLASOVI AMRE, AMELE, ISPUNJAVAJU
SOBIČAK. I KROZ OTVOREN PROZOR, ŠIRE SE GRADOM. SREĆA JE
ŽIV STIĆI DO PRVE LINIJE. SREĆA JE OTVORITI KONZERVU.
SREĆA JE PISMO SINA, DOBITI. LUDILO JE ČUTI: TATA, JEL' JOŠ KOJI
PEDERSKI METAK U SOBU, UŠO ?! - JESU LI GELERI SLJIVU, OTRESLI ?

VALOVI I MUZIKA, UZBUĐUJU ME. DIŠEM. GUTAM ZRAK. ŠIRIM
RUKE. HUMI MJE BOGZNA KAKVA. ZADNJA KONZERVA, ZELENA,
MASNIH SLOVA - POKLON TALIJANSKE VLADE - DONO DEL GOVERNO
ITALIANO', PUKLA JE SINOĆ UZ UNHKR LUK I PIVO MALO SARAJEVSKO.
ROK UPOTREBE KONZERVE DAVNO JE PROŠAO. ROK UNIŠTENJA GRADA,
NJEGOVOG DUHA, MLADOSTI, ZNANJA JE GOSPODO EUROPEJCI, ISTEKAO.
VAŠE OGLEDALO I VAŠ JUTARNJI LIK U NJEMU NIKAD NEĆE BITI TAKO
LIJEPO, KAO ŠTO JE TO DANAS PROBUĐENI STANOVNIK SARAJEVA.
NI SLOMLJENO OGLEDALO, NE MOŽE SAKRITI LJEPOTU NJEGOVOG LICA
SJAJ U OČIMA.
DANAS SLAVIMO, DANAS JE OPET EUROPA TU I MI U NJOJ.
DANAS SMO PONOVO NA VALOVIMA RADIO 99.

KRONIKA UŽASA
(12 DNEVNIKA SLUŠAMO NA ČEKANJU)

ZAGREB: - IZVJEŠTAJ SA SLUŽBENOG PUTA - PRIHVAĆEN. RIZNICA PERA
JA POTPISA PRIMJERA, DEKLARACIJA - BOGATIJA ZA DVA PERA.
- ŠKOLSKA GODINA JE DUGA, A PERA TE TROŠE!

MOSTAR: - ŽIVO ODUŠEVLJENJE POZDRAVOM, POTPISIVANJE - GRANATAMA!
MOSTARKE DUŠE I DANAS OTIŠLE U NEBO.

PALE: - PALEOLITI' DVIJE LINIJE RAZGRANIČENJA OTVORILI PRIMIRJE.
- GRANATAMA I SIMIĆHA STAVLJEN JE POTPIS SIGURNO.

BIHAĆ: AUTONOMAŠI BEZ REFERENDUMA.

BANJA LUKA: UHVAĆEN ZEC! RADOVAN RUČAGU U BOSNI.
- KOSTI POKUPILI BOJOVNICI PRAVOSLAVLJA 'I ODNIJELI NA NAJVIŠI

EEZ: PARLAMENT GLASAO ZA VOJNU INTERVENCIJU! HAFAAJ

SARHONIKA: - U GRADU SU SAFARI - MENJOVI! ČUVAJTE SE!   PAZI NA
- USKORO OKLOPNI VLAK ZA ZENICU!   HLOR!
- NA SKENDERIJI - DVA FRANCUZA U MILJACKI!
- NAKON BURNE NOĆI - BILO JE TO JUČER SVAJLJESTI!
- TKO NE ZNA TENIS IGRATI - MOŽE DA UĐU UZ TENIS 2.
- KONVOJI ZA 15 DANA - INSALAH!!!

VRIJEME JE POTPISA - IDITE MATIČARU !

"LEO NEWS" Kulag3

"VIJESTI" "BESTI" IZVJEŠĆA

308 PETAK 29/01/93

DANAS JE 290-ti DAN,
KAKO JE OVAJ MALI GRAĐANIN
SARAJEVA, OTIŠAO U
EUROPU.

OTIŠAO JE, A U PISMU PIŠE:

"STALNO MISLIM NA TEBE,
DRAGI MOJ TATA, NA MOJE
SARAJEVO I NA MOJU BiH."

NE OKREĆI SE SINE!

SARHONIKA: NA KONFERENCIJI ZA TISAK I RTV,
VRLI NAM G. HAMO PORUČUJE:

"SABUR - SELANET" *

EKSKLUZIVNO

★ VIDI A. ŠKALJIĆ - TURCIZMI U SH STR 539
- U VELJAČI BIT ĆE I SOMUNA.

.L.N. BUDITE PAŽLJIVI: OVO NIJE
LED, NIJE NI SNIJEG. OVO SU
DUŠE STANOVNIKA SARAJEVA.

- IZ VIK'a : OSTAVI PREDU, Mr. GURM.
FAĆAJ SE METLE I ČISTI SVOJU
AVLIJU.

- IRFO : NEŠ TI MENI PREDU.
HAMO, PREDO & A.J. FURAMO
NA EUROVIZIJU '93.

.L.N. : STA JE SA JUKINOM RAJOM ?

"LEO NEWS"
kul a93

ANKETA - BR. 3.
UPIŠITE!

ZAŠTO SMO
SE BORILI?

VETERANI

ZA DANE RADOSTI

a) ZA SLOBODU...

b) ZA JEDINSTVENU BH-A...

c) ZA POSLOVNI PROSTOR...

D) ZA DRŽAVU TRI DRŽAVE...

ZA KANISTER S VODOM,
AKUMULATOR I KONZERVU
BEZ KRMETINE!

P.S. DA ODEM NA MORE!
DA POSTANEM PILOT I DA OTKAČIN GNJIDE OD LJUDI

TER ESSERE LIBERI DI RITORNARCI INSIEME SOTTO UN CIELO STELLATO

— Da gori odjeca od mene !!!

— Da što prije odem odavde

— Za definitivni dokaz da su Mravojedi najljepši i da tao takvi trebaju ići papa

— Za

— ZA POSLOVNI PROSTOR ISTAN I TAKO DALJE

— DA NEMAMO STRUJE!

— Za čuvanje ženske djece od 17-24 godine

SLOBODNA DALMACIJA

broj 14878

subota, godina XLIX cijena 15 dinara

ISSN 0350-4662

utorak 2. srpnja 1991.

Pomaže li zdrav razum?

SLOBODNA DALMACIJA 5

UTORAK, 2. SVIBNJA 1991.

novosti

KONFERENCIJA ZA NOVINARE STJEPANA MESIĆA

IMAMO ŠANSU ZA OPSTANAK

Rastanimo se kao ljudi

PJEŠICE U RAT

ŠTO DALJE OD SMRTI, TRKOM

Ibro, vrati zlato!

PORIJEKLO ZLATNIH LJILJANA

LJILJAN

GLINA:
PROPADANJE U
RATNO ŽIVO BLATO
LJUDI KAO
»GLINENI GOLUBOVI«

...rljava politika

...lefoni ...ekidu | Otvoreno šest prijelaza

»Letimo svi skupa!«
Nema predaje

»Europo,
zaustavi rat!«

OD LISTOPADA POSVE SLOBODNI

»Dječja
ambasada«

ATLAS

PESCARA
8. 7. 91.

BOL — JELSA

LASTOVO

NOVO — NOVO — NOVO

TEMPERATURE MORA

SOS za Sv. Petra

NIŠTA OD KOMIŽE 92!
20. 07. 92.

Kula 92

ABOVE: CLOCKWISE FROM TOP LEFT

IT'S NOT IMPORTANT TO WIN—BUT TO SURVIVE
Enis Selimović
Sarajevo, 1995

Baron de Coubertin, the founder of the modern Olympics, stated that, "The important thing in the Olympic Games is not winning, but taking part." Enis Selimović reinterprets this slogan in this unpublished poster he shared with us. The moustachioed Baron grasps one of Trio's postcards with the slogan *Best Memories of Sarajevo*.

DO YOU REMEMBER SARAJEVO?
Trio
Sarajevo, 1992

Trio produced a series of posters bearing this slogan. Vučko, a friendly wolf, was the official mascot of the XIV Sarajevo Winter Olympics in 1984, and became a much-loved symbol of the city. Vučko was a popular Yugoslav cartoon created by the Croatian artist Nedeljko Dragić before the Olympics. The Slovenian painter Jože Trobec reinterpreted it for the Games.

THE IMPORTANT THING IS WINNING
Trio
Sarajevo, 1994

One of Trio studios redesigns using Baron de Coubertin's famous quote.

OPPOSITE
1984 SARAJEVO 1994
Trio
Sarajevo, 1994

This postcard marks the tenth anniversary of the Winter Olympic Games in Sarajevo. Two years before this card was produced, the city's Olympic Museum was hit by Serb incendiary shells; it burned to the ground along with all its artefacts.

1984 SARAJEVO 1994

Design "Trio" Sarajevo

Began Turbić—whose original, hand-painted posters feature heavily in this book—was born in 1939 near Gradačac in the Tuzla Canton. He studied at the School of Applied Arts in Sarajevo and the Academy of Applied Arts in Belgrade. A member of Bosnia's Association of Fine Artists, in 1994 he was elected assistant professor of Art Culture with Methodology at Tuzla's Department of Classroom Teaching and Preschool Education, Faculty of Philosophy. When we met Began Turbić in 1998, he generously shared much of his passionate wartime work with us.

OPPOSITE: CLOCKWISE FROM TOP LEFT
BULLFIGHT
Began Turbić
Tuzla, 1992
Bosnia is depicted here as a bull in a bullfight, pierced by two knives—one Serbian, the other Croatian—and stuck by the lances of the international community.

UN—BAD MANDATE, GOOD APPETITE
Began Turbić
Tuzla, 1992
In this unpublished poster, the double-headed eagle of Serbia is perched atop a crumbling symbol of the UN. Note how the artist has turned the Serb emblem into a swastika. During the war, the popular sentiment in Bosnia was that the United Nations favoured the aggressors rather than those under attack.

WE ARE PRISONERS OF THE UN
Began Turbić
Tuzla, 1992
In this poster, Bosnian civilians are handcuffed by the United Nations and held captive by a Croatian barrier, a Serb dagger, and the barrel of a Yugoslav People's Army tank. The falling loaf of bread represents the highly criticised UN aid programme, which was considered a poor substitute for real intervention.

UN—WHO SAYS THEY'RE NOT MOVING A FINGER FOR BiH
Began Turbić
Tuzla, 1992
Turbić singles out the British and French for special ridicule in their handling of the Bosnian crisis. Among many destructive acts, Great Britain—led by Prime Minister John Major—repeatedly blocked attempts to lift the arms embargo against Bosnia-Herzegovina, thus making it much harder for Bosnia to defend itself. Meanwhile, France—under President François Mitterrand—appeared to favour extreme Serb nationalists and yet-to-be-indicted war criminals.

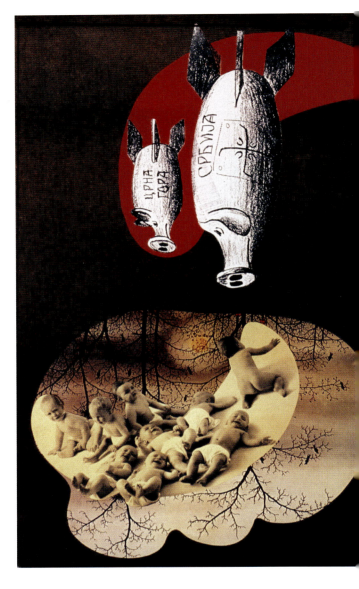

ABOVE
MONTENEGRO—SERBIA
Began Turbić
Tuzla, 1992
One of the few posters that refers to Montenegro, an early but short-lived partner of Serbia in the war. Both countries are predominantly Orthodox Christian, hence the symbolic images of pigs—animals considered unclean by Muslims.

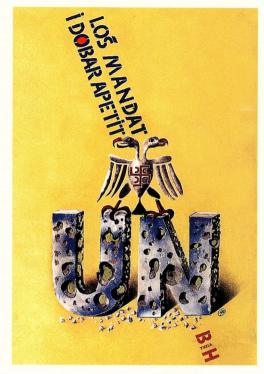

LOŠ MANDAT I DOBAR APETIT

UN

B-H

KO KAŽE DA NE MRDAJU NI PRSTOM ZA BOSNU I HERCEGOVINU

UN

UN

MI SMO ZATOČENICI UN-a

RIGHT

WORKING FOR PEACE
United Nations
Place and date unknown

A UN poster for its Protection Force displaying an asinine and tepid design concept. The poster seems to be as lacking in enthusiasm—to protect Bosnia-Herzegovina's people—as UNPROFOR seemed to be on the ground during the war. Nobody was sorry to see the back of UNPROFOR when, after the Dayton Agreement was signed in 1995, NATO took over peacekeeping operations.

OPPOSITE

UN ARE TO BE BLAMED FOR MY STEP
Began Turbić
Tuzla, 1992

The vast majority of Bosnians, of all ethnicities, would agree with the sentiment in this poster and those by Began Turbić on the previous page—that the UN shares responsibility for what happened in Bosnia.

OPPOSITE: TOP TO BOTTOM

OMARSKA—NAME OF THE ROSES IN BOSNIA
Art Publishing
Sarajevo, 1994

The Serb-run internment camp at Omarska was located in an abandoned mining complex. This poster features the floor plan of the buildings and takes its title from Umberto Eco's epic novel about a series of murders in a labyrinthine medieval monastery. Omarska was surrounded by three rings of guards, and only two people are known to have escaped. Prisoners were separated into categories. "Category A" inmates consisted of intellectuals, Muslim community and religious leaders— as well as volunteers in any of the Muslim militias or Bosniak Territorial Defence forces. These prisoners were generally executed in the Red House *(Crvena Kuća)* upon arrival. Prisoners were beaten in the White House *(Bijela Kuća)*. Art Publishing, which has several posters featued in this book, was a group of three visual artists working in Sarajevo during the siege: Bojan Bahić, Sanda Hnatjuk and Zoran Buletić.

THE CAMPS REMAIN—EVERYTHING PASSES
Dani magazine
Sarajevo, January 1995

This cover contrasts two pictures of camps: one from World War II, the other from Bosnia. The slogan on the left reads, The Camps Remain; the one on the right, Everything Passes.

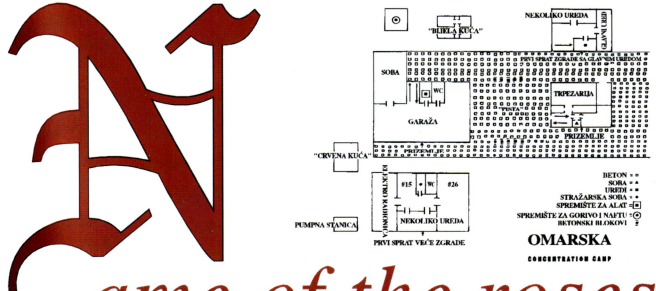

CAME of the roses

IN BOSNIA

SARAJEVO 31.01.1995, No 28, YEAR IV, PRICE 2 DM.   SARAJEVO 31.01.1995, BROJ 28, GODINA IV, CIJENA 2 DM

KOMISIJI ZA ISTRAŽIVANJE RATNIH ZLOČINA U BOSNI I HERCEGOVINI
RATNI ZLOČINAC
TO THE COMMISION FOR THE INVESTIGATION OF THE WAR CRIMINALS IN BOSNIA AND HERZEGOVINA
WAR CRIMINAL

RADOVAN KARADŽIĆ, predsjednik terorističke Srpske demokratske stranke.
Rođen 19. 6. 1945. Mjesto rođenja Šavnik, SR Jugoslavija. Zanimanje - neuropsihijatar.
Direktno odgovoran za organizovano naoružavanje i obuku članova SDS-a s ciljem zauzimanja teritorija RBiH i proglašenje jednonacionalne tzv. Srpske
Republike BiH. Pripremao dovođenje arkanovaca, šešeljevaca, Belih orlova, rojalista i drugih plaćenih kriminalaca iz Srbije i Crne Gore s ciljem
provođenja etničkog čišćenja teritorija. Naredio da se napadnu Bijeljina, Foča, Sarajevo, Široki Brijeg, Odžak, Višegrad i mnogi drugi gradovi. Naredio
da se neosvojena mjesta blokiraju radi izgladnjivanja stanovništva i izvrgnu artiljerijskim napadima kao i djelovanju snjaperista. Naredio otvaranje
logora za muslimansko i hrvatsko stanovništvo. Do sada odgovoran za smrt 127.448, ranjavanje 129.000 lica, za progon sa svojih ognjišta 700.000 ljudi
unutar BiH i preko 800.000 van granica BiH, što je u skladu sa njegovom najavom o nestanku sa lica zemlje, "cijelog jednog naroda".
Odgovaraće za početak rata u BiH, masovna ubistva, silovanja, mučenja, poniževanja, genocid - djela koja su u međunarodnom pravu svrstana u kategoriju
ratnih zločina. Odgovaraće i pred sopstvenim narodom jer ga je naveo u zločin.

RATNI ZLOĆINAC

TO THE COMMISION FOR THE INVESTIGATION OF THE WAR CRIMINALS IN BOSNIA AND HERZEGOVINA

WAR CRIMINAL

RATKO MLADIĆ, a JNA officer, the ex-commander of the 2^{nc} Military Region with the Headquarters in Sarajevo.
He carried out armament of the SDS by all kinds of weapons from the magazines of the ex-JNA. He trained the SDS extremists in handling the armament of the ex-JNA in the military grounds. He ordered the concentration of Serbian terrorist units around Sarajevo and other towns, on which he planned the attacks. He ordered the acctive assistance of JNA units to chetniks in their attacks on inhabited places. Together with a group of officers he ordered the attack on Sarajevo, on April, 6", 1992. He directed missiles, both to the selected buildings of industrial, cultural, historical and humanitarian inportance and to the civilians. He had previously, organized and placed groups of snipers. He ordered setting fire to more significant buildings and then the use of the artillery in order to prevent the extingushing fires. He ordered the firing of places, where citizens gatnered in order to buy food. He is responible for the death and permanent disability of thousansds of people. Due to the use of forbidden methods of war waging defined by the Geneva Convelion from 1949

WAR CRIMINAL: RADOVAN KARADŽIĆ
Trio
Sarajevo, 1992
This unofficial Wanted poster reads:

Radovan Karadžić, president of the terrorist Serbian Democratic Party. Born: 19.6.1945. Place of birth: Savnik, Socialist Republic of Yugoslavia. Occupation: neuropsychologist. He is directly responsible for arming and training members of the SDS to capture the territory of the Republic of Bosnia-Herzegovina and declare the mono-national Serb Republic in Bosnia-Herzegovina. He organised the movement of Arkan's men, Šešelj's White Eagles, and the royalists, as well as other paid criminals from Serbia and Montenegro, with the aim of ethnically cleansing territories. He ordered the attacks on Bijeljina, Foča, Sarajevo, Široki Brijeg, Odžac, Višegrad, and many other towns. He ordered the blockade of unconquered towns to starve the population and attacked them with artillery and snipers. He ordered the opening of camps for the Muslim and Croat populations. He has been responsible for the deaths of 127,448 people, the wounding of 129,000 people, the displacement of 700,000 people from their homes within BiH, and the expulsion of 800,000 people from the republic. This is all in line with his announcement that a whole nation will "disappear from the face of the earth". He is responsible for starting the war in BiH, mass murder, rape, torture, humiliation, and genocide: acts that, under international law, fall into the category of war crimes. He will also be responsible before his people, as he led them into crime.

Karadžić, the self-declared "leader of the Bosnian Serbs", was finally arrested in Belgrade in July 2008. After evading capture for many years, he was discovered living in Belgrade disguised as a long-haired and bearded new-age healer. Karadžić was transferred to the International Criminal Tribunal for the Former Yugoslavia in The Hague on 30 July 2008 where he was tried for genocide, crimes against humanity and other war crimes committed in Bosnia. Found guilty on most charges, he received 40 years in prison. After an unsuccessful appeal, however, this was increased to a whole-life sentence. Finally, something like justice had been done.

WAR CRIMINAL: RATKO MLADIĆ
Trio
Sarajevo, 1992
Accusations against Ratko Mladić, the head of the Bosnian Serb Army, were printed in English. Both these unofficial posters were displayed just a few months after the start of the Bosnian War, and a full three years before the International Tribunal in The Hague officially indicted Mladić and Karadžić. Mladić was finally captured in northern Serbia in May 2011, almost three years after Karadžić was also unearthed. Like Karadžić before him, Mladić was speedily extradited to The Hague, where he was eventually found guilty of genocide, crimes against humanity and violations of the laws and customs of war. After a lengthy trial he was sentenced to life in prison but, like Karadžić before him, he appealed the sentence. On 8 June 2021, however, in a near-unanimous decision by the judges, his appeal was rejected.

OPPOSITE
TRNOPOLJE
Asim Đelilović
Travnik, 1993
Trnopolje was a Serb-run transit camp that held Bosnian prisoners who had survived the death camps and were waiting to be exchanged for Serb prisoners. Conditions at Trnopolje were as grim, however, as those at Omarska and other internment camps; detainees were routinely mistreated, tortured, and killed.

TR**NO**POLJE

RIGHT: TOP TO BOTTOM
19641994—TUZLA PORTRAIT GALLERY—30 YEARS
Edin Derviševic
Tuzla, 1994
Tuzla was proud of its cultural institutions and the fact that they not only survived the war but were active throughout it.

4 APRIL '92
Forum of Tuzla Citizens
Tuzla, 1992
Bosnia's Presidency (headed by President Alija Izetbegović) mobilised all territorial defence forces on 4 April 1992. Tuzla, an industrial centre in the northeast of the country with a population of around 115,000, is Bosnia's third-largest city after Sarajevo and Zenica. The symbol of Tuzla is a goat since during the Austro-Hungarian occupation goats were forbidden; they were seen as a threat to the forests as they eat saplings and all new growth. Legend has it that there was only one goat in Tuzla, but the people still had plenty of cheese and milk—the parable being that resilient Tuzlans can not only survive external interference, but thrive during it. On 4 April 1992, this poster infers, Tuzla was ready. The following day, two young women were shot dead by snipers in Sarajevo (see page 98)—and the day after that, 6 April, marks the beginning of the Bosnian War. The idea to use a goat in many Forum of Tuzla Citizens' posters was Jasminko Artautović's, the lead graphic designer at the Forum. The goat in this poster was sketched by Ismet Hrvanović, who has other hand-drawn posters in this book.

OPPOSITE
EVIL DOESN'T LIVE HERE
Edin Derviševic
Tuzla, 1992
The history of opposition to nationalism in Tuzla dates back to World War II. Then, as now, the citizens of Tuzla stood for the right of all ethnic groups to coexist peacefully. Tuzla's ideals were vociferously championed by Mayor Selim Bešlagić (1990–2001) who earned international fame for his success in holding Tuzla's ethnic mix together. It has been reported that Tuzla had more Muslim-Orthodox-Catholic interfaith marriages than any other city in Bosnia. Tuzla is also unique in that it never fell under the control of any one nationalist party—and that's what this poster communicates.

OPPOSITE: TOP TO BOTTOM

15 MAY '92
Forum of Tuzla Citizens
Tuzla, 1992

On 15 May 1992, the 92nd Motorized Brigade of the Yugoslav People's Army (JNA) left their garrison near the centre of Tuzla. They attempted to remove weapons previously entrusted to them by local defence forces, to whom the weapons constitutionally belonged. Their presumed plan was to encircle the city before shelling it into submission—a strategy they had employed repeatedly in Bosnia (including in Sarajevo the previous week). Unlike many other Bosnian population centres, however, Tuzla had anticipated this likely Serb tactic. An assortment of local Bosnian armed groups—including the Patriotic League, Green Berets, and armed police units—managed to block the convoy's forward movement on Brčanska Malta street. Before long the entire column of vehicles was in flames. It was later verified that at least 92 JNA soldiers were killed and 33 injured. This was a significant defeat for the JNA in Bosnia and one that undoubtedly saved Tuzla from the full force of Serb military aggression. Indeed, so significant a defeat was it that for the next 24 years Serbia would (largely unsuccessfully) attempt to prosecute for war crimes Ilija Jurišić, the local commander of the Bosnian forces involved in the attack.

9 MAY—VICTORY OVER FASCISM DAY?
Forum of Tuzla Citizens
Tuzla, 1992

In many European countries, the 9th of May is celebrated as the day fascism was defeated; it was the day in 1945 when the Allies took Berlin. Here the European Union flag is juxtaposed with a scene from *Guernica*, Pablo Picasso's 1937 painting of the horrific Spanish Civil War bombardment (below). The poster's title queries whether fascism has been defeated. Echoes of Picasso's masterpiece can also be see in another Bosnian poster on page 111.

The following eight propaganda posters (ending on page 143) were commissioned in 1993 by the Ministry of Information of Republika Srpska, in Banja Luka. They were distributed as part of a campaign that aimed to gain international sympathy for the Serb cause. According to Draško Mikanović, one of the designers who contributed to the series, "The posters are just poor attempts to say the things that were not presented to the world in the way they should have been." Mikanović claimed that these were the only propaganda posters the Bosnian Serbs produced during the war, and although he did not initially want to design them, he felt he had to. "We were blown away with the Croatian propaganda, and some coming from the Muslim side", he told us. The posters were drawn with gouache and each was printed in an edition of 500 copies. There was a plan to continue printing them, but the designers were disgusted when they found they were being sold locally instead of being distributed for free to Serbian communities abroad. According to Mikanović, this profiteering mentality resulted in the Serbs losing the Bosnian propaganda war. Three designers who collaborated with Mikanović on these posters asked not to be credited.

OPPOSITE: CLOCKWISE FROM TOP LEFT

YOU'LL LISTEN TO THE SNAKE—EVE DID THE SAME
Draško Mikanović et al.
Banja Luka, 1993
The snake is painted in Croatia's national colours and is crawling into the heart of the European Union. All three posters on this page express anti-Croat themes that were prevalent in Serbia during the war.

THE BEAST IS OUT AGAIN
Draško Mikanović et al.
Banja Luka, 1993
This poster refers to the fascist state of Croatia that existed during World War II. Croatia was allied with Nazi Germany between 1941–45. The beast of Croatian fascism was so ferocious that even the Nazis were shocked by atrocities committed against hundreds of thousands of Serbs and other minorities. Tuđman's election as president of the first independent Croatian state since 1945 spread fear among Serbs in Croatia because the memory of World War II was very much alive. This fear was exploited by the regime in Serbia, which went on to annex Serb-populated areas of Croatia.

NASTY KID OF A NASTY MOTHER
Draško Mikanović et al.
Banja Luka, 1993
Here Croatia is the blond kid and Germany the nasty mother. An important part of modern nationalist thinking in Serbia is that Croatia is Germany's puppet and, as a result, Serbs tend to blame Germans for the Bosnian and Croatian wars.

ABOVE
EXPELLED SERBS
Anonymous (Public Domain)
Croatia, July 1941
In the 1990s, Serbs' fears about Croatia's intentions, methods, and prejudice against them were partly based on historical facts that are impossible to deny. This photograph shows Serbs being forced to flee with their belongings in the fascist Independent State of Croatia during World War II. Extensive pogroms and terrible atrocities were committed against Serbs (and other ethnic minorities) between 1941–45. When Franjo Tuđman came to power in Croatia in 1990, fear grew among the Serb minority that his nationalism spelled existential disaster for them.

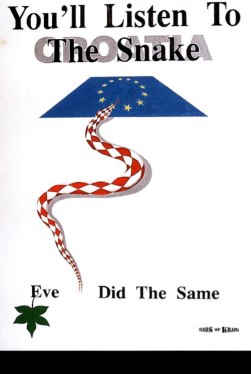

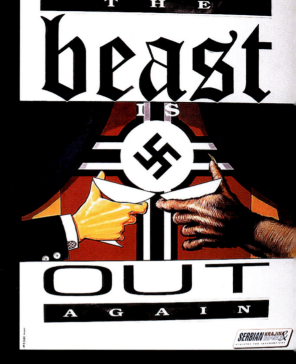

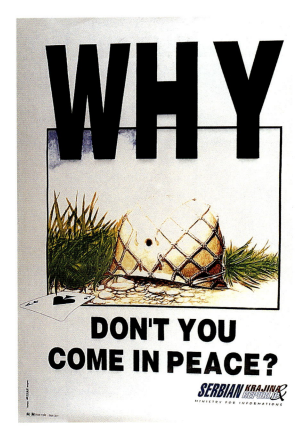

YOU CAN PREVENT THIS
Draško Mikanović et al.
Banja Luka, 1993
An American war widow receives the Stars and Stripes. Both posters on this page were meant as a warning to the international community in general, and the US in particular, to keep out of Bosnia.

WHY DON'T YOU COME IN PEACE?
Draško Mikanović et al.
Banja Luka, 1993
This image of an American helmet from the Vietnam era is a crude warning to the international community to keep out of the Bosnian War. It reflects the commonly-held Serbian view that UN and NATO peacekeeping forces were actually aggressors in disguise.

THIS IS NOT A PAINT COMMERCIAL—THIS IS FUTURE
Draško Mikanović et al.
Banja Luka, 1993
The colour green is identified with Islam. This poster implies that the whole of Europe is in danger of being Islamicised, starting with Bosnia. Throughout its history, Serbia has seen itself as the defender of Christian Europe against the Muslim hordes from the east.

THIS IS NOT A PAINT COMMERCIAL

THIS IS FUTURE

RIGHT
PER SERBIAN GRAVES—AD ASTRA
Draško Mikanović et al.
Banja Luka, 1933

This Bosnian Serb poster has a double meaning: the term *Ad Astra* ("to the stars" in Latin) implies the Serbian victims of the war will have a glorious future in heaven. On the other hand, the stars are arranged in the same position as they occur on the European Union flag, suggesting that the EU was somehow responsible for the war. Anti-EU feeling was common among Serbs at the time of the war.

OPPOSITE
YOU HAVE VICTIMS FOR ENEMIES
Draško Mikanović et al.
Banja Luka, 1993

This poster expresses the view, still prevalent in Serbia, that Serbs are innocent victims of an international conspiracy. This image works on a semi-religious level, too—bringing to mind a traditional Orthodox icon of Madonna holding the Christ Child.

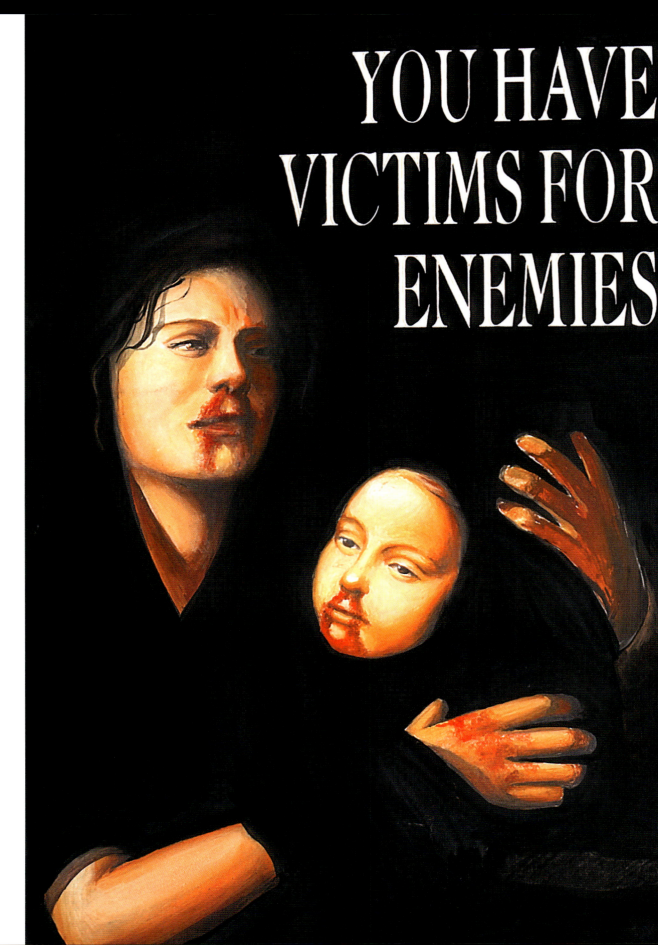

TO BE
Enis Selimović
Sarajevo, 1994

Sarajevo Winter Festival, headed by Ibrahim Spahić (who is also director of the International Peace Centre in Sarajevo), commissioned and printed many original posters throughout the siege of Sarajevo. This one was inspired by the soliloquy given by Prince Hamlet in William Shakespeare's play.

OPPOSITE
WHO'S NEXT?
Art Publishing
Sarajevo, 1994

Masaccio was a 15th century Florentine Renaissance artist. His painting of Adam and Eve's expulsion from paradise was the source of inspiration for this poster.

FOLLOWING SPREAD
TWILIGHT ZONES
Dani magazine (front and back covers)
Sarajevo, May 1994

This cover—from the popular Sarajevo news magazine *Dani*—associates Bosnian cities designated as "Safe Areas" by the UN with the European and American cities which were key players in the international response to the war. This image made the point that the fate of these Bosnian Twilight Zones depended on political decisions made elsewhere. Srebrenica and Žepa were ethnically cleansed by the Bosnian Serbs in 1995, and thousands were murdered, while the international community did nothing. One is eerily reminded of a line from *Looking Back on the Spanish Civil War,* by George Orwell: "The outcome of the Spanish war", he wrote in 1942, "was settled in London, Paris, Rome, Berlin—at any rate not in Spain."

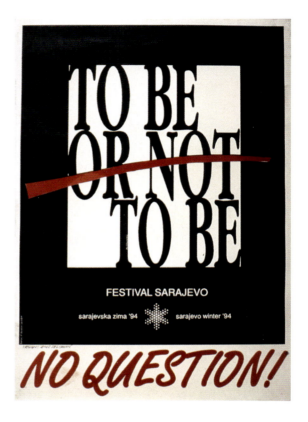

WHO'S NEXT?

"Adam & Eva" by Masaccio, redesign Art Publishing

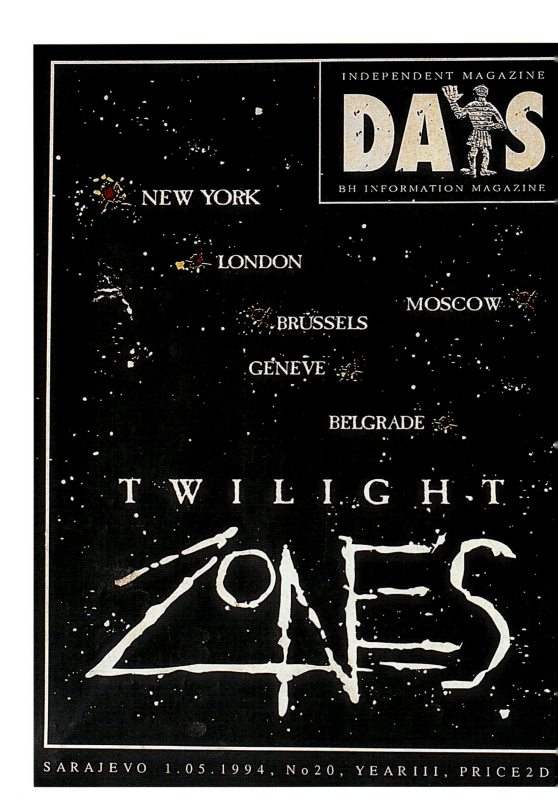

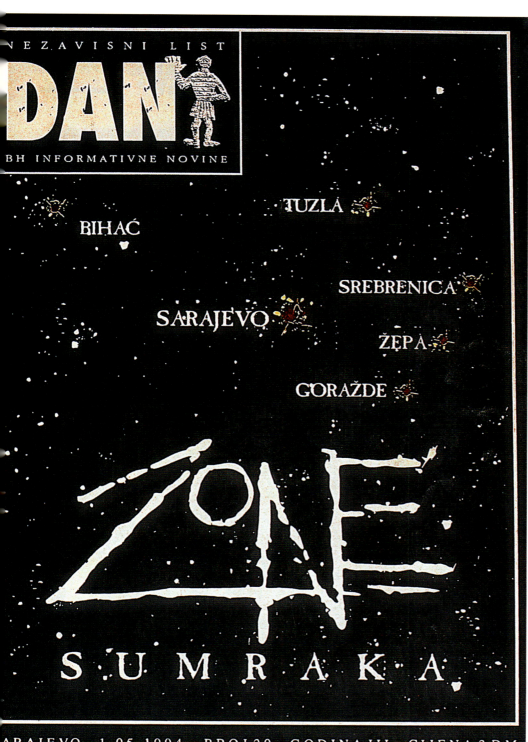

Asim Đelilović is a highly productive and greatly respected Bosnian visual artist. He splits his time between Sarajevo and Travnik. Đelilović creates books, posters, and graphic design; he also makes art objects and installations—all with a social and political theme. He teaches design in Sarajevo and is the director of the *Museum in Exile* project.

OPPOSITE: TOP TO BOTTOM
UH!
Asim Đelilović
Travnik, 1993
Tensions between Bosnian Croats and Muslims in central Bosnia and in Herzegovina turned into full-scale war in April 1993. This poster expresses the shock and horror that Muslims living there felt when their former allies, and lifelong neighbours, turned against them. The Muslim-controlled part of Bosnia was now blockaded on all sides. Asim Đelilović shapes the red and white Croatian chessboard *(šahovnica)* into the letter "U", a reference to the *Ustaša:* Croatian fascists of the Nazi period. The word itself—"Uh!"—the author explained to us, mimics the sound someone makes when they are punched hard in the stomach.

LOVE ME!
Asim Đelilović
Travnik, 1993
When fighting broke out between Bosnian Croats and Muslims, Đelilović was expelled by Croatian forces from Vitez, a small town in central Bosnia. He and thousands of Muslims fled toward Travnik, the main town in the region. This poster plays on the word love, which in Bosnian means to hunt. Đelilović said that on the road to Travnik he was stopped and beaten by soldiers of the HVO (Croatian Defence Council). While this was happening, Đelilović remembers thinking about the word love in both languages: "Why don't these people love me?" and "Why are they hunting me?" In Bosnian language the word love means to hunt.

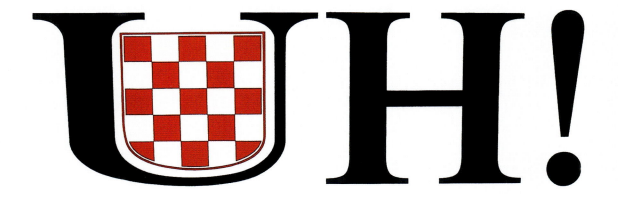

RIGHT
THE HSP HAND CAN SAVE YOU
HSP
Photograph by Daoud Sarhandi
Croatia, 1998

This poster was photographed on a wall in Zagreb, Croatia. HSP stands for *Hrvatska stranka prava* (Croatian Party of Rights) and is an ultra-nationalist Croat party based in Zagreb. HSP was established in 1990 by Dobroslav Paraga and modelled on a party of the same name that existed in the late 19th century. It still exists today and has a virulent nationalistic website (it's essentially a fascist organisation). HSP believes that all Croats should be united in one state—thus justifying the taking of land from neighbouring countries. In the early 1990s, HSP had a large paramilitary wing called HOS, which stands for Croatian Defence Forces. The texts on the top left- and right-hand part of the poster read:

> GOD AND CROATS
> READY FOR HOME

OPPOSITE: LEFT TO RIGHT
HOS—READY FOR HOME
HOS
Mostar, 1993

The literal translation of this title is Ready for Home, but the real meaning of this slogan, to Croats, is Ready to Defend the Homeland. This slogan was used by Croatia's fascist *Ustaša* regime during World War II. Although it sounds innocent enough, it was a battle cry during one of the most brutal periods in Croatian history. The slogan's reappearance during the breakup of the former Yugoslavia caused widespread fear among Croatian Serbs.

HOS
HOS
Mostar, 1993

This poster appeared before the Muslim-Croat split in Herzegovina in 1994. Note the Bosnian *fleur-de-lis* at the top of the poster, alongside the red and white Croatian *šahovnica*. After the split, Bosnia's emblem was no longer used by Croats. The text reads:

> HOS WILL LIBERATE YOU
> BUT YOU ALONE MUST DECIDE
> IN WHAT KIND OF COUNTRY YOU WISH TO LIVE

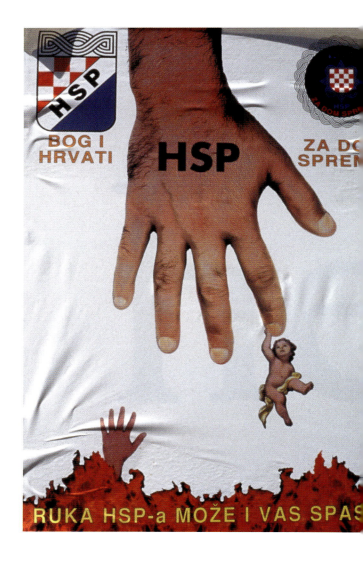

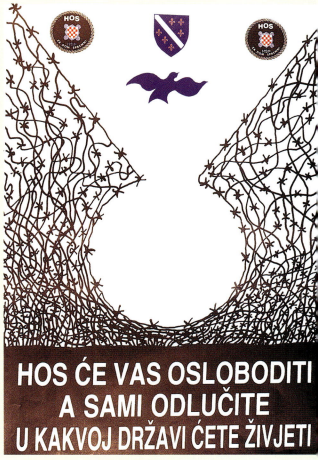

HRVATSKO

SPONZORI PLAKATA: Zavičajni klub »KUPRES

UVIJEK
HRVATSKI
KUPRES

HRVATI, KUPREŠACI,
SVI PRIJATELJI KUPRESA,
UČINIMO SVE,
VRATIMO MIR I BLAGOSTANJE
NA NAŠ KUPRES,
S BOŽJOM POMOĆI,
JEDNOM ZA SVAGDA!

Gabrijel Jurkić: VISORAVAN U CVATU
motiv kupreškog polja naslikan 1914 godine

KUPREŠKA
BOJNA

KUPRES

E OBRANE
A KUPRES

BRIGADA
KRALJA TOMISLAVA

HRVATSKA TISKARA« Zagreb, »VEČERNJI LIST« Zagreb, REPROSTUDIO d.o.o. ing. DRAGO REPAR, Petrova 88, Zagreb

PREVIOUS SPREAD
KUPRES—ALWAYS CROATIAN
HVO (Kupres Battalion)
Croatia, 1993
Kupres is a town in central Bosnia-Herzegovina with a
large Croat population. It was much fought over in 1992
and became a symbol of Croatia's territorial ambitions. In
the winter of 1992 Croatian President Tuđman installed
Mate Boban, an ultranationalist warlord, in power. Boban
then set up the Bosnian Croat parastate Herceg-Bosna,
which in line with Tuđman's ambitions for controlling
Herzegovina openly rejected any union with Bosnia.
Instead, Boban attempted to remove the region from
Bosnia altogether and join it up with Croatia. This opened
a new and vicious front in the war, between Bosnian
Croats and Muslims.

RIGHT
HVO—LOVE FOR THE HOMELAND
Art Forces
Mostar, 1993
Ljubav za dom (Love for the Homeland) was a fascist
Ustaša slogan popular during World War II.

OPPOSITE
THIRD CIM BRIGADE
HVO (Cim Brigade)
Mostar, 1993
Cim is a neighbourhood on the outskirts of Mostar. When
Serbia invaded Croatia in 1991 many Bosnian Croats
from Herzegovina joined the fight against them. They
returned as seasoned fighters and prepared to defend
their communities against subsequent Serb attacks
in Bosnia. They were altogether better organised and
equipped than the Bosnian Muslims. From April 1992
onward, Bosnia's President Izetbegović was concerned
with the Serb onslaught in eastern Bosnia and his
priority was defending Sarajevo. Meanwhile, the HVO
(Croatian Defence Council) was expected to counter the
Serb offensive in Herzegovina. Initially, many Bosnian
Muslims enlisted in the HVO and fought alongside the
Bosnian Croats. This relationship collapsed, however, as
Croat claims to an ethnically pure Croatian mini-state in
Herzegovina grew.

CIMSKA
III
BOJNA
2. BRIGADA

ALL FOR HERCEG-BOSNA—FOR FREEDOM
HVO
Croatia, 1992

Herceg-Bosna was an unrecognised mini-state in western Bosnia that Croatia established in 1991. It continued to be expanded until it occupied about 30% of Bosnia's territory. At first, Croat forces fought against the Bosnian Serbs alongside Bosnian Muslims, but this alliance eventually ruptured when the Bosnian Croats attacked their former Muslim allies. The brutal Croat-Bosnian war lasted from October 1992 until February 1994. Although Franjo Tuđman was never indicted by the International Criminal Tribunal for the Former Yugoslavia (and he died in 1999) in 2017 the Tribunal upheld findings that he and other leading Croat politicians were responsible for crimes committed in the Herceg-Bosna parastate. Herceg-Bosna was eventually assimilated into the legally constituted Muslim-Croat federation, although surprisingly Herceg-Bosna wasn't formally abolished until 1999, four years after the Dayton Agreement ended the Bosnian War.

HVO RECRUITMENT
HVO
Mostar, 1993

The text on the lower part of this poster (by an exiled Croatian writer murdered in Paris in 1978 by the Yugoslav secret police) reads:

> *Every Croat, no matter in what part of the world he is, no matter what his personal political views are, past faults and misconceptions were, today wants to establish a sovereign, free state of Croatia. (Ante Bruno Bušić)*

Ironically, the soldier in the upper half of the poster stands in front the Stari Most, the Old Bridge linking east and west Mostar. It was destroyed by Croat forces in November 1993 in a senseless act of vandalism. Although the bridge was eventually rebuilt, Mostar is still a divided city: west Mostar is almost exclusively Croat, while east Mostar is predominantly Muslim Bosniak. The lower half of the poster depicts Međugorje, a Catholic place of pilgrimage in Herzegovina, where sightings of the Virgin Mary were frequently reported. Međugorje and the surrounding towns are the heartlands of hard-line Croatian nationalism. In the tourist shops of Međugorje, religious souvenirs are openly sold alongside images of Ante Pavelić, the *Ustaša* leader of Croatia's World War II fascist state.

HITLER
Anonymous, place and date unknown

The red and white Croatian *šahovnica* (chessboard), transformed into a powerful critique of Croatian policy towards Bosnia.

**SVE ZA
HERCEG - BOSNU**

POKAŽIMO SVIMA DA JE NAŠA SOLIDARNOST I HUMANOST
SNAŽAN PUT ČEŽNJE
ZA SLOBODOM
Vaša sredstva možete uplatiti na račun HVO - glavni sanitetski stožer
Herceg-Bosne dinarski račun   30114-621-79-013600-2350468745
NE SUTRA — NEGO DANAS

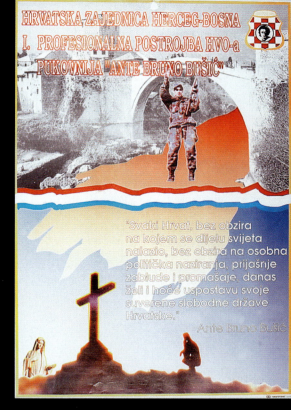

HRVATSKA ZAJEDNICA HERCEG-BOSNA
I. PROFESIONALNA POSTROJBA HVO-a
PUKOVNIJA "ANTE BRUNO BUŠIĆ"

"Svaki Hrvat, bez obzira
na kojem se dijelu svijeta
nalazio, bez obzira na osobna
politička naziranja, prijašnje
zablude i promašaje, danas
želi i hoće uspostavu svoje
suverene slobodne države
Hrvatske."

Ante Bruno Bušić

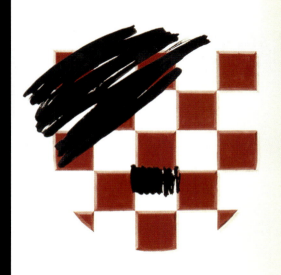

DESTROYED OLD BRIDGE; *Photograph by Daoud Sarhandi; Mostar, January 1996*
Apart from being a crossing point between east and west Mostar, the Stari Most (Old Bridge) symbolised the ancient fusion of eastern and western cultures in Bosnia. The bridge was eventually rebuilt by UNESCO, and inaugurated in 2004.

DO NOT FORGET
Radio Television Mostar
Mostar, 1994
A poster for an exhibition of drawings by Tahir Kosović in the last year of the war, organised by Radio Television Mostar.

WE ARE THE FRIENDS FROM MOSTAR—FREEDOM IS CREATED BY ALL TOGETHER
Nedžad Pašalić Paša
Mostar, 1993
The first part of this slogan was taken from a football chant for the local team, Velez, and is well known to the people of Bosnia.

HOMAGE TO MOSTAR
Salim Obralić
Sarajevo, 1994
A poster for an exhibition devoted to Mostar's Stari Most (Old Bridge). After the bridge's destruction, this exhibition was held in Sarajevo as a homage to Mostar's much-loved architectural symbol of unity; 25 artists participated.

BiH—IN THE HEART OF THE WORLD
Hamza Filipović
Mostar, 1993
The author of this poster died during the Muslim-Croat war.

200,000 SOLDIERS OF THE BOSNIAN ARMY GUARANTEE THE STATE
Čedomir Hadžić
Mostar, 1994
Only 25 copies of this poster were printed, we were told.

IZLOZBA ULUBIHa
HOMAGE MOSTARU
JANUAR 1994

200000 boraca
armije
bosne i hercegovine
garant
državnosti

OPPOSITE: CLOCKWISE FROM TOP LEFT

AGAINST EVIL—FOR A FREE BiH
Ismet Hrvanović
Tuzla, 1992
A defiant early pro-Bosnian propaganda poster.

LET'S OVERRUN THEM!
Anonymous
Zenica, 1994
A later pro-Bosnian propaganda poster, with one golden lily.

BOSNIAN ARMY ON BOSNIA'S BORDERS
Bosnian Army (ABiH) Press Centre
Sarajevo, 1993
We came across this poster in the house of a collector, Zlatko Serdarević, on the east side of Mostar, which was and still is predominantly Muslim. Serdarević rummaged around for quite a while before digging out this work from his large stock of posters and war memorabilia. Above Serdarević's head, we noticed a large, badly fixed hole in the ceiling. A mortar had hit his house in 1994, passing through the roof and embedding itself in the floor. Indeed, its tail and fins were still sticking out of the carpet.

LET'S DIG TO VICTORY
Bosnian Army (ABiH) Press Centre
Sarajevo, 1992
This poster was produced to encourage young Bosnian fighters to defend themselves on the front lines by digging trenches. Many died out in the open because they didn't appreciate the point of this basic military technique, which offers protection against sniper fire and shrapnel.

PROTIV ZLA — ZA SLOBODNU BOSNU I HERCEGOVINU

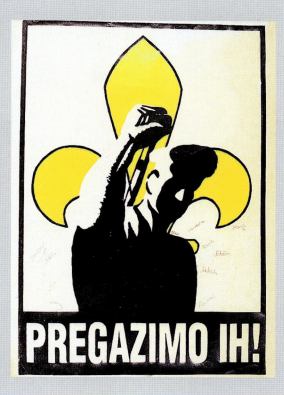

PREGAZIMO IH!

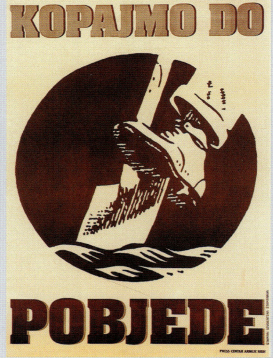

KOPAJMO DO POBJEDE

BOSANSKA VOJSKA NA BOSANSKIM GRANICAMA

OPPOSITE: LEFT TO RIGHT
15 APRIL—REPUBLIC OF BiH ARMY DAY
Salim Obralić
Sarajevo, 1994
A dreamy image of Bosnia's mountain terrain contrasts with the harsh reality of celebrating the armed forces.

FREEDOM
Zdravko Novak
Tuzla, 1992
The juxtaposition of a dream-like bird with a mortar bomb could not be more stark. The bird holds the lily of Bosnia in her beak.

FOLLOWING SPREAD: LEFT TO RIGHT
CRIMINALS—THEY WILL NOT FORGIVE YOU
Territorial Defence (TO)
Photograph by Kemal Hadžić
Sarajevo, 1992
This poster was produced by Sarajevo's Territorial Defence as a warning that organised criminals operating within the city would not be tolerated. The little girl is the daughter of the photographer who took the picture.

DEDICATED TO VASE MISKIN STREET—STREET OF SPITE
Territorial Defence (TO)
Sarajevo, 1992
Seventeen people were killed on 27 May 1992 in a narrow Sarajevan street while they lined up for bread. Television pictures of the atrocity were broadcast around the world. It was the first event that brought the brutal reality of the Bosnian War into Western living rooms. The Serbian leadership denied that Serb forces fired the mortars and claimed that Muslim paramilitary units had shelled Sarajevo themselves, for publicity purposes, and had even swapped the bodies of the real Serb victims for Muslim and Croat corpses. To make matters worse, this cynical lie was reported internationally, thereby giving it limited credibility. The red rose symbolises the splatter pattern mortars make when they hit asphalt.

SARAJEVO ROSE
Photograph by Rupert Wolfe Murray
Sarajevo, 2021
A mortar-shell splatter pattern from the siege years—locally known as a Sarajevo Rose—memorialised with coloured resin. These urban scars are now protected monuments in Sarajevo.

NO ONE'S (CANDLE) EVER BURNS UNTIL DAWN
Territorial Defence (TO)
Sarajevo, 1992
This slogan is derived from a popular expression, meaning "nothing lasts forever". The candles are labelled JNA (Yugoslav People's Army) and CCCC. In Serbian Cyrillic, "C" is the equivalent of "S". The slogan reads *Samo Sloga Srbina Spasava,* meaning Only Unity Saves the Serbs. This design is based on a celebrated Polish poster; thanks to Jan Nuckowski for pointing this out.

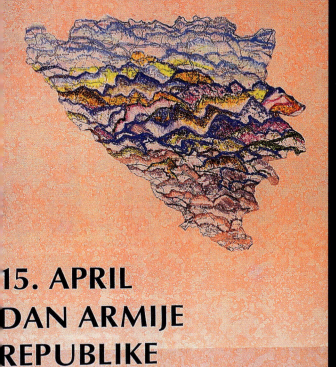

15. APRIL
DAN ARMIJE
REPUBLIKE
BOSNE I HERCEGOVINE

SLOBODA

ZLOČINCI,
ONI VAM NEĆE
OPROSTITI !

TO BiH

ULICI VASE MISKINA

Sarajevo, 27.maja '92

CRNQ

ULICI PRKOSA

TO BiH

Ničija nije
do zore gorjela!

TO BiH

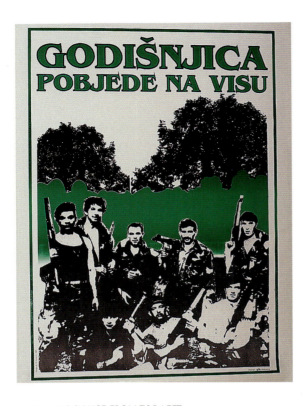

ABOVE: CLOCKWISE FROM TOP LEFT
BiH VICTORY ANNIVERSARY AT VIS
Nijaz Omerović
Gračanica, 1993

BiH—OUR HOMELAND
Irfan Handukić
Zenica, 1994

LET'S ALL JOIN IN TO DEFEND BiH
Irfan Handukić
Zenica, 1994
The caption at the bottom reads:

> THIS IS HOW THOSE WHO DIDN'T SUCCEED IN
> DEFENDING THEMSELVES ENDED UP

OPPOSITE: TOP TO BOTTOM
HAPPILY TOWARDS FREEDOM
Fuad Kasumović
Tuzla, 1995
A chilling contrast between the word "happy" and the
image of a rocket propelled grenade launcher.

DEFEND BOSNIA AND HERZEGOVINA
Irfan Handukić
Zenica, 1994
This ABiH poster features jet fighters and is a call for
foreign military intervention.

ARMIJA
REPUBLIKE BOSNE I HERCEGOVINE
15. april '92. 15. april '95

Sretno do slobode

ODBRANIMO BOSNU I HERCEGOVINU
DEFEND BOSNIA AND HERCEGOVINA

DAN ARMIJE
REPUBLIKE
BOSNE I HERCEGOVINE

15. APRIL

CRNI LABUDOVI 4.4.'94.

1993

DISUNITED NATIONS OF
BOSNIA AND HERZEGOVINA

PREVIOUS SPREAD: LEFT TO RIGHT
ARMY DAY
Bosnian Army (ABiH) Press Centre
Sarajevo, 1996
This Bosnian Army propaganda poster shows a group of soldiers looking remarkably casual, and also rather undernourished.

BLACK SWANS
Anonymous
Tuzla, 1994
The Black Swans were an infamous paramilitary unit. They operated primarily in central Bosnia, where they were exclusively Croat and were accused of appalling acts of brutality and terror. In the Tuzla region, however, the Black Swans consisted of Muslim and Croat irregulars who covertly fought alongside the official government forces of the ABiH.

ABOVE
DISUNITED NATIONS OF BiH
Trio
Sarajevo, 1993
This redesign of the UN logo was created after the Vance-Owen Peace Plan of January 1993 was proposed—a plan that didn't create peace and seriously worsened the war. Briton David Owen represented the European Community, and American Cyrus Vance was a UN Special

Envoy. Their plan proposed the division of Bosnia into ten semi-autonomous ethnic cantons that would be governed by the majority ethnoreligious populations in each: Serbs, Croats, and Bosniaks (Muslims). Although this plan was never implemented, it had the effect of speeding up ethnic cleansing by Serbs and Croats, who attempted to homogenise what they saw as "their territories" before the prospective canton borders were put in place.

OPPOSITE
THIS IS MY HOMELAND!
Bosnian Army (ABiH) Press Centre
Sarajevo, 1993
During the Bosnian War, foreign powers presented various peace plans; they all proposed partitioning the country along ethnoreligious lines. Democratic Bosnians everywhere, however, were adamant that Bosnia should not be divided. The map in the top right-hand corner depicts a peace plan of August 1993 proposed by Thorvald Stoltenberg and David Owen. As described in the previous caption, Owen was the British author of an earlier failed peace plan. The map in the opposite corner appears to be the Contact Group (United States, Russia, Great Britain, France, and Germany) plan of July 1994. The slogan over both maps reads: This is Not My Homeland. Eventually, of course, a de facto partition of Bosnia did occur as a result of the Dayton Agreement of 1995.

**OVO NIJE
MOJA DOMOVINA...**

**NI OVO NIJE
MOJA DOMOVINA...**

OVO JE
MOJA DOMOVINA!

PRESS CENTAR ARMIJE RBiH

Štampa : JP GEODETSKI

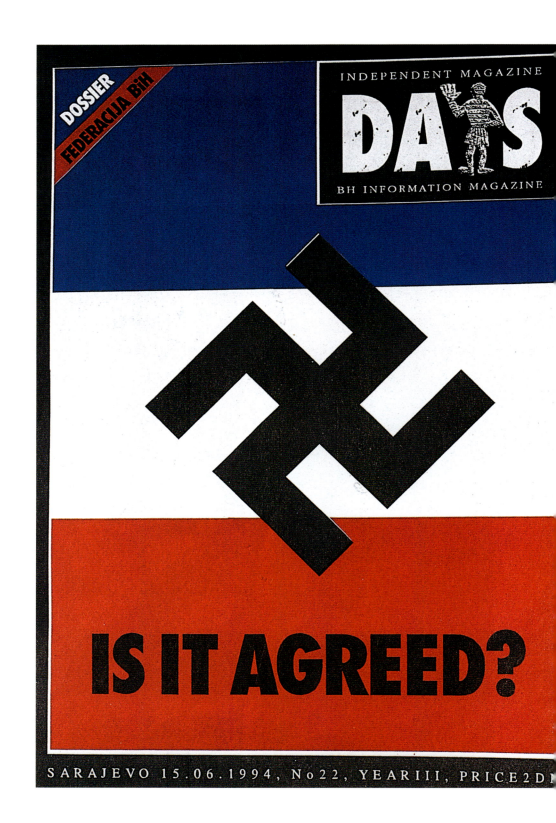

PREVIOUS SPREAD
IS IT AGREED?
Dani magazine (front and back covers)
Sarajevo, June 1994
The Muslim-Croat federation was formed in 1994. Although controversial, it did end the fighting between Croats and Muslims and enabled both parties to combine and fight Bosnian Serb forces, which in this cover image are associated with Nazism.

RIGHT
UNTOUCHABLE
Art Publishing
Sarajevo, 1994
This poster is a homage to the work of the German photographer August Sander, who took humane photos of mainly working people, and then categorised them into seven broad categories; marginalised people he placed in a category he called "The Last People". In this poster, they have been renamed UNtouchable—a play on the name for the lowest social caste in India combined with the acronym for the United Nations. This thought reflected many Bosnian's perceptions of the UN's attitude to them.

OPPOSITE
PIPE OF PEACE
Art Publishing
Sarajevo, 1994
This poster makes a play on Rene Magritte's famous surrealist painting *Ceci n'est pas une pipe* (This is not a pipe). The year of the poster's creation coincides with the peace that was declared between Croatia and Bosnia, that resulted in the Muslim-Croat federation.

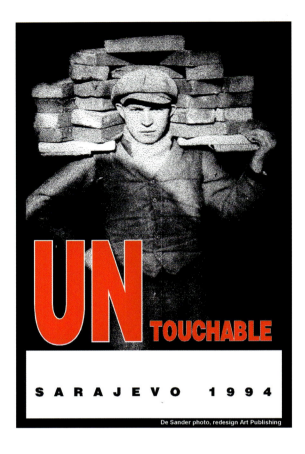

SARAJEVO 1994

De Sander photo, redesign Art Publishing

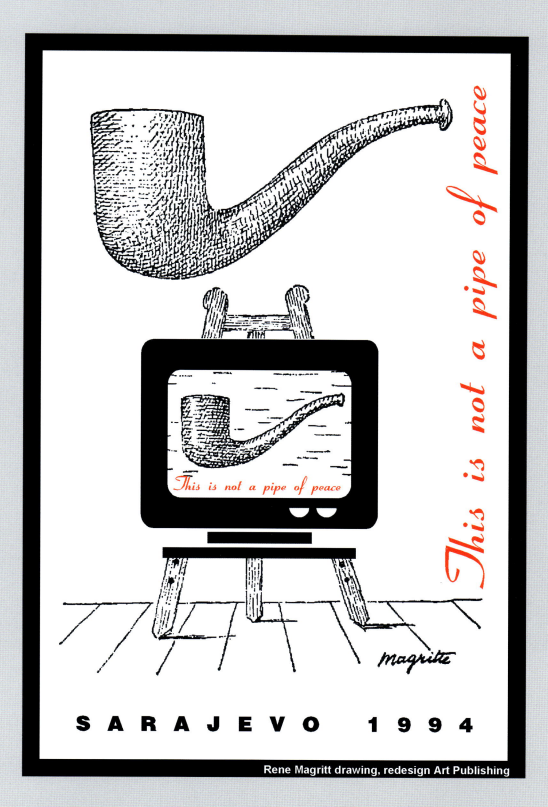

This is not a pipe of peace

This is not a pipe of peace

SARAJEVO 1994

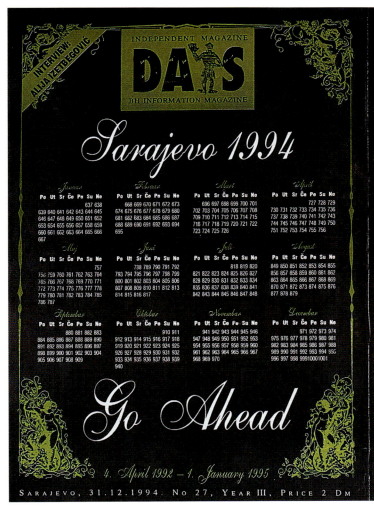

PREVIOUS SPREAD: LEFT TO RIGHT
OLYMPICS SPORTS COMPLEX
Photograph by Master Sgt. Michael J. Haggerty
Sarajevo, 1995

The 1984 Olympics Sports Complex was turned into an improvised cemetery to accommodate victims of the siege of Sarajevo.

SARAJEVO 1994—SARAJEVO 1995—GO AHEAD
Dani magazine **(front and back covers)**
Sarajevo, December 1994

This magazine cover, designed by Trio, features a calendar that highlights the day-count of the Sarajevo siege, thus showing the first day of 1994 as 637—the number of days the siege had been in place up to that date. The siege lasted from 2 April 1992 to 29 February 1996: three years, ten months, three weeks, and three days. It continued beyond the formal end of hostilities brought about by the Dayton Agreement, making it the longest siege in the history of modern European warfare.

OPPOSITE
WHO FUCKED THE CULTURE UP?
Trio
Sarajevo, 1995

This poster was produced for the Sarajevo Winter Festival, an arts event held at the beginning of each year. The festival began in 1984—the year the Winter Olympics took place in Sarajevo—and was held each year of the siege, against overwhelming odds. Sarajevo is home to most of Bosnia's artists and designers. Although many left during the war, many also stayed and contributed to the city's rich and varied artistic life. Inevitably, images of war and death occupied a central place in the art produced during this time. Much of the work protests against the injustice of the war and calls for international attention. Many foreign artists, writers, theatre directors, actors, musicians, and designers responded to this call—visiting Sarajevo and lending their talents and voices to those who lived there. Although this meant that Sarajevo was creatively highly fertile, the wall-to-wall international publicity the city received left other Bosnian cities in relative obscurity.

ABOVE
SARAJEVO WINTER '95
Fuad Hadžihalilović
Sarajevo, 1995
Sarajevans reaching for the stars. A promotional image for the Sarajevo Winter Festival.

OPPOSITE
SARAJEVO ALPHABET
Trio
Sarajevo, 1994
A play on an 18th century image of artillery, which was a new science at the time, and a one-handed sign language alphabet. Was the designer trying to say that the situation in Sarajevo was as surreal as this image suggests, or that nobody seemed to be listening to Sarajevo's desperate plight, or that Sarajevo had one hand tied behind its back?

All the images on this and the following two spreads are publicity posters for the Sarajevo Winter Festival (run by the International Peace Centre) or specific festival events. Ibrahim Spahić has been the indomitable General Director of the festival since it started in 1984 following the Winter Olympics of that year. Spahić envisages the Sarajevo Winter Festival as an open Balkan space for the arts, and it never missed one edition during the siege of Sarajevo. All these posters were produced by a variety of artists working with the festival, and their images need little or no literal interpretation.

RIGHT
ENRICO BAJ, HERVÉ DI ROSA
Trio
Sarajevo, 1993
An event showcasing the work of two artists: the Italian Surrealist Enrico Baj, and the French painter Hervé Di Rosa.

OPPOSITE
STOP
Enis Selimović
Sarajevo, 1994
Inspired by the German medieval painter Albrecht Dürer.

FOLLOWING SPREAD: LEFT: CLOCKWISE FROM TOP LEFT
UNTITLED
Mehmed Zaimović
Sarajevo, 1996

UNTITLED
Fikret Libovać
Sarajevo, 1995

UNTITLED
Amer Bakšić
Sarajevo, 1994

SARAJEVO—CULTURAL CAPITAL OF EUROPE
Dino Malović
Sarajevo, 1994

FOLLOWING SPREAD: RIGHT
SARAJEVO WINTER '94
Dino Malović
Sarajevo, 1994
This design appears to be based on a celebrated Polish poster; thanks to Jan Nuckowski for pointing this out.

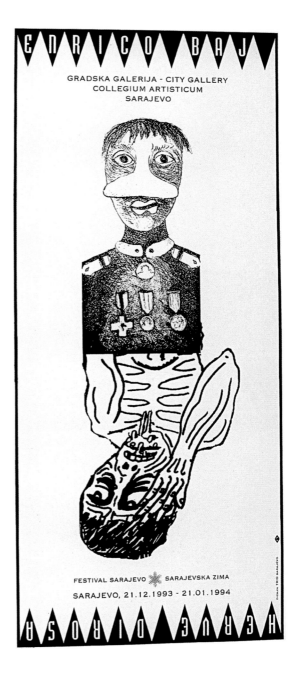

SLOBODA

HOW *BOSNIAN WAR POSTERS* CAME TOGETHER
A NOTE FROM THE AUTHOR

When I started collecting the posters that eventually became *Bosnian War Posters*, I was far from being a writer or a graphic designer. I was a documentary film editor. In 1995, however, I put my career on hold and went to Bosnia with a burning sense of outrage at the genocidal events taking place in the heart of Europe.

In Tuzla, northeastern Bosnia, I met an actress and theatre director called Baisa Baki. She was trying to stage a version of Shakespeare's *A Midsummer Night's Dream* with a youth drama company she had assembled. I returned to England in mid-1996 in order to fundraise, so I could make a documentary film about her play.

Corin Redgrave (Vanessa Redgrave's brother) at the Royal Shakespeare Company invited me to give a talk to actors in Stratford-Upon-Avon. And the immensely talented and beautiful Julie Christie sent me one hundred pounds! Although my fundraising petered out unsuccessfully, I wasn't deterred. I got hold of a Sony Hi-8 camera, a microphone, and two boxes of video cassettes. And with Julie Christie's £100 cheque (which I had half a mind to frame, not bank) I bought a bus ticket back to Bosnia. I was going to make my documentary after all ... I thought. Wrong! Baisa never managed to get her Shakespearian production off the ground.

Then one day in the winter of 1997, I had an idea: why not tell the story of the war through posters? Baisa laughed, told me it was impossible and advised me to forget it. But I couldn't get the idea out of my head. And with the help of Alina Boboc and Steven Gordon—and the support of Rupert and Stephanie Wolfe Murray (the founder of Canongate Publishing)—over the next year we tracked down and photographed around 700 posters, magazine covers, and postcards.

Much later, the challenge was to select these powerful works of art and shape them into a coherent story of the war. Here, my film editing skills came in useful. I put *Bosnian War Posters* together in much the same way as a film is cut: poster-by-poster (i.e. "shot-by-shot"), section-by-section (i.e. "scene-by-scene"), from the "first act" to the "dénouement". The book's captions work as a kind of "voice-over", guiding the reader on an informational level in contrast to the images that work on a more emotional one.

When I edit film, I sometimes feel I am sculpting with images, sounds, and text. When I edited *Bosnian War Posters* I had a similar sensation, only without the sound. I hope that when the book is browsed (even without reading any of the texts) it provokes an emotional response in the reader and stimulates personal thoughts, memories, and reflections—in much the same way as a great movie can impact the viewer.

Fortunately, I had the great luxury (encouraged by Interlink Publishing) to edit and design the book myself. And I did this slowly, over more than a year—taking infinite care with each visual juxtaposition as well as the overall tonal composition of the book. When designing the book, if I felt I needed a photograph, I commissioned it or searched for one in an archive. If I sensed I had a hole in the story, I went back to my poster collection and found a suitable one to plug the gap. Caption texts were written as the book expanded visually. And those texts were then rewritten many times with investigative rigour. My Introduction was the first long text to be completed (along with first drafts of the captions), followed by three Prefaces and four Afterwords. All texts have been translated into Bosnian, since I very much wanted the book to be understood in ex-Yugoslavia, too.

All things considered, buying that bus ticket back to Bosnia was money well spent. *Bosnian War Posters* was published, and a key part of a country's heritage was saved for future generations. If you're reading this, Julie Christie, once again I'd like to say Thanks!

D. J. Simon.

FREEDOM. By Zdravko Novak, Tuzla, 1992. The juxtaposition of a dream-like bird with a mortar bomb and other weapons could not be more stark. The bird holds the *fleur-de-lis* medieval emblem of Bosnia in her beak.

FESTIVAL SARAJEVO

sarajevska zima '94　　　　　sarajevo winter '94

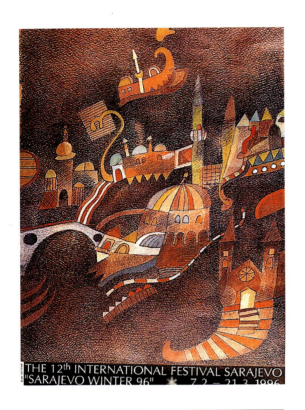

THE 12th INTERNATIONAL FESTIVAL SARAJEVO
"SARAJEVO WINTER 96" ✳ 7.2 – 21.3.1996

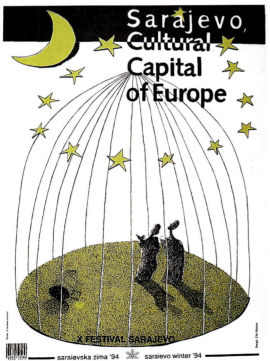

Sarajevo, Cultural Capital of Europe

X FESTIVAL SARAJEVO
saraievska zima '94 ✳ saraievo winter '94

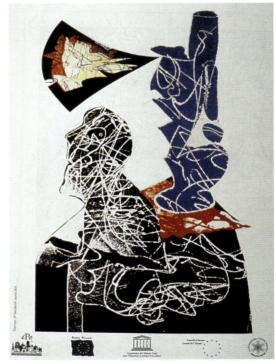

X FESTIVAL SARAJEVO

sarajevska zima '94   sarajevo winter '94

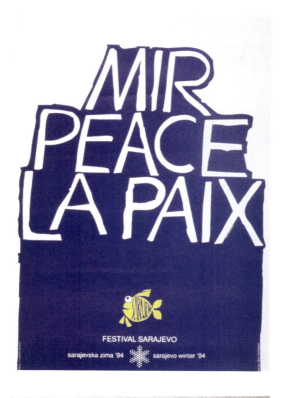

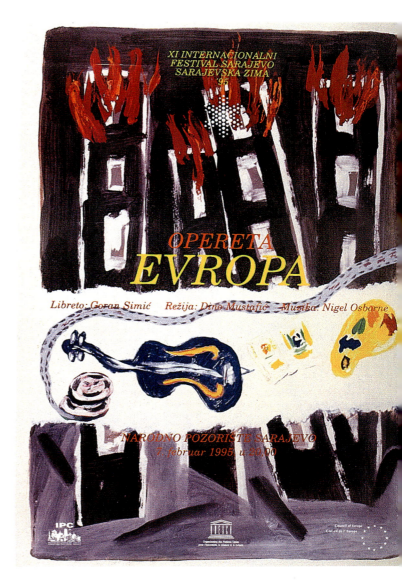

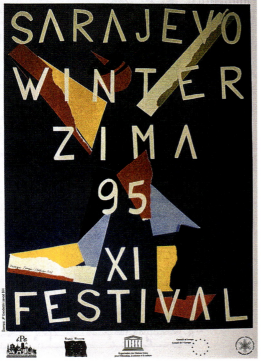

EVERYTHING IS POSSIBLE!!!
Art Publishing
Sarajevo, 1995

I NEED SARAJEVO WINTER
Stjepan Roš
Sarajevo, 1994

SARAJEVO WINTER '95
Avdo Žiga
Sarajevo, 1995

SARAJEVO WINTER '95
Andreas Pfeiffer
Sarajevo, 1995

PREVIOUS SPREAD: RIGHT: CLOCKWISE FROM TOP LEFT
PEACE
Enis Selimović
Sarajevo, 1994

OPERETTA EUROPA
Nusret Pašić
Sarajevo, 1995
A poster for an opera written by Goran Simić and directed by Dino Mustafić—with music by Nigel Osborne, a Scottish composer, teacher and aid worker.

SARAJEVO WINTER '95
Tanja Roš and Stjepan Roš
Sarajevo, 1995

OPPOSITE: TOP TO BOTTOM
SAR-AJ-EVO 1992 '93
Enis Selimović
Sarajevo, 1993
"AJ" communicates an expression of physical pain or shock, similar to the English "Ouch!"

ARTISTS OF SARAJEVO FOR A FREE BiH
Dževad Hozo
Sarajevo, 1992
The artists listed on this poster held a joint exhibition of work in Sarajevo at a gallery belonging to the Bosnian Army. This was a symbolic way for them to declare their support for the country's legitimate armed forces and the elected government in Sarajevo in their fight against Serb aggression. Heavy shelling on the day this photograph was taken prevented many more artists than appear on the poster from reaching the Sarajevo Academy of Fine Arts, where the picture was taken.

UMJETNICI SARAJEVA ZA SLOBODNU BOSNU I HERCEGOVINU

Mustafa Skopljak Salem Obralić   Čulić Dragan   Sućeska Hasan
Seid Hasanefendić Pašić Nusret   Avdo Žiga   Mirsada Baljić   Sead Čizmić   Dževad Hozo   Edin Numankadić
                                    Esad Muftić

Arifović Nedim   Alma Suljević
Acković-Čišić Nina   Ljubović Ibrahim
Bostandžić Smail   Malović Edin
Češljar Suad   Muhić Hamzalija
Gavrić Alma   Mujezinović Saida
Gavrić Stijepo   Kalcina Ivan
Hozo Irfan   Kovač Ana
Karamatić Renata   Ramić Afan
Karišik Husein   Tadić Radoslav
Kasapović Mile   Vrana Elma
Libovac Fikret   Zaimović Mehmed

                                                                                        Walldeg Petar

To raise awareness about Sarajevo's desperate situation during the siege, Trio studios came up with the concept of redesigning many design icons from a wide variety of genres. Most of these images were eventually printed as postcards (generically known as *Greetings from Sarajevo*), taken out of the city by journalists and aid workers, and then posted all over the world. Before long, Sarajevo became known as a hip European city in mortal danger.

ABOVE: LEFT TO RIGHT
SUPERMAN
Trio
Sarajevo, 1994
The DC Comics character and Superman logo—"S" stands for Sarajevo.

SARAJEVO'S CONDENSED
Trio
Sarajevo, 1994
Andy Warhol's iconic Campbell's soup can, reinterpreted here with bullet holes.

OPPOSITE
HOPELESS (FRONT AND BACK)
Trio
Sarajevo, 1994
Roy Lichtenstein's famous Pop Art image, rephrased.

FOLLOWING SPREAD: LEFT TO RIGHT
SCREAM
Trio
Sarajevo, 1993
A redesign of Edvard Munch's existentialist painting.

MONA LISA
Trio
Sarajevo, 1993
After Leonardo da Vinci, with a teardrop.

Lichtenstein's "Hopeless" - Redesign by "Trio" - Sarajevo

"opeless" – Roy Lichtenstein
designed by **"TRIO" Sarajevo**

PRODUCTION **"FABRIKA"** PRINTED BY **MÜLLER** SARAJEVO

This document has been created in war circumstances.
(No paper, no inks, no electricity, no water. Just good will.)

X FESTIVAL SARAJEVO

"Scream" redesign by "Trio" - Sarajevo
Štampa JP Gevdetski zavod B.H.

sarajevska zima '94 sarajevo winter '94

"Mona Lisa" redesign by "Trio" - Sarajevo

SARAJEVO 1993

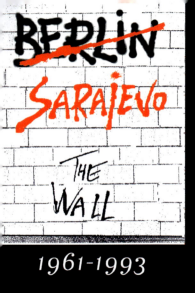

BERLIN ~~SARAJEVO~~

THE WALL

1961-1993

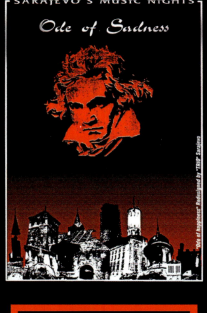

SARAJEVO'S MUSIC NIGHTS

Ode of Sadness

"Ode of happiness" Redesigned by "TRIO" Sarajevo

SOME LIKE IT
– in Sarajevo –

NEVER MIND
THE BOLLOCKS

HERE'S THE
SaR aJEVO

"Never mind..." Redesigned by "TRIO" Sarajevo

GOD Save THE SaR aJEVO

Sex Pistols

SARAJEVO 1993

"God Save the Queen" Redesigned by "TRIO" Sarajevo

I WANT YOU
TO SAVE SARAJEVO
NEAREST RECRUITING STATION

"I WANT YOU" – redesign by "Trio" - Sarajevo

"That's one small
step for Sarajevo,
but one giant leap for mankind..."

Neil Armstrong, at 4.17 p.m.

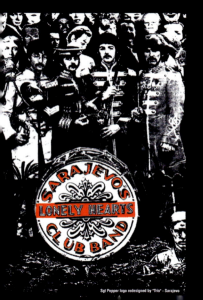

Sarajevos
LONELY HEARTS
CLUB BAND

Sgt Pepper logo redesigned by "Trio" - Sarajevo

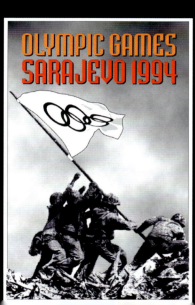

OLYMPIC GAMES
SARAJEVO 1994

ABSOLUT
Country of Bosnia
SARAJEVO

Absolut Sarajevo is made from
Authentic Bosnian citizens:
Muslims, Serbs, Croats,
Jewish and Special blends,
born in rich Country of Bosnia.
The Spirit of togetherness
is an age-old Bosnian
tradition dating back more
than 800 years.
Sarajevo has been sold under
the name Absolute Since 1992.

80 PROOF

IMPORTED

ABSOLUT VODKA

WELCOME TO OLYMPIC GAMES

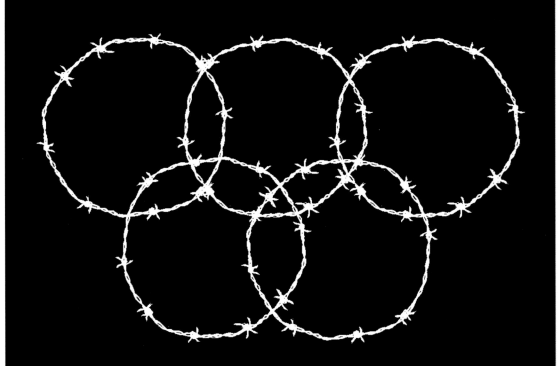

SARAJEVO
1984-1994

Design "Trio" Sarajevo

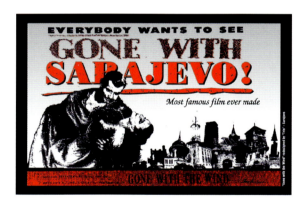

GREETINGS FROM SARAJEVO (REDESIGNS)
Trio
Sarajevo, siege years

While editing this book in 2021 Bojan Hadžihalilović—one of the founding members (along with Dada Hadžihalilović and Lejla Mulabegović) of Trio design studio in Sarajevo—sent us the complete set of Trio's wartime redesigns, allowing us to present them here in all their glory. Trio's redesign concept has been recognised as an extraordinary 20th century visual communication campaign—one conducted, moreover, under the most difficult circumstances (a siege) and with one of the most ambitious aims: to avert the destruction of a people, a city, and a way of life. The obvious should also be stated: that it was a project conducted prior to the Internet and before the birth of social media. It was a paper and ink campaign (when paper and ink were also very hard to find)—which, in today's digital world, seems like a concept from another civilisation. Several of the Trio redesigns share the same Sarajevo city skyline graphic that appears as a logo for the International Peace Centre.

It's
sad,
so sad
It's a sad,
sad situation
And it's getting
more and more absurd...

SARAJEVO,

seems to be the hardest word...

TITO'S FUNERAL
Anonymous (Public Domain)
Yugoslavia, May 1980

Tito, born in 1892, was interred in the House of Flowers mausoleum in Belgrade on 8 May 1980, the day after what would have been his 88th birthday. He was the last of the great allied wartime leaders to pass away. And if anyone doubts that he was one of the most respected, too, they only need to take note of how many international dignitaries attended his funeral. Heads of state: 39 (notably, US President Jimmy Carter and Cuba's Fidel Castro did not attend); 21 heads of government or vice-heads of state; 19 deputies or foreign ministers; 48 other state delegations; 54 delegations of political parties and organisations. Almost every country in the world sent a representative of some kind, while the outpouring of national grief seemed to be without precedent. How, one wonders, did things go so badly wrong, and so fast, for the country Tito left behind? Political greed, rampant corruption, economic mismanagement, and surging ultra-nationalism is the fatal combination of factors most commonly blamed. Whether Tito himself can be faulted for leaving Yugoslavia in such a dire situation is a question still keenly debated, as is the possible meddling in Yugoslav affairs by outside powers.

IT WAS HONOURABLE TO LIVE WITH SARAJEVO
Dani magazine poster
Sarajevo, 1993

The slogan "It Was Honourable To Live With Tito" became popular after the death of Yugoslavia's leader in 1980. In this poster, Tito's coffin is replaced with a bombed out Sarajevo skyline. In the lower part of the poster, standing around this skyline, is a cluster of Yugoslav People's Army officers. The vast audience is a photomontage of faces relevant to the times, among them: Vojislav Šešelj, Radovan Karadžić, and presidents Slobodan Milošević, Franjo Tuđman and Alija Izetbegović. A bored-looking British Prime Minister John Major and a gloating French President François Mitterrand—two politicians whose strategies did untold damage during the Bosnian War—can also be spotted on the far right of the group. (It's not clear what Madonna is doing there, but she was perhaps the best-known iconoclast of that era.) This poster was distributed as a free pull-out in a 1993 edition of *Dani* magazine.

BILO JE ČASNO
ŽIVJETI SA SARAJEVOM...

GREETINGS FROM SARAJEVO
Trio
Sarajevo, 1994
Three Cupid marksmen aiming at the same Sarajevo city skyline graphic that is used as a logo for the International Peace Centre. Cupid is said to be the mythological son of Mars, the god of war, and Venus the goddess of love. Here this progeny of opposing forces targets a besieged Sarajevo with golden bows and arrows.

OPPOSITE
BACK TO THE FUTURE
Art Publishing
Sarajevo, 1994
Albert Einstein, the famous physicist, said "I know not with what weapons World War III will be fought, but World War IV will be fought with sticks and stones." What makes this poster particularly poignant is that soldiers in the Bosnian Army were obliged to use old-fashioned and even handmade weapons, and tactics like World War I-style trenches since they started the war essentially unarmed; they were the only combatants that didn't have a neighbouring state supplying them with weapons. Here the tip of the archer's arrow is one of Bosnia's traditional *fleur-de-lis.*

FOLLOWING SPREAD
FARCE? NATO
Dani magazine (front and back covers)
Sarajevo, November 1994
By late 1994 there was increasing pressure for NATO to finally intervene in Bosnia and stop the war. Limited airstrikes began, primarily to enforce the no-fly zone established by the UN Security Council. The airstrikes didn't achieve what the citizens of Bosnia were hoping for, however, and were stopped when hundreds of UNPROFOR peacekeepers were taken hostage by Bosnian Serbs forces. The farcical aspect of this was that the world's greatest military alliance couldn't stand up to a ragtag force of extreme Serb nationalists. The image shows the array of sophisticated weaponry that NATO had at its disposal, and also makes a mockery of the alliance's acronym.

PAGES 208–209
MAYBE AIRLINES
Sanjin Jukić
Sarajevo, 1995
A poster for an art exhibition in Graz, Austria, entitled Sarajevo Ghetto Spectacle, organised by the Obala Art Center in Sarajevo. These huge Ukrainian transport planes were hired by the UN and used to supply food to Sarajevo during its four-year siege.

BACK TO THE FUTURE

IN BOSNIA

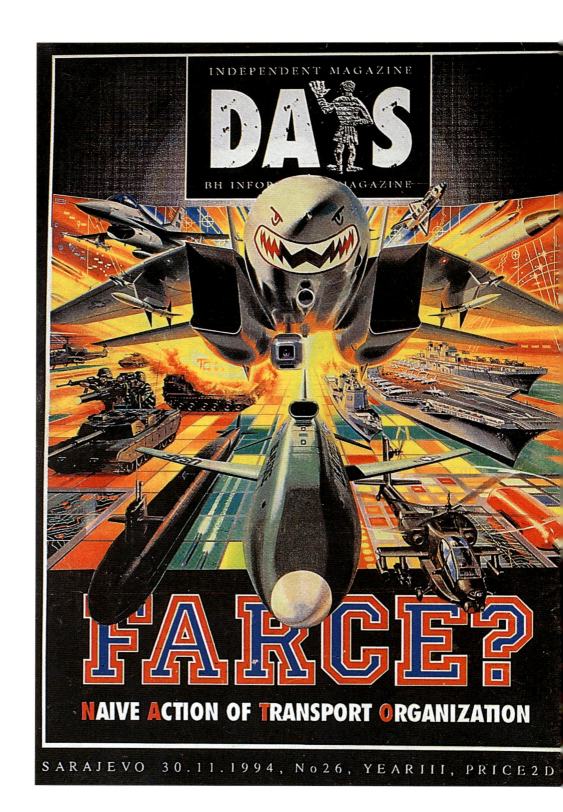

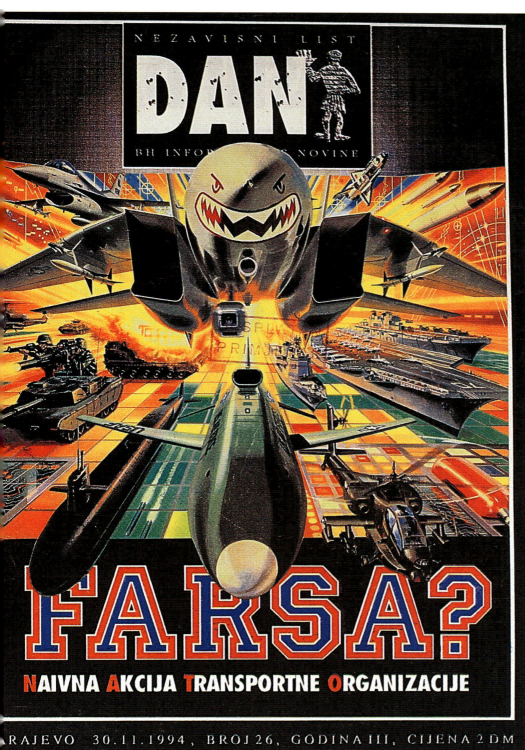

Only we fly to Sarajevo

MAYBE AIRLINES

KAPIJA
Edin Derviševič
Tuzla, 1995

At 9 p.m. on 25 May 1995 Serb forces in the hills above Tuzla fired an artillery shell that landed in a part of the old town known as Kapija. This was where young people regularly gathered to chat and drink coffee. The shell exploded in their midst. The square was more crowded than usual since it was National Youth Day. (Ironically, it was also the day Yugoslavia had celebrated Tito's "official" birthday.) Seventy-one young people died that night in Tuzla—most were between the ages of 18 and 25—and 240 were injured. A young American journalist called Chris Mathieu later blogged about the full horror of the scene (extract):

> That night I walked into the main hospital in the town of Tuzla in northern Bosnia.
>   I entered the building to the sounds of screaming and crying and total chaos. I recoiled, quickly stepping out of the way of a hospital orderly walking toward me in a shoe-deep river of blood in the lobby.
>   He was pushing a broomstick with a window-washing squeegee attached, redirecting the flow of blood to the outside of the front entrance, where it smacked the pavement like several litres of water tossed from a bucket.
>   The blood was flowing on the tile floor from several operating rooms, and from panic-filled hospital corridors.
>   Later, I watched a technician at the morgue weeping as he piled the heads of some of the victims in a corner after identifying the ethnicity of each one—all teenage girls—as Croats, Muslims, and Serbs.
>   "They were all Bosnians," he said, tears streaming down his face. "Why were they killed?"

Novak Đukić, a former Army of Republika Srpska officer, was found guilty in 2008 of ordering the shelling of Kapija; he was sentenced to 25 years in prison.

KAPIJA
Photograph by Rupert Wolfe Murray
Tuzla, 2021

The site where the shell landed is now marked with a plaque bearing a poem by Bosnia-Herzegovina's most lauded poet, Mak Dizdar:

> Here one does not live
> just to live
> Here one does not live
> just to die
> Here one also dies
> to live

OPPOSITE
25 MAY 1995–96 (FIRST ANNIVERSARY)
Printcom
Tuzla, 1996

So appalling were the news images of what has come to be called the "Tuzla massacre"—as Chris Mathieu's important blog, quoted above, makes clear—that TV broadcasters and publications around the world chose not to show them. As a result, the shelling of Kapija received little international attention.

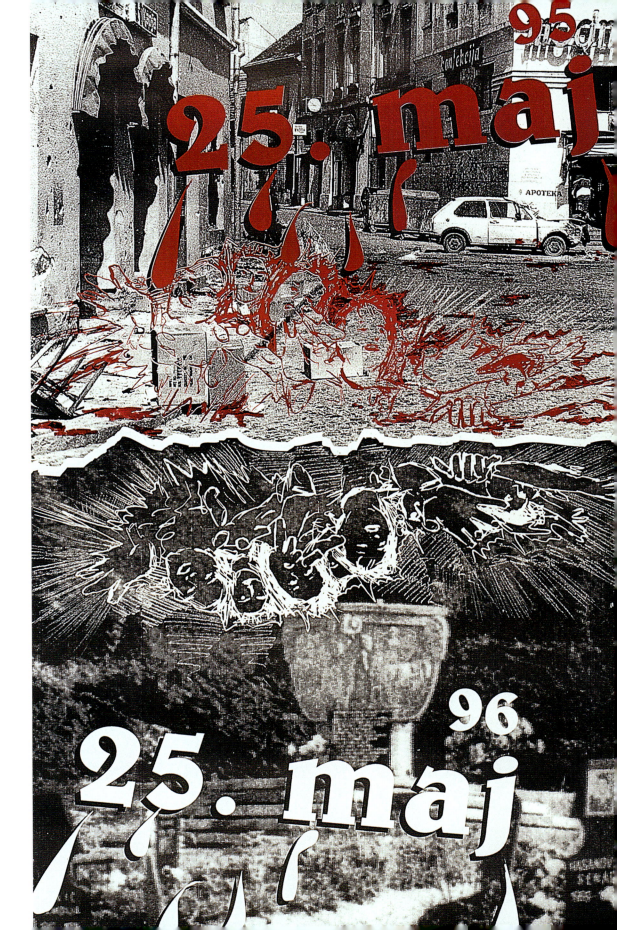

SLANA BANJA CEMETERY; *Photograph by Rupert Wolfe Murray; Tuzla, 2021*
Fifty-one of the 71 young victims killed in the Kapija attack were interred in a memorial cemetery created in a Tuzlan park. The other 20 were buried in family graves.

VICTORY!
Dani magazine (front and back covers)
Sarajevo, May 1995
Less than three weeks before the shelling of Tuzla (detailed on the previous two spreads) and several months before the decisive events in Srebrenica and Žepa depicted opposite, Dani published this alarmingly direct comparison between Nazism and Serb nationalism. The cover was a response to the Bosnian Serb Army's ultimatum, issued on 17 April, that said all Muslim fighters and civilians should leave Srebrenica within 24 hours.

OPPOSITE: TOP TO BOTTOM
EXPELLED
Dani magazine (front and back covers)
Sarajevo, August 1995
Areas with a majority of Bosnian Muslims were put under siege by Serbian forces at the start of the war. A year later, in April 1993, the UN designated the first Safe Area in Bosnia: the town of Srebrenica. Three weeks later, five more towns and cities were declared Safe Areas: Bihać, Goražde, Tuzla, Sarajevo, and Žepa. They turned out to be some of the least safe places in Bosnia. On 11 July 1995 Serb forces led by General Ratko Mladić overran the town of Srebrenica; the Dutch UNPROFOR troops who were stationed there offered no resistance. Twenty-three thousand Muslim women and children were expelled and Srebrenica is now inside Republika Srpska. When Srebrenica was taken, rumours of a massacre of the male population abounded; these rumours were soon confirmed true.

ONCE AGAIN!
Dani magazine (front and back covers)
Sarajevo, September 1995
On 28 August 1995 Serb forces besieging Sarajevo fired five mortar shells into the busy market square: 43 people were killed and 75 injured. This was the second fatal attack on the same location in less than 18 months. Three days later—after years of international indecision—NATO began bombing Serb military targets around Sarajevo and throughout Serb-held Bosnia.

EXPELLED

SARAJEVO AUGUST 1995, No 34, YEAR IV, PRICE 2 DM

PROGNANI

SARAJEVO AVGUST/KOLOVOZ 1995, BROJ 34, GODINA IV, CIJENA 2 DM

ONCE AGAIN!   PONOVO!

SARAJEVO   SEPTEMBER 1995, No 35, YEAR IV, PRICE 2 DM   SARAJEVO SEPTEMBAR/RUJAN 1995, BROJ 35, GODINA IV, CIJENA 2 DM

UN PROTECTION FORCE
Photograph by Stef Adjuc
Srebrenica / Potočari, 1993

Shortly after Srebrenica was declared a UN Safe Area, a Dutch Battalion (known as Dutchbat) took over UNPROFOR peacekeeping duties in Srebrenica. Their mission ended in disaster for the civilian population. In 2002, following a seven-year investigation in the Netherlands, Dutchbat were accused of being criminally negligent for not preventing the massacre of more than 8,300 civilians. In fairness to the performance of Dutchbat, however, the UN high command also failed to protect the people or back up its own peacekeepers. (This photograph shows a French UNPROFOR soldier in Srebrenica, before the arrival of the Dutch Battalion in 1994.)

RIGHT

DUTCHBAT
Photograph by Rupert Wolfe Murray
Srebrenica / Potočari, 2021

As Bosnian Serb forces launched their final assault on Srebrenica in July 1995, civilians flocked to this UN military base. They were not given the protection they sought. Worse, Dutchbat soldiers have been accused of assisting the Serbs in the ethnic cleansing that subsequently took place. Concrete security blocks in this photograph, marked DUTCHBAT, have been conserved—as a monument to political and military failure, perhaps.

OPPOSITE

ETHNIC CLEANSING
Anonymous
Srebrenica, 1995

This photo collage shows a Bosnian boy on board a truck, in the process of being transported out of Srebrenica when it was ethnically cleansed.

KANTONALNI ODBOR
SDA TPK

TUZLA

VRATIMO IM VJERU U ŽIVOT

ABOVE

LET'S GIVE THEM BACK THEIR FAITH IN LIFE
Adin Šadić
Tuzla, 1995

The vast majority of refugees from Srebrenica ended up living in the Tuzla region. This poster was commissioned by Bosnian President Alija Izetbegović's ruling Party of Democratic Action (SDA).

OPPOSITE

BIRDS
Forum of Tuzla Citizens
Tuzla, 1995

The Forum of Tuzla Citizens' main graphic designer, Jasminko Arnautović—whose posters address issues of nationalism, secularism, and tolerance—was questioned by police about this image since it appeared shortly after the exodus of Bosniak citizens ethnically cleansed from Srebrenica and Žepa. Bosnian authorities believed that the black crows symbolised refugees harassing Tuzla (since many came to the city), and that the poster was a sarcastic retort to one by Adin Šadić (above). Arnautović insists, however, that he meant it as a warning against the danger posed by nationalism in general, as well as other hardships Tuzla had to deal with. He remembers that in an earlier, unpublished version of the poster the birds had labels hung around their necks stating these

hardships clearly: "Nationalism", "Hunger", as well as "International Community" since it was felt at the time (and still is) that it had failed Bosnia. The labels were presumably removed to make the birds more open to symbolic interpretation, and inspiration for this poster must have come from the Hitchcock film of the same name. It was produced in collaboration with the Forum of Tuzla Citizens. The figure in the poster is a statue of Atlas that stands in the centre of Tuzla; the figure appears in many Forum of Tuzla Citizens posters. For example, on the right we see the same statue used symbolically to address other sociopolitical issues. The first of them, as were many other Forum of Tuzla Citizens posters, was produced in collaboration with the European Parliament's PHARE Programme for aspiring EU states, and Helsinki Citizens' Assembly. From top to bottom: SHIP speaks about Tuzla as an example of secularism and tolerance, ahead of the rest of the country, pulling it forward; LIBERTY expresses the idea that Tuzla is an example of hope and tolerance, in the mold of western secular democracies; U SURU? expresses something more complex. During the first municipal elections after the war, one candidate frequently used the expression, "I'm going to put Tuzla *in order.*" *U Suru* translates as "order", in the way animals are herded together. He meant to force the people to accept an order based on nationalistic principals.

THIS SPREAD
ENDGAME; *Photograph by Rupert Wolfe Murray; Sarajevo, 2021*
After the genocidal events in Srebrenica and Žepa fully came to light in the summer of 1995, followed by another marketplace massacre in Sarajevo, the international community—largely at the insistence of President Bill Clinton's administration—finally decided to bomb Bosnian Serb forces. The Bosnian War was reaching its endgame. A sustained NATO bombing campaign, called Operation Deliberate Force that lasted between 30 August and 20 September 1995, struck around 340 Bosnian Serb targets. Heavy weapons that had ringed Sarajevo for more than three years were destroyed or withdrawn. The ferocity of Operation Deliberate Force sidelined Radovan Kadadžić and drove Serbia's President Slobodan Milošević to the negotiating table in Dayton, Ohio. It was rightly asked, however—and still is—why Operation Deliberate Force couldn't have happened years earlier, thus saving countless lives and halting the wholesale destruction of Bosnia-Herzegovina?

FOLLOWING SPREAD
THE END OF THE WAR; *Asim Đelilović; Travnik, 1997*
In Bosnian, the word *rat* means war. Đelilović uses the word graphically in this poster to mimic the sound a machine gun makes: rat-a-tat. The exclamation and question marks express the scepticism felt by many Bosnians about the peace that the Dayton Agreement. The Dayton Agreement was finalised at Wright-Patterson Air Force Base, Ohio, on 21 November 1995, and formally signed in Paris on 14 December that year. Overseen by US President Bill Clinton, Presidents Milošević of Serbia, Tuđman of Croatia, and Izetbegović of Bosnia-Herzegovina were co-signatories. Although Dayton stopped the war, in the years that followed many people would come to see it as a failed political experiment.

SIGNING THE DAYTON PEACE AGREEMENT; *Anonymous; Paris, 14 December 1995 (Public Domain)*
A round of applause hardly seemed to fit the occasion of the Paris Peace Conference for the ex-Yugoslavia—especially applause by and for some of the statesmen assembled here. Seated (left to right): President of Serbia, Slobodan Milošević; President of Croatia, Franjo Tuđman; President of Bosnia-Herzegovina, Alija Izetbegović. Standing (left to right): Spanish Prime Minister Felipe González; US President Bill Clinton; French President Jacques Chirac; German Chancellor Helmut Kohl; UK Prime Minister John Major; Russian Prime Minister Viktor Chernomyrdin.

EX-YOUGOSLAVIE

m e

SARAJEVO

rry

mas

PREVIOUS SPREAD
MERRY XMAS SARAJEVO; *Trio; Sarajevo, 1995*
Against all odds, Sarajevo—marked for destruction by Bosnian Serb forces—had survived.

THIS SPREAD
GRBAVICA; *Photograph by Lt. Stacey Wyzkowski; Sarajevo, March 1996*
After the Dayton Agreement was signed at the end of 1995, a strange kind of peace settled over Sarajevo since it remained under siege until February 1996. This photo, taken in Grbavica—a downtown part of the city occupied by the Bosnian Serb Army during the war—shows the scale of destruction after the siege of the city was finally lifted. Meanwhile, approximately 60,000 foreign troops from all corners of the globe poured into the country. At the time, it was difficult to drive anywhere in Bosnia without being stuck behind long columns of slow-moving military vehicles. These troops were under the command of NATO, a more respected military entity than the UN's derisory peacekeeping force.

BOSNIA
Čedomir Kostović
USA, 1995

A wry and moving comment on post-Dayton Bosnia. Kostović's poster compares the dissection of a violin with the dismemberment of Bosnia into three ethnic parts (Muslim, Serb, and Croat). It might still be recognisable as a violin, but it certainly can't be played.

BOSNIA

SUPERMAN
UNICEF
Bosnia-Herzegovina, 1996
As a result of the war, Bosnia-Herzegovina was littered with landmines and other unexploded munitions. A massive de-mining campaign began and UNICEF, in collaboration with other organisations, came up with this public awareness poster. It was printed in both Latin and Cyrillic scripts. A popular quips was, "What took you so long?"

DAYTONATION
Asim Đelilović
Travnik, 1996
This poster plays on the words Dayton, spelt phonetically as it would be in Bosnian, and detonation—suggesting that the peace deal might set off another conflict, rather than resolve the recent one. (As the 1919 Treaty of Versailles had set the clock ticking for World War II.) The 1995 Dayton Agreement guaranteed the right of more than two million displaced Bosnian people to return to their pre-war homes. But as 1996 came and went, it became obvious that this was probably not going to happen. Extreme nationalists and war criminals were still in power all over the country, especially in Republika Srpska (Serb Republic) which has an equal say in running the country. Many of the local entities the peace treaty assumed would cooperate with each other were still run by the same people who had fought so ruthlessly to create ethnically pure mini-states. They had no intention of allowing refugees from other ethnic groups to return to their homes. The locations listed in this poster became flashpoints as refugees attempted to return: there were riots in Stolac and Jusići, which were under the control of Croats and Serbs respectively. In Mostar, the Croats continued to expel Muslims from the western part of the city. Brčko was a special case: it was the only city in Bosnia whose status was left open at Dayton—i.e. it was not placed under the jurisdiction of Republika Srpska or the Muslim-Croat federation; instead, it was placed under the temporary supervision of the international community. Today, Brčko is considered the only self-governing free city in Europe. It is similar to the Baltic city of Gdansk which, as Danzig, was run independently of Poland and Germany between the two world wars.

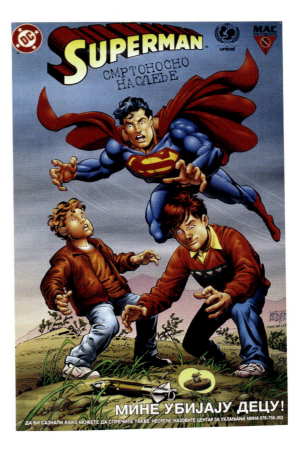

DE**j**TONACIJE

Stolac,Jusići,Mostar,Brčko...

ABOVE
SREBRENICA GRAVESTONES
Photograph by Rupert Wolfe Murray
Srebrenica/Potočari Genocide Memorial Cemetery, 2021
There are 6,504 gravestones at the Genocide Memorial
Cemetery. More will be added as bodies are identified.
Every year, thousands of people from all over the world
visit the graveyard and pay their respects.

OPPOSITE
SREBRENICA REMBRANCE DAY
Anonymous
Tuzla, 1996
One year after the genocidal events in Srebrenica and
Žepa, thousands of refugees were living in Tuzla. Over the
years many Bosniaks have returned to Srebrenica, and
they seem to be accepted by local Serbs and mosques
have been rebuilt. On a Republica Srpska political level,
however, tensions still exist. The text on the poster reads:

WE DON'T FORGET THE DEAD
WE THINK OF THE LIVING

BELOW
POTOČARI MEMORIAL WALL
Photograph by Rupert Wolfe Murray
Srebrenica/Potočari Genocide Memorial Cemetery, 2021
There are 8,372 names engraved on the memorial
wall of mainly men and boys murdered in and around
Srebrenica following its fall to Bosnian Serb forces.

NE ZABORAVIMO MRTVE
MISLIMO NA ŽIVE
SREBRENICA

11. JULI
1995.
DAN SJEĆANJA

NO TEETH...?
A MUSTACHE...?
SMEL LIKE SHIT...?

BOSNIAN GIRL

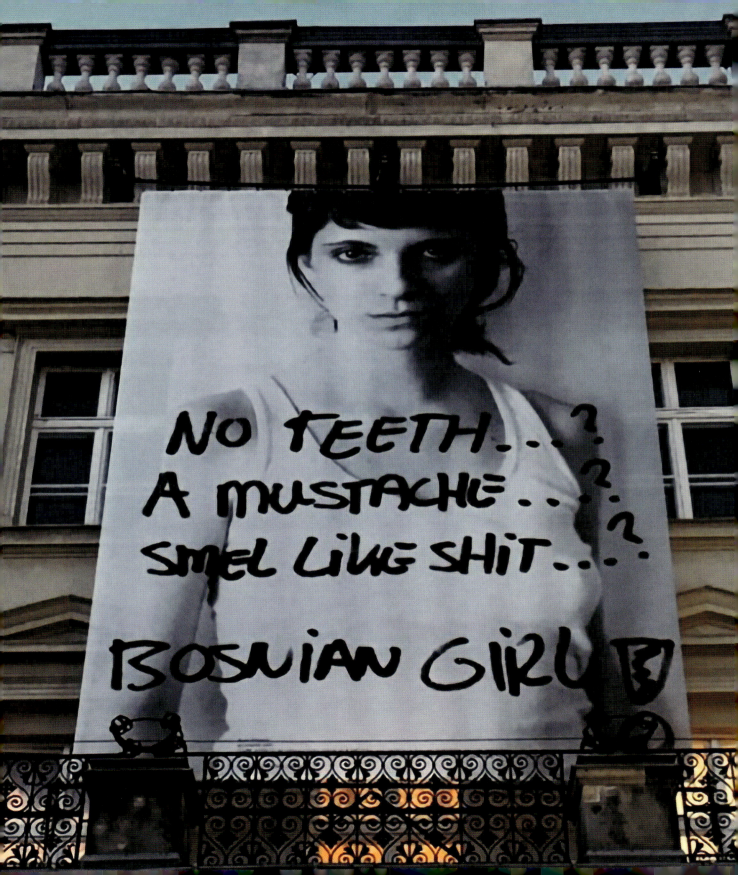

BOSNIAN GIRL
Anonymous
Srebrenica, date unknown
Photograph by Rupert Wolf Murray
Srebrenica/Potočari Genocide Memorial Cemetery, 2021
Various graffiti daubed by Dutchbat peacekeepers on the walls of their base in Srebrenica were discovered after they left. The graphics have been preserved in the visitor exhibition centre of the memorial cemetery. This is one of the most shocking.

BOSNIAN GIRL
Šejla Kamerić
Photograph by Zivazava
Sarajevo, 2003
Šejla Kamerćc subverted the "Bosnian Girl" UN graffiti by superimposing it over a self-portrait. This gigantic copy of her poster was displayed at the Maxim Gorki Theatre, Berlin, between October-November 2019.

OPPOSITE
BRČKO—THE TEST OF HUMANITY
Forum of Tuzla Citizens
Tuzla, 1998
Brčko is a city-region in the north of Bosnia, near the border with Croatia. Before the war it had a majority Muslim population, with sizable Croat and Serb minorities. During the war, Serb forces expelled all non-Serbs from the area, killing thousands. The entire Brčko district forms a corridor linking the eastern and western parts of Republika Srpska. Brčko is also of vital strategic importance to the Muslim-Croat federation, as it connects the Federation of Bosnia-Herzegovina to Croatia: its main access point to the world. These geopolitical demands make Brčko one of the most strategically complex regions in Bosnia. In March 1999 the international community proclaimed Brčko to be a "special" multi-ethnic district, to be administered internationally. Many Serbs, as well as Muslims, reacted angrily against this ruling. In October 2000 there was a serious outbreak of violence: thousands of Serb students rampaged through Brčko city, smashing Muslims' property and demanding their expulsion. Things have quietened down in recent years, however, and a certain amount of reintegration has been achieved. The three butterfly nets in this poster represent the interests of the main ethnoreligious groups in Bosnia (Muslim, Catholic, and Serb Orthodox). The butterfly represents the vulnerability of a multi-ethnic community when overshadowed by nationalist forces (the butterfly also graphically forms the accent on the letter "Č" upon which it is perched). This is one of many human rights posters commissioned by the Forum of Tuzla Citizens and designed by Jasminko Arnautović.

ABOVE
DESTRUCTION
Photograph by Brian D. Thompson
Brčko, 1996
Bosniak men repairing their home, destroyed by Bosnian Serb forces during the war.

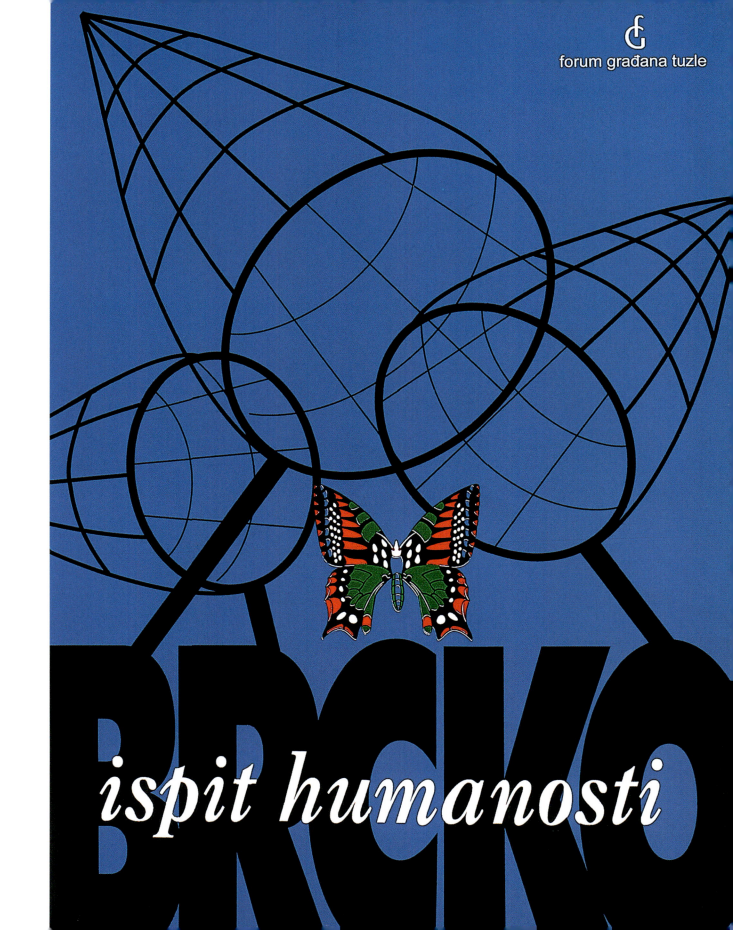

forum građana tuzle

BRCKO

ispit humanosti

RIGHT

BRČKO IS SERBIAN AND IS GOING TO STAY SERBIAN—WE KEEP OUR WORD
SSJ
Brčko, 1996

After the war, the notorious Serb warlord Arkan (written here in the Cyrillic alphabet: *APKAH)* metamorphosed into a politician, complete with a suit, tie and a winning smile. After years of conducting mass murder campaigns in Bosnia and Croatia with his Tigers death squad, incredulously he received funding for his political party— Party of Serbian Unity (SSJ)—from the European Union and ran in the first Bosnian elections, held in September 1996. He was later banned from political office in Bosnia, however, and the shame-faced international community withdrew his funding. Subsequently, he took part in the war in Kosovo, before being assassinated in a gangland-style hit in the lobby of a hotel he owned in Belgrade.

OPPOSITE

ARKAN ELECTION POSTERS
SSJ
Photograph by Alina Wolfe Murray
Republika Srpska, 1996

Despite his reputation of cruelty and the trail of death he left behind him, Arkan remained immensely popular among many Serbs in Bosnia—almost a national hero. These posters of a baby-faced Arkan on a house in the Serb Republic show that ordinary Serbs bought Belgrade's propaganda line: that he was a defender of Serb rights against invading Muslim hordes. The graffiti in this image includes his name in Cyrillic, the Serb nationalist slogan (CCCC) and the acronym, also in Cyrillic, of Arkan's post-war political party: Serbian Unity.

THE NEW FACE OF SARAJEVO
Dani magazine
Sarajevo, March 1998

Overt Islamic practices such as wearing the burka were outlawed by Tito. The appearance of fully veiled Muslim women in Bosnian cities was relatively new after the war. It was unheard of in urban areas before 1992 but during the war women started dressing and appearing in public in this way. After the war, the increased spread of such practices (although the Burka is still far from a common sight on the streets of Bosnia) marked a new phase in the development of Bosnian society. These practices were criticised by westernised Bosniaks who saw them as a worrying sign of the possible ethnic and social ghettoisation of the country.

OPPOSITE: LEFT TO RIGHT
ARMY DAY
Bosnian Army (ABiH) Press Centre
Sarajevo, 1998

Soon after the Dayton Agreement was signed, the Army of Bosnia-Herzegovina (ABiH), which had fought through the war with very few weapons, suddenly got international funding and training. Guns and uniforms flowed into the country and the ABiH was restructured as the Army of the Federation of Bosnia and Herzegovina (AFBiH). The hope was that they would be able to defend the Muslim-Croat federation in the event of further Serb aggression. It is interesting to note the minaret and other symbols of Islamic culture Photoshopped into the background of this poster. This seems odd, considering that the army had fought to preserve religious diversity in Bosnia.

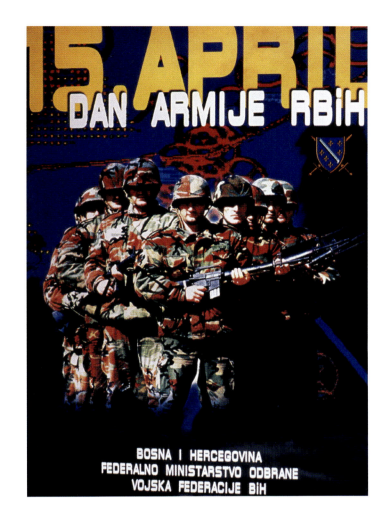

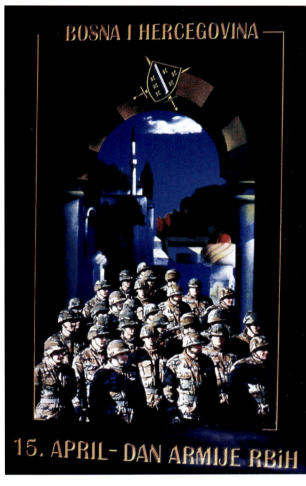

RIGHT
REFUCHESS
Art Publishing
Sarajevo, 1994

A pun on the word refugees and a statement about how complicated it was, after the war, for displaced Bosnians (and especially Bosnian Muslims) to return to their homes.

OPPOSITE
LET ME GO HOME!
Forum of Tuzla Citizens
Tuzla, 1998

More than two million people were made homeless during the fighting in Bosnia. This poster speaks about the complications for refugees and the internally displaced to return home. It was produced in early 1998, more than two years after the Dayton Agreement was signed—an agreement that granted all Bosnians the right to go home. Those brave enough to attempt this in Serb and Croat controlled areas, however, had to cope with a complex bureaucracy and hostile local authorities. This poster was commissioned by the Forum of Tuzla Citizens; Tuzla was one of the few areas where internally displaced people were allowed home. On another level, the non-return of refugees has played a large part in the steady decline in Bosnia's population—as has the lack of employment opportunities. Moreover, this economic and social insecurity has also ensured that fertility is at an all-time low. For all these reasons, it is estimated that contemporary Bosnia has more than one million fewer citizens than just before the war, with more deaths than births occurring every year since 2009. This poster was designed by Jasminko Arnautović.

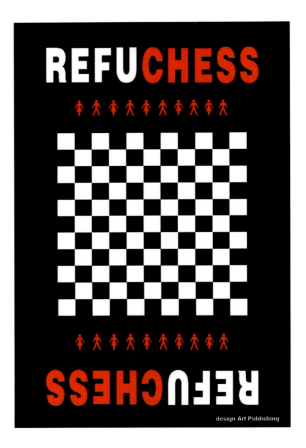

RADO-OUT
Novi Prelom magazine
Banja Luka, 1996

The slogan at the bottom of this image is a play on Radovan Karadžić's first name, broken into two parts: "Rado" and "van". Van means go in Bosnian. *Novi Prelom* (New Breakthrough) was an independent news magazine published in Banja Luka, the capital of Republika Srpska, that was often critical of the nationalist Bosnian Serb leadership. The magazine was shut down during the war but reopened in late 1995 (the status of this publication at the time of editing this book in 2021 is unknown). The image is a photomontage of Radovan Karadžić's face on the left, and Biljana Plavšić's on the right—strangely similar when juxtaposed in this way. Plavšić was a staunch Karadžić ally throughout the war. When the war ended and Karadžić was indicted for war crimes, Plavšić seized leadership of the SDS (Serbian Democratic Party). She became president of Republika Srpska in 1996 and was supported by the international community, which saw her as more cooperative than other Bosnian Serb politicians despite the fact that she held views so distasteful that even Milošević once said she should be locked up. Plavšić was a practising biologist before the war, as well as a professor of biology at the University of Sarajevo, and is quoted as saying that Muslims are "genetically inferior" to Serbs and that ethnic cleansing is a "natural phenomenon". After losing the elections in 1998 Plavšić voluntarily turned herself over to the International Criminal Tribunal for the former Yugoslavia, correctly assuming that her name was on a secret list of wanted war criminals. She was the only woman involved in the war to be indicted, and was found guilty of war crimes. In 2003, Plavšić received a prison sentence of 11 years, but was released early in 2009. Milorad Dodik—a nationalist Bosnian Serb politician (of the Alliance of Independent Social Democrats) who at the time of writing is a member of Bosnia's tripartite Presidency—provided a Republika Srpska jet to pick Plavšić up from prison and arranged a hero's welcome for her when she got home.

WE DID NOT BLEED IN VAIN
Draško Mikanović
Banja Luka, 1996

This poster shows rare and powerful criticism from Republika Srpska journalists of the policies and leadership of the Serbian Democratic Party. Referencing the large-scale corruption among the party's leadership (especially by Radovan Karadžić, Biljana Plavšić, and Momčilo Krajišnik). The slogan at the bottom reads:

THE D CASHED IN

In 2006 Krajišnik was convicted of war crimes, for which he received 20 years in prison. He was released early in 2013 and returned to Republika Srpska; he died of Covid-19 in 2020.

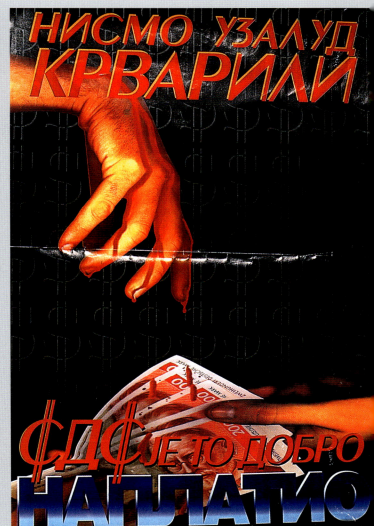

RIGHT

LAW

Office of the High Representative (OHR)
Sarajevo, 22 July 2021

The glorification of war criminals and the denial of their crimes were made criminal offences on 22 July 2021 by Valentin Inzko, Bosnia-Herzegovina's outgoing High Representative. Inzko—who held the position for 12 years—said, "My conscience dictates that I have no right to end my term while the convicted war criminals are being glorified." The Bosnian Serb leadership immediately cried foul, of course, and promised to defy the law. To stamp out this socially and politically corrosive behaviour, this law should have been enshrined immediately after the Dayton Peace Agreement was signed. While to be loudly applauded now, it is proving very difficult to enforce and is being flouted in many parts of the country.

OPPOSITE: TOP TO BOTTOM

HE MEANS PEACE!/DON'T TOUCH HIM!
SDS
Photographs by Daoud Sarhandi
Republika Srpska, 1997

After the Bosnian War ended and Radovan Karadžić was indicted for war crimes, his political power waned—although he remained at large. As a gesture of support for the warlord, pro-Karadžić posters began to appear, some of which were in English and were aimed at the international community (NATO forces were supposedly on the lookout for him). Since the Dayton Agreement barred indicted war criminals from holding political office, however, none of the posters carried the logo of the SDS (Serbian Democratic Party), the party which Karadžić formerly led. It is widely believed, however, that these posters were produced by the SDS. Karadžić was caught in 2008 and sent to the International Criminal Tribunal for the former Yugoslavia in The Hague. He is currently serving life in prison for genocide and other war crimes.

FOLLOWING SPREAD: LEFT TO RIGHT

WITH TRADITION INTO THE FUTURE
SDS
Republika Srpska, 1998

The faces on the screen are those of three famous Serbs: Saint Sava (the patron saint of Serbs), Nikola Tesla (the Serbian-American electrical engineer, whose name now graces flashy electric cars), and Vuk Karadžić (a 19th century linguist and nationalist writer). The fingers of the child's right hand form the traditional three-fingered Serb salute that became associated with the worst excesses of contemporary nationalist politicians and their death squads. This linking together of past and present continues the tendency of much Serbian propaganda, as seen in other examples earlier in this book.

HAPPY PEACEFUL NEW YEAR '96
Novi Prelom magazine
Banja Luka, 1996

The traditional three-fingered Serb salute: injured, but still defiant.

LAW

ON AMENDMENT

TO THE CRIMINAL CODE OF BOSNIA AND HERZEGOVINA

Article 1

(Amendment to Article 145a)

- In the Criminal Code of Bosnia and Herzegovina (Official Gazette of BiH Nos. 3/03, 32/03, 37/03, 54/04, 61/04, 30/05, 53/06, 55/06, 32/07, 8/10, 47/14, 22/15, 40/15 and 35/18) in Article 145a, after paragraph (1) new paragraphs (2) to (6) shall be added to read:

"(2) Whoever publicly incites to violence or hatred directed against a group of persons or a member of such a group defined by reference to race, colour, religion, descent or national or ethnic origin, when that behaviour does not constitute the criminal offence from paragraph (1) of this Article, shall be punished by imprisonment for a term between three months and three years.

(3) Whoever publicly condones, denies, grossly trivializes or tries to justify a crime of genocide, crimes against humanity or a war crime established by a final adjudication pursuant to the Charter of the International Military Tribunal appended to the London Agreement of 8 August 1945 or by the International Criminal Tribunal for the former Yugoslavia or the International Criminal Court or a court in Bosnia and Herzegovina, directed against a group of persons or a member of such a group defined by reference to race, colour, religion, descent or national or ethnic origin, when the conduct is carried out in a manner likely to incite to violence or hatred against such a group or a member of such a group, shall be punished by imprisonment for a term between six months and five years.

(4) Whoever perpetrates the criminal offence referred to in paragraphs (1) to (3) of this Article by public dissemination or distribution of tracts, pictures or other material, shall be punished by imprisonment for a term not less than one year.

(5) If the criminal offence referred to in paragraphs (1) to (3) of this Article is carried out in a manner likely to disturb public peace and order or which is threatening, abusive or insulting, the perpetrator shall be punished by imprisonment for a term not less than three years.

(6) Whoever gives a recognition, award, memorial, any kind of memento, or any privilege or similar to a person sentenced by a final judgement for genocide, crimes against humanity or a war crime, or names a public object such as a street, square, park, bridge, an institution, building, municipality or a city or similar, or registers a brand, after or under a name of a person sentenced by a final judgement for genocide, crimes against humanity or a war crime, or whoever glorifies a person sentenced by a final judgement for genocide, crimes against humanity or a war crime in any way, shall be punished by imprisonment for a term not less than three years."

- Paragraph (2), which shall become paragraph (7), shall be amended to read:

"(7) A perpetrator of the criminal offence referred to in paragraphs (1) to (4) of this Article who is an official or responsible person or employed in an institution of authority or any body financed through public budget, shall be punished by imprisonment for a term not less than three years."

 **DON'T TOUCH HIM !**
HE IS  FREEDOM !

Српска Демократска Странка
(српских земаља)

С ТРАДИЦИЈОМ У БУДУЋНОСТ !

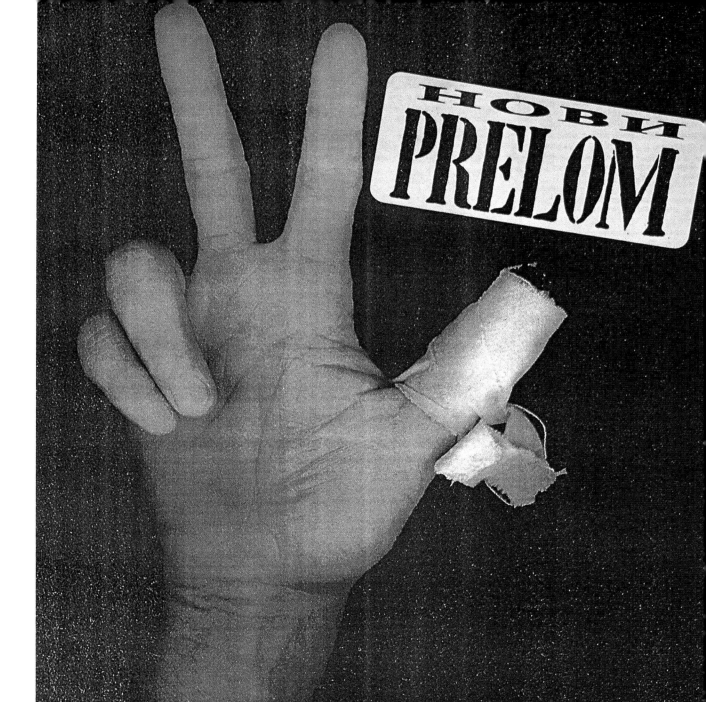

НОВИ PRELOM

Срећна и мирна '96.

МОЖЕМО

ОД УСАМЉЕНОГ О

ИЗБОРИ 7

13.09.-14.09.1997.

PREVIOUS SPREAD
CAN WE DO BETTER THAN BEING A LONELY ISLAND IN THE OCEAN?
Građanski glas
Banka Luka, 1997

A pessimistic and, with hindsight, alarmingly prophetic poster produced in Republika Srpska for the first elections after the end of the war—held during the dates in yellow. Did a scene from Andrei Tarkovski's *Solaris* (the great Russian film director's 1972 sci-fi classic, illustrated below) serve as inspiration for this poster's image?

OPPOSITE
WANTED—PERSONS INDICTED FOR WAR CRIMES
ICTY
The Hague, February 1998

This poster was released by the International Criminal Tribunal for the former Yugoslavia (ICTY) three years after the war ended. Faces were filled in as photographs were acquired. The poster was aimed at NATO peacekeepers since they were in a position to make an arrest; it would have been fatal for locals to approach the armed bodyguards who accompanied these criminals everywhere. The poster appeared in public places and at checkpoints across Bosnia-Herzegovina. Unfortunately, there was a lack of political will on the part of the NATO member states to enforce these arrest warrants, mainly for fear of upsetting the Bosnian Serbs. Two of the most important fugitives, Radovan Karadžić (second row, third from left) and General Ratko Mladić (fourth row, second from right) were eventually caught in Serbia, however, sent for trial in The Hague, convicted, and imprisoned for life for genocide and other war crimes. At the time of writing, they are still in prison. Most of the other men on this poster were either captured or turned themselves in. Some were acquitted, but most were found guilty and imprisoned for varying lengths of time. While this version of the poster names 50 wanted individuals (of which the overwhelming majority are described as Bosnian Serb) overall the ICTY indicted 161 people for their actions in all the former Yugoslav conflicts. Since 2011, nobody indictees remain at large, and having completed its work the Tribunal was dissolved in 2017.

ABOVE
RADOVAN KARADŽIĆ
ICTY
The Hague, 2008

This photograph shows Radovan Karadžić at his trial in 2008—a decade after the poster opposite was issued.

PERSONS INDICTED FOR WAR CRIMES
WARRANTS FOR THEIR ARREST ARE HELD BY THEIR RESPECTIVE CAPITALS

**IF YOU ENCOUNTER ANY OF THESE INDICTED WAR CRIMINALS IN THE COURSE OF YOUR REGULAR DUTIES
AND THE SITUATION PERMITS, DETAIN THEM AND CONTACT YOUR CHAIN OF COMMAND!**

Updated as of: 12 Feb 98 — Updated as of: 12 Feb 98

MIRKO BABIĆ	NENAD BANOVIĆ	PREDRAG BANOVIĆ	GORAN BOROVNICA	RANKO ČEŠIĆ	DAMIR DOŠEN	DRAGAN FUŠTAR	MOMČILO GRUBAN

JANKO JANJIĆ	ČOJKO JANKOVIĆ	RADOVAN KARADŽIĆ	DUŠAN KNEŽEVIĆ	DRAGAN KONDIĆ	MILOJICA KOS	PREDRAG KOSTIĆ	RADOMIR KOVAČ	DRAGOLJUB KUNARAC

DRAGAN KULUNDŽIJA	MIROSLAV KVOČKA	GORAN LAJIĆ	ZORAN MARINIĆ	MILAN MARTIĆ	ŽELJKO MEAKIĆ	SLOBODAN MILJKOVIĆ	RATKO MLADIĆ	MILE MRKŠIĆ

DRAGAN NIKOLIĆ	NEDELJKO PASPALJ	MILAN PAVLIĆ	DRAGOLJUB PRCAĆ	MILUTIN POPOVIĆ	DRAŽENKO PREDOJEVIĆ	MLADEN RADIĆ	MIROSLAV RADIĆ	IVICA RAJIĆ

DRAGOMIR ŠAPONJA	ŽELJKO SAVIĆ	DUŠKO SIKIRICA	BLAGOJE SIMIĆ	MILAN SIMIĆ	VESELIN ŠLJIVANČANIN	RADOVAN STANKOVIĆ	MIROSLAV TADIĆ	NEDELJKO TIMARAC

STEVAN TODOROVIĆ	ZORAN VUKOVIĆ	SIMO ZARIĆ	DRAGAN ZELENOVIĆ	ZORAN ŽIGIĆ

WANTED — **WANTED**

Although there are no posters to illustrate the fact, it would not be right to suggest that war crimes were not committed in Bosnia by non-Serbs, too. They were—although on a smaller scale than those committed by Serb forces. For example, there was a notorious Bosniak-Croat camp situated at Čelebići, a village in the Konjic region of central Bosnia. This detention facility was established right at the beginning of the war, and closed at the end of 1992. Many of the Serb detainees who filled the camp (400–700, it is estimated) were civilians with no connection to Bosnian Serb military forces. Three former soldiers were tried and convicted at the ICTY in 1996 for war crimes committed at Čelebići. They were: camp commander Zdravko Mucić (a Bosnian Croat), the vicious deputy commander Hazim Delić (Bosniak), and a particularly sadistic guard named Esad "Zenga" Landžo (Bosniak). Another smaller camp, used to detain both Serb and Croat prisoners, was Musala: a former sports hall in Konjic. Musala was run by the Bosnian Army from 1992–94, and ICTY convictions were eventually secured against two Bosniaks who served there.

SERB PRISONERS AT ČELEBIĆI
ICTY (photographer unknown, Public Domain)
Čelebići, 1992
The Čelebići camp was a former Yugoslav People's Army site. It comprised of various hangars. Males were held in some of the buildings, and females in others. Conditions at the camp and the treatment of all detainees was horrendous. Čelebići camp was known to and used by the Bosnian Ministry of the Interior, Croatian Defence Council, and Bosnian Territorial Defence. Čelebići served no legitimate military purpose.

ABOVE
THE HAGUE TRIBUNAL—ANTI-CRIMINAL!
Forum of Tuzla Citizens
Tuzla, 1997
The Forum of Tuzla Citizens printed more copies of this poster (3,000) than any of its others. It was designed by Jasminko Arnautović. At the time, many people felt that the ICTY was against their ethnoreligious group. The poster states, however, that it was: Not ANTI-SERB. Not ANTI-CROAT. Not ANTI-BOSNIAK. Only ANTI-CRIMINAL!

RIGHT

FATHER CHRISTMAS, DON'T STRAY FROM YOUR PATH!
Forum of Tuzla Citizens
Tuzla, 1996

The title of this poster is drawn from a popular Yugoslav-era children's song that celebrated Christmas. The signpost points to:

DEMOCRACY
MULTICULTURALISM
SECULARISM!

In the winter of 1996 President Alija Izetbegović advised Muslims in Bosnia not to celebrate the Christian festival of Christmas. Comically, several Bosnian men who dressed as Santa Claus—and had done so for years—were arrested. Most Muslims in Bosnia found this completely ludicrous. In the former Yugoslavia, and especially in Bosnia with its ethnically entwined population, celebrations for all the different faiths had been acknowledged by people of the other faiths. Bosnian Muslims almost unanimously ignored Izetbegović's appeal, and it became much lampooned. There was, however, a more serious side to Izetbegović's pronouncement: it seemed to indicate that the Bosnian (SDA) leadership in Sarajevo tacitly recognised that Bosnia was now divided along religious lines. Both posters on this page were designed by Jasminko Arnautović and illustrated by Jusuf "Juka" Jaganjać

OPPOSITE

DRAGONS
Forum of Tuzla Citizens
Tuzla, 1997

The poem in the bottom left corner, by the distinguished Herzegovinian poet Mak Dizdar, reads:

Bread is the word for bread
For wine it is wine
For water it is
Water

The image shows Bosnia being dismembered by three dragons of nationalism. The green (Muslim) dragon blindfolds the country to truth; the red and white (Croat) dragon stabs Bosnia in the back; the red and blue (Serb) dragon chops up the country with an axe. This poster was controversial at the time, as it implied that none of the dominant parties in Bosnia were interested in protecting the country's multi-ethnic character. The Dizdar poem references the fact that the truth is the truth (bread cannot be called wine, nor wine water)—and that truth cannot be reshaped to fit fascistic or nationalistic lies. In standing up for the truth, and challenging those lies, Bosnia here is being butchered.

Za riječ da hljeb je hljeb
Da vino je vino
A voda da je
Voda

RIGHT
HOW CAN WE LIVE WITHOUT SANTA CLAUS?
Dani magazine
Sarajevo, January 1997
Dani magazine's humorous retort to President Alija Izetbegović's intention to do away with public displays of Christian symbols in Bosnia after the war—including Santa Claus, a harmless figure beloved by children of all faiths.

OPPOSITE
LET THE WESTERN TRASH HANG
Dani magazine
Caricature by Enes Huseinčehajić
Sarajevo, October 1998
Another wry take on the shifting religious and political discourse taking place in Bosnia. Once one starts removing western cultural references, this cover implies, where does one stop: is even Mickey Mouse not safe from being lynched? Art direction of this cover was by Trio studios.

FOLLOWING SPREAD: LEFT TO RIGHT
CHOOSE THE BEST
OSCE / Trio
Sarajevo, 1996
This poster was commissioned by the OSCE (Organization for Security and Co-operation in Europe) which, among its other missions, had the responsibility to organise and oversee democratic elections in Bosnia-Herzegovina; the first post-war elections were held in September 1996. Trio studios designed a series of posters of fruits and vegetables with the same design format as this one. The slogan subliminally asks the electorate to ignore a candidate's nationality and simply choose the best person for the job. Although this campaign was widely ridiculed, it was a well-intentioned and intelligent one— but perhaps too subtle for some people. By eliminating all political symbols, on the one hand the OSCE intended to underline its own impartiality, and on the other hand wanted to encourage citizens to ignore nationalist rhetoric and focus on more substantial issues.

CHOOSE THE BEST
Dani magazine
Sarajevo, September 1996
Dani produced an irreverent take on the OSCE's original slogan.

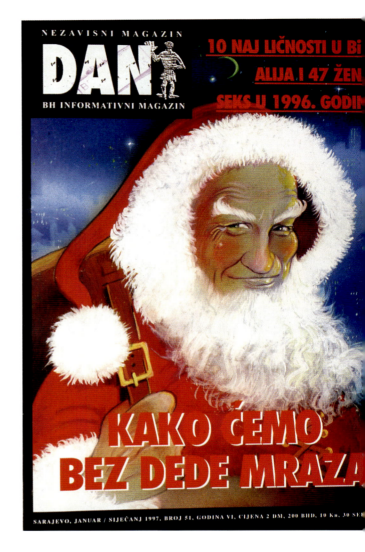

NEZAVISNI MAGAZIN

DANi

BH INFORMATIVNI MAGAZIN

www.bhdani.com

ZA DANE
GOVORE:

JASNA ŠAMIĆ

SENAD HADŽIFEJZOVIĆ

DAMIR ABDULKERIM MIRKOVIĆ

VERAN MATIĆ

MILOŠ VASIĆ

DEJAN DUKOVSKI

ROBERTO CIULLI

BORBENI
POKLIČ NOVIH
BOŠNJAČKIH IDEOLOGA:

NEKA VISI ZAPADNO SMEĆE!

DANI U DUBROVNIKU: LEJLA MEĐU ARIJEVCIMA

SARAJEVO, 26. OKTOBAR / LISTOPAD 1998, BROJ 87, GODINA VII, CIJENA 2 KM, 12 Kn, 350 SIT, 15 YUD, 4.90 DEM, 36 OS, 4 SF, 16 FF, 100 BF, 100 FLUX, 6.10 HFL, 4.600 LIT, 28 SEK

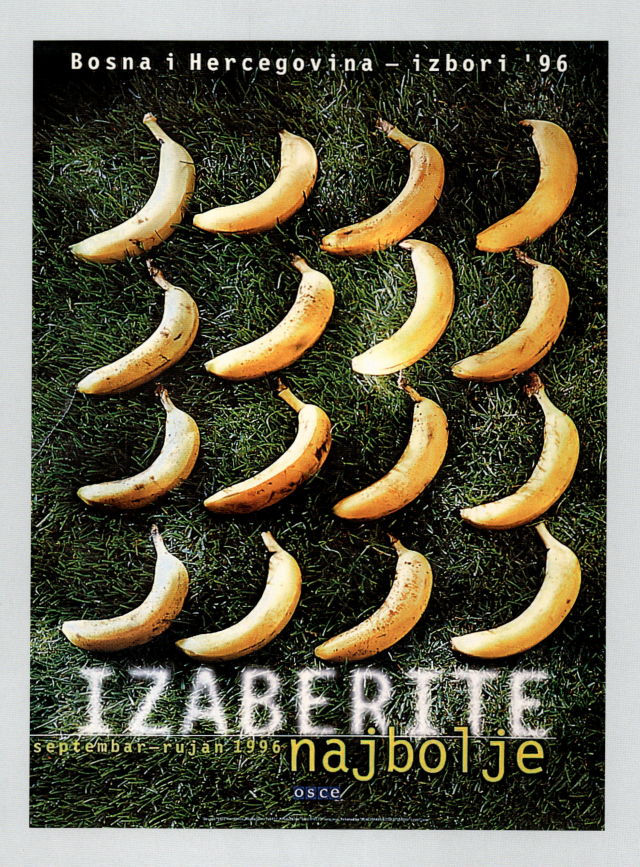

NEZAVISNI MAGAZIN

DAN

BH INFORMATIVNI MAGAZIN

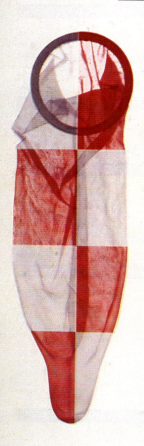  

IZABERITE NAJBOLJE

SARAJEVO, SEPTEMBAR/RUJAN 1996, BROJ 47, GODINA V, CIJENA 2 DM, 200 BHD,10 Kn, 30 SEK, 300 SIT

CHOOSE THE BEST
Polikita magazine poster
Lukavac, 1997
Polikita was a satirical magazine produced by Samir Šestan in Lukavac, near the Bosnian city of Tuzla. It parodied *Politika*, the most widely read daily newspaper in Serbia. Every issue of Šestan's *Polikita* contained a free humorous poster. When this one was designed, there were still hundreds of thousands of refugees abroad with no homes in Bosnia to return to. Others displaced in Bosnia and elsewhere in the former Yugoslavia were desperate to emigrate to any country that would take them; few countries would.

CHOOSE WELL
Anonymous
Photograph by Daoud Sarhandi
Tuzla, 1998
This even more cynical take on the Choose The Best slogan (observed on a wall in Tuzla) shows just how much faith had been lost in post-war Bosnian politics. It reads:

THERE ARE NO BAD FISH—THERE IS ONLY BAD BAIT

The examples of "bad bait" on display are:

The bait of the nation
Civil bait
Socialist bait
Patriotic bait

Democratic bait
Economic bait
Social bait
Liberal bait

Social-democratic bait
Secessionist bait
Unitarian bait
The bait of the independent candidate

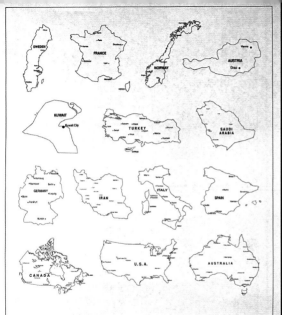

IZABERITE NAJBOLJE

IZBORI '98

Muotne mamje   *Građanski mamac*   *Socijalistički mamac*   *Patriotski mamac*

Demokratski mamac   *Ekonomski mamac*   *Svojski mamac*   *Liberalni mamac*

Socijal-demokratski mamac   *Nacionalni mamac*   *Unitaristički mamac*   *Mamac Nezavisnog kandidata*

NE POSTOJE LOŠE RIBE - POSTOJE SAMO LOŠI MAMCI!

IZABERITE DOBAR

RIGHT
BOOKSTALL
Photograph by Rupert Wolfe Murray
Tuzla, 2021
Biographies on sale at an open-air bookstall in Tuzla about President Alija Izetbegović and Naser Orić, the legendary Bosniak defender of Srebrenica, who was charged with war crimes against Serbs in eastern Bosnia.

OPPOSITE
THE WILL OF THE PEOPLE WON
Dani magazine
Sarajevo, June 1998
As the post-war years passed, Alija Izetbegović— president of the Social Democratic Action party and a member of Bosnia's post-Dayton tripartite Presidency until 2000—was criticised for being authoritarian and aloof. Izetbegović died in 2003. In recent years, discontent with mainstream politics has become endemic among Bosnia's citizens, and one detects that there is now a certain amount of nostalgia for Izetbegović.

NEZAVISNI MAGAZIN

DANI

BH INFORMATIVNI MAGAZIN

www.bhdani.com

SARAJEVO, 22. JUNI/LIPANJ 1998. BROJ 78. GODINA VII. CIJENA 2 KM. 12 KN. 350 SIT. 15 YUD. 4.90 DEM. 36 OS. 4 SF. 16 FF. 100 BF. 100 FLUX. 6.10 HFL. 4.600 LIT. 28 SEK

POBIJEDILA VOLJA NARODA

ABOVE: LEFT TO RIGHT

NUMBER PLATES
Samir Plasto
Sarajevo, 1996

In 1996 the OHR (Office of the High Representative) organised a poster competition called *Bosnia and Herzegovina 2000,* asking for designers to imagine the future of the country. This poster, the winner of the competition, took car number plates as its theme. It dealt with a serious problem that existed in Bosnia until 1998. Each region of Bosnia issued its own number plates, the tags identifying the town where the owner lived and which ethnic-religious group was in power there. For instance, "SA" stood for Sarajevo, and the lilies showed that the car came from the part of the city which was under Bosniak control. This seriously hindered freedom of movement in Bosnia. Eventually, the OHR enforced an anonymous car numbering system that protected the driver's location and presumed ethnic identity.

FLINTSTONES
Dejan Vekić
Sarajevo, 1996

The Flintstones in Bosnia. Mosques, synagogues, and churches can be seen through the window—ironically suggesting the fabled return of religious harmony in an otherwise Stone Age country of the future.

OPPOSITE: LEFT TO RIGHT

LABYRINTH
Šejla Kamerić
Sarajevo, 1996

Prophetically true: the Dayton Agreement produced a political labyrinth in which Bosnia remains lost to this day. How the absurdities of Bosnia's current tripartite political structure will be ironed out is still anyone's guess.

BEWARE! SNIPER
Alma Fazlić
Sarajevo, 1996

During the war in Sarajevo, the slogan *Pazi Snajper* (Beware Sniper) would be daubed at all the main intersections. This poster replaces the word *Snajper* with the date 2000. Although the Dayton Agreement ended the worst excesses of ethnic cleansing, the political reality it established has never been able to resolve the underlying cause of the conflict: a relentless ambition by Bosnian Serb politicians for a state, detached from Bosniaks and Croats and possibly attached to Serbia proper. Dayton entrenched this nationalist ambition by rewarding Serb nationalist politicians with their own quasi-ministate: Republika Srpska. So, while war did not break out again in the year 2000—as this poster seemed to suggest—the possibility of armed conflict in the future cannot be excluded.

BOSNA I HERCEGOVINA

POSTER COMPETITION OHR AND ALU
"BOSNIA & HERZEGOVINA 2000" July 1996.

OHR

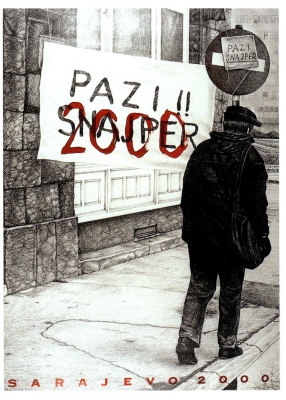

SARAJEVO 2000

AFTERMATH BOSNIA
Asim Đelilović
Travnik, 1997

Looking at the image opposite, one sees a strange kind of hope expressed by Đelilović. The green shoots of recovery are sprouting out of the "perpetrators" of the carnage, represented by the axe still embedded in Bosnia's truncated remains. If this was Đelilović's hope, it has unfortunately not come to pass; Republika Srpska, as well as Serbia proper, has not yet owned up to its disproportionate share of blame for what happened in Bosnia in the 1990s—quite the opposite: one might interpret the shoots as the regrowth of Serb (and perhaps Croat too) expansionist aspirations. At the time of writing, we can only wait to see what happens in Bosnia-Herzegovina—and hope that things do not progress from bad to worse, and then to another catastrophe.

As we edit this book to go to press—the world is in the grips of the Coronavirus pandemic. Apart from causing a global health crisis, Covid-19 is also impacting politics around the world; Bosnia's fragile political landscape is highly vulnerable. Bosnia is also experiencing internal pressure from the wave of immigrants crossing her territory as they look for a better life in the EU—a Union to which Bosnia-Herzegovina has no realistic chance of being admitted. These issues are coupled with a dangerous revisionist approach to the dissolution of the former Yugoslavia by some political actors in the Western Balkans (see Introduction footnote #21 on page 43). There is also constant agitation for independence by officials in Republika Srpska, the Serb-controlled part of Bosnia. Indeed, on 5 May 2021, there appeared in the *Washington Post* extracts from an extremely frank interview with the outgoing High Representative for Bosnia and Herzegovina—Valentin Inzko, responsible for the implementation of the Dayton Agreement since 2009. The article ("International Official: Bosnian Serbs Seek to Split Country", by Edith M. Lederer) states:

> He [Valentin Inzko] *said the Bosnian Serbs' actions have "poisoned" the political atmosphere and sidelined reforms at a time when the country is "in the grip" of the Covid-19 pandemic. Bosnia should be firmly on the path to membership in the European Union, he said, "but here we are today and one of its political leaders is openly advocating dividing the country, disparaging and mocking the EU in the process."*
> *Inzko warned that even if a breakup is prevented, the Serbs' aim is "a perpetually dysfunctional" country. That is already happening "in the near-paralysis of the highest institutions ... including the presidency, the Council of Ministers and the Parliamentary Assembly," he said.*
> *He said Bosnia's multi-ethnic and diverse society that existed before the war "has all but disappeared" and defending multi-ethnic spaces has become more difficult than creating single ethnicity ones.*

> *"Hate speech, the glorification of war criminals, and revisionism or outright genocide denial, despite the verdicts of international judicial bodies, remain very common in political discourse," he said.*

Later, in the autumn of 2021, Republika Srpska leader and member of Bosnia's tripartite Presidency, Milorad Dodik, ramped up the pressure further by threatening to withdraw Serb soldiers from the Bosnian army, with the aim of once again creating a separate, ethnically pure Bosnian Serb army. Dodik also planned to disengage from the judiciary, the tax administration, and the intelligence and medicine agencies. The new, recently appointed, High Representative, Christian Schmidt, gravely warned that Dodik's actions were "tantamount to secession without proclaiming it", representing an "existential threat" to Bosnia.

We invited Asim Đelilović, the author of this poster—which was inspired by the work of the great Japanese graphic designer Shigeo Fukuda—to redesign it for the cover of this book. Credit for the idea to convert the circular tree trunk into the form of Bosnia's external borders goes to Carolina Rivas.

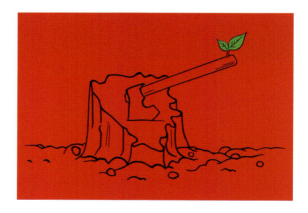

I am struck by the coincidence that nearly 30 years prior to Đelilović's redesign—and entirely unbeknown to Carolina or Asim—the Bosnian artist Began Turbić drew Bosnia as a three-legged wooden stool (also see page 52) supported by her three nationalities and faiths.

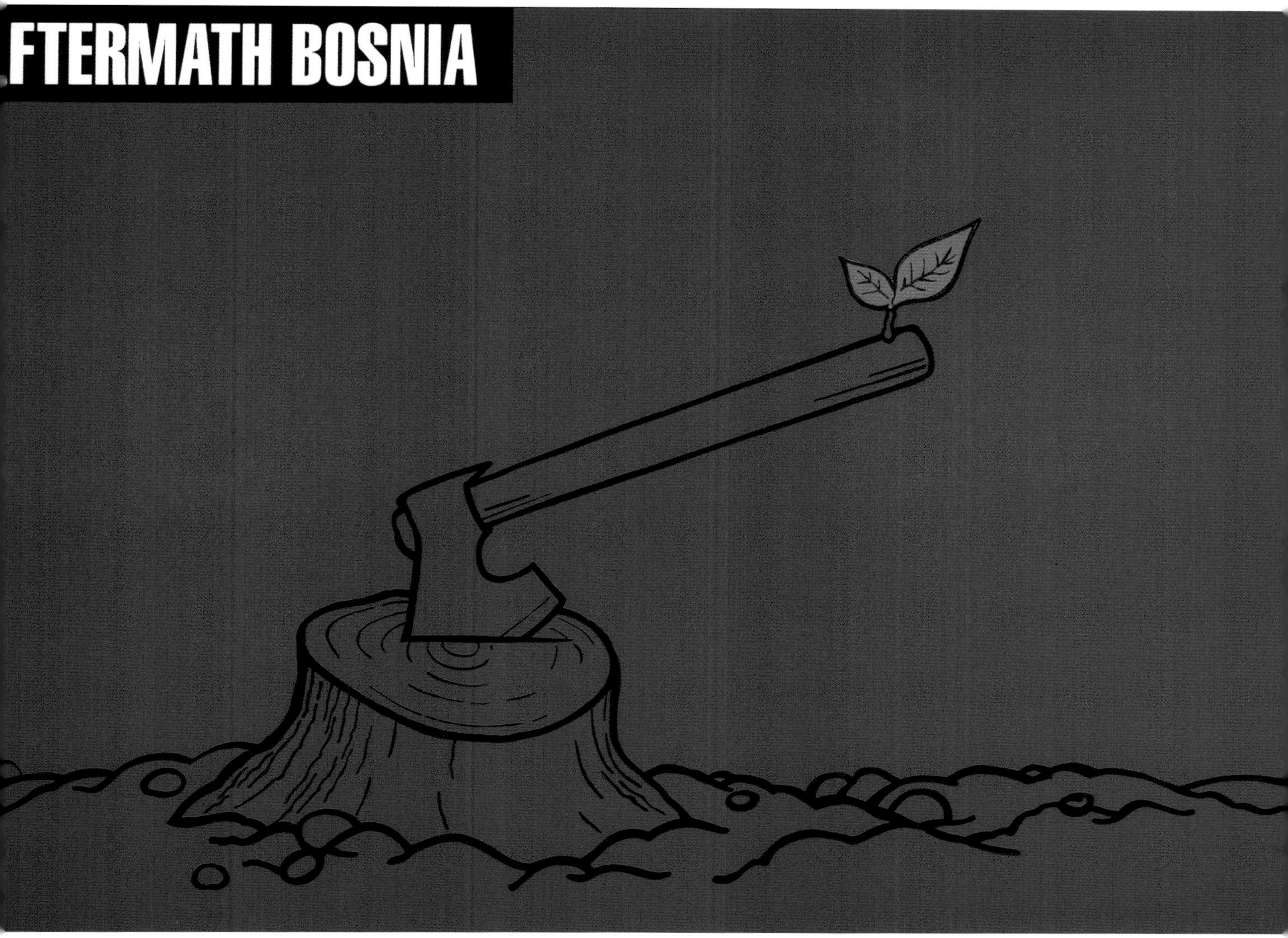
FTERMATH BOSNIA

INDEX TO DESIGNERS

AFTERWORDS

TUZLA'S ATLAS; *Photograph by Rupert Wolfe Murray; Tuzla, 2021*
At the four corners of Kipovi bridge in Tuzla stand four statues of the ancient Greek god Atlas, whose mythological responsibility was holding up the celestial heavens. This statue was chosen by the Forum of Tuzla Citizens as a symbol of the city. The original graphic idea was Slobodan Stuhli's, and it appears in many of the Forum's pro-democracy posters (see page 219). Most of the Forum's posters were designed by Jasminko Arnautović.

AFTERWORD
HOW THIS BOOK CAME TOGETHER
Rupert Wolfe Murray

In the following pages, you'll hear from the people who made *Bosnian War Posters* happen. My role in the book's production isn't easily explained, at least not in publishing terms. The best description I can come up with is "Producer": as in an executive film producer who stumps up the cash to make a movie happen.

But what was I doing in Bosnia just after the war? And how did I have enough money to fund two people to collect war posters and another to photograph them?

The fact that I had any money at all was almost miraculous. I had arrived in Bosnia flat broke, by bus, at the end of the war. Luckily, my mother had met an inspiring Bosnian designer—Jasminko Arnautović, whose name crops up frequently in this book—and she had his phone number. I called him, he invited me to stay in his flat in Tuzla, and I spent the last of my money getting a bus there from Sarajevo. Jasminko fed me, housed me, and even got me an unpaid job as writer-of-letters-in-English for the Mayor of Tuzla—the legendary Selim Bešlagić, who defended Tuzla's great human rights record throughout the war.

Not far from where I was absorbing Jasminko's incredible war stories (and his dirty jokes!) the Americans had landed. Tuzla's old airport had become the new base for thousands of US troops. They were setting up shop as NATO's Implementation Force (IFOR).

Two ideas then formed in my mind: one, Americans tend to have little awareness of anywhere outside their home state—their grasp of world geography is atrocious; two, my mother (Stephanie Wolfe Murray)—only recently retired from publishing—had

helped an eccentric journalist publish *Cry Bosnia*—a good photo book of the war that wasn't selling well.

"Why not sell *Cry Bosnia* to the Americans?" I shouted down an old-fashioned telephone in Tuzla's post office. "They've probably got no idea what planet they're on. It might help them learn something about where they are and what's been going on here."

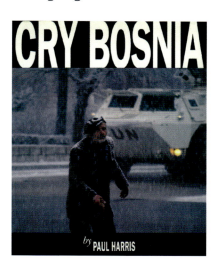

Bosnia's postal service barely functioned in those days, but my mother managed to send me a box of *Cry Bosnia* through Edinburgh Direct Aid—a friendly Scottish aid agency. Having failed to convince her to come out and sell the books herself, I was landed with the task. I then spent weeks trying to gain access to the American base, which was so over-fortified it was a joke; the soldiers seemed to be expecting an attack from the Bosnian Muslims, even though they showed nothing but gratitude for saving them from the Serbs.

When I eventually managed to make contact with the cheery American who ran the PX shop (slang for Post Exchange) he told me he loved *Cry Bosnia,* and he immediately bought the whole box. He also did something very unusual in the book trade: he paid cash on delivery. And not only that: he ended up buying the entire print run. And before long we had enough money to pay for a reprint. In the network of PX shops in the American military bases in the region, *Cry Bosnia* was the only book on the war, sitting alongside soft porn and pulp fiction paperbacks.

"Why don't we do a photo book about the Americans?" I suggested to my mother on a call from the post office. "We could photograph them at work, find out what they're doing, and also meet the other armies that are here under the NATO flag. It'd sell like hotcakes."

Finding a photographer was easy, as I was friends with a great one: Steve Gordon. Steve was also at a loose end in Tuzla. But getting permission from the Americans was difficult, as their fortress in Tuzla was designed to keep out writers, journalists and photographers—as well as would-be suicide bombers. A chance meeting with the US Commander, General Nash, however, suddenly opened doors.

A couple of years later, we had two bestselling documentary books under our belts: *IFOR on IFOR* and *The Road to Peace.* And we were sitting on a pile of cash. So, when Daoud Sarhandi came up with the idea for this poster book, I was able to support its initial costs—buying time so he and Alina could find the material and Steve could photograph it.

I was now in a position to run a small charity with my mother, without having to spend all our time thinking up fundraising wheezes and filling in complex bureaucratic forms for international donors. For several years, we funded Bosnians who had been wounded in the war and wanted to set up

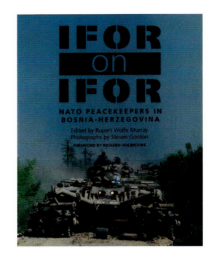

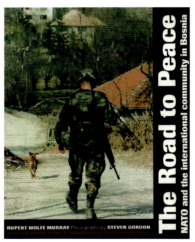

PREVIOUS PAGE
CRY BOSNIA
Published by Interlink Books, 1995
Paul Harris (Author and Photographer);
David Rieff (Introduction)

ABOVE: TOP TO BOTTOM
IFOR ON IFOR: NATO PEACEKEEPERS IN BOSNIA-HERZEGOVINA
Published by Connect Trading, 1996
Rupert Wolfe Murray (Editor); Steven Gordon (Photographer); Richard Holbrooke (Foreword)

THE ROAD TO PEACE: NATO AND THE INTERNATIONAL COMMUNITY IN BOSNIA
Published by Connect Trading, 1998
Rupert Wolfe Murray (Editor); Steven Gordon (Photographer); General George A. Joulwan, Supreme Allied Commander, Europe (Foreword)

their own business. We also bought a white van and distributed second-hand English books (which my mother collected in Britain) to schools and libraries all over Bosnia.

By this time I was renting a house in Tuzla. My girlfriend and soon-to-be wife, Alina Boboc, came down from Romania in her old Ford Fiesta. She quickly learned Bosnian and was looking for something to do with her journalistic skills. Around this time we also met Daoud—another Briton who was friends with Jasminko and looking for things to do in Tuzla—and I asked him to help us by driving around the country: delivering English books to libraries as well as copies of my books to military bases.

Perhaps this crazy routine of constantly motoring around Bosnia made us realise, in logistical terms at least, that publishing a book of propaganda posters from the war was possible.

Now, more than twenty years later, I am delighted that Daoud has brought us all together again to produce this book. I hope it reaches libraries all over Bosnia, the Bosnian diaspora all over the world, and the general reader everywhere—and that it will remain in print for many years to come. There is so much here that can't be found in any other book about the Bosnian War.

Rupert Wolfe Murray is the author of 9 Months in Tibet. *For many years he ran aid projects in Central and Eastern Europe.*

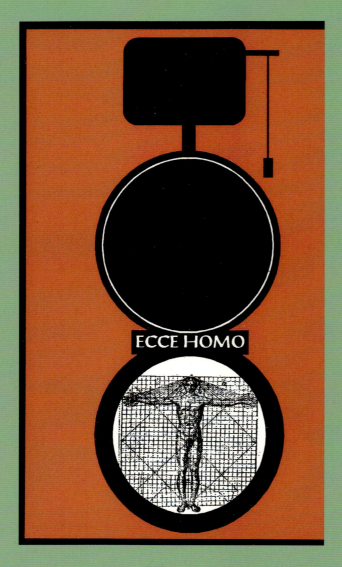

ECCE HOMO; *Art Publishing; Sarajevo, 1994*
The words *Ecce Homo*—Latin for "Behold the Man"—were uttered by Pontius Pilate when he paraded a bleeding Jesus before a hostile crowd prior to his crucifixion. Pilate wanted to underline that Christ, under his crown of thorns, was no deity, but merely flesh and blood that could suffer and bleed. At the end of the 15th century, Renaissance Man—with his divine geometry—was drafted by Leonardo da Vinci. This perfect man embodies strength, functionality, and beauty—a combination of essential qualities esteemed by the Roman author, architect, and civil and military engineer known as Vitruvius. (The version of "Vitruvian Man" shown floating in Art Publishing's toilet bowl was drawn by Cesare Cesariano in 1521). Since the intellectual basis of the Renaissance period was its acceptance of humanism as a guiding doctrine, this graphic intends to tell us that the atrocities of the Bosnian War—and the siege of Sarajevo where this image was produced—render post-Renaissance European history and values (modernity) null and void—ready to be flushed away. I am very grateful to Bojan Bahić, one of the original members of Art Publishing, whose concept this poster was and who sent me this postcard version printed in Sarajevo in 1994. Thanks also to Ibrahim Spahić at the International Peace Centre, Sarajevo, for bringing this graphic to my attention in 2021, and to Carol A. Wells at the Center for the Study of Political Graphics, Los Angeles, for helping me to contextualise it.

AFTERWORD
BOSNIA: A LOVE LETTER
Daoud Sarhandi

Some projects mean the world to their authors. This book is one of those for me. I remember nearly everything about its origins as if those events happened a few short weeks ago. In fact, nearly 25 years have passed since one cold day in 1997—in Tuzla, northeast Bosnia—I had the idea for this book. It was one of those ideas that strike like lightning, and that I couldn't give up on once it had. Many people thought the project impossible to accomplish, but thankfully Rupert Wolfe Murray believed in it and financed the research, and his fiancé Alina Wolfe Murray (Alina Boboc, as she then was) dedicated a year of her life to working with me with a tenacity that impressed greatly. Without Alina the investigation and collection of posters never would have been completed. I must also once again thank all the Bosnians who shared posters with us. Without their trust and generosity nothing would have resulted from our efforts.

After all the painstaking and often physically draining research, Steven Gordon travelled around the region with us taking slide photographs of posters retained by their authors or owners. This was still the analogue age of photography, and I had to develop those slides in Serbia since in Bosnia it was impossible. It was also still the pre-digital age of communication. Old-fashioned legwork, endless driving around, and crackly analogue telephone calls were the means of our research. One also needs to remember that Bosnia's overall infrastructure was still shattered. In short, nothing about this project was simple.

When I look at *Bosnian War Posters* today, it fills me with a whole range of emotions. Of course, there are the personal ones connected with doing this work, and all that implied in my life. At the time, I knew nothing much about research, or writing, and even less about graphic design. I certainly didn't do this as some kind of professional stepping stone since creatively I was, and predominantly still am, a filmmaker.

I got involved with Bosnia on a political level, and emotionally too. Like many foreigners who went there during the war, I was bewitched by the country, horrified by what was happening, and fast became obsessed by playing my little part in righting such a huge and glaring wrong. It may sound rather twee to put it like this, but looking back, I see that I fell in love with Bosnia. I think I'm still trying to understand exactly why and how that happened. Perhaps it was connected with my complex mixed-faith and multiracial background; perhaps it was an aching desire to be on the humane side of history. I know that at times I would gladly have given my life to try to save Bosnia.

Finally, I gave both less and more than my life. I have given her this book. It is, if you like, my love letter to this complex and beautiful country.

And here we are in 2021: so much older and wiser. Or at least we should be, as so much has happened personally and on the international stage since we collected the material. Take the United States, for example: Bill Clinton went out; George W. Bush came in; the Twin Towers came down; wars were launched in Afghanistan, Iraq, and Libya. Exit Bush; enter and exit Obama; hello and goodbye Trump; Covid-19.

And during all this time Bosnia has advanced very little since in late 1995 the US, alongside the presidents of Bosnia, Croatia and Serbia, forged a peace agreement at Wright-Patterson Air Force Base in Dayton, Ohio. Connected with that event, I feel it's worth quoting one paragraph of a text that reads more prophetically today than it did when it appeared in *The Daily Telegraph* in December 1995. The British historian and Bosnia-aficionado Noel Malcolm wrote:

> *The new Bosnia [...] will be the geopolitical equivalent of an artwork by Damien Hirst. Hirst takes a cow, saws it in half, and pickles each half in formaldehyde. It may be an ingenious work of art, but is it still a cow? Similarly with the new Bosnia. It may have the cleverest of constitutions, but is it still a country?*

For me, the poster that expresses this idea most poignantly is Čedomir Kostović's dissected violin. Malcolm and Kostović are right: Bosnia has become one of the most politically dysfunctional states in the world. An indefinite peace is still not guaranteed. The good news (if there is any) is that so far there has been no more sniping and bombing and internment and rape camps have not returned—although neither have the majority of displaced and ethnically cleansed citizens.

In short, Bosnia still needs all the help it can get, and I hope this book plays its part.

RIGHT: TOP TO BOTTOM
BOSNIA
Čedomir Kostović
USA, 1995
Caption on page 230.

GENERAL RATKO MLADIĆ—SERBIAN
Serbia, 2006
Photograph by Wolfgang Kuhnle
As this poster photographed on a wall in the region shows, in the post-war period, Serb war criminals are still venerated by certain sections of the population. It is a disturbing practice that continues to this day—but one that in Bosnia, at least, was made illegal in 2021.

THE LOOK—ISLAMADE; *Draško Mikanović et al.; Banja Luka, 1993*
A poster equating Serbia with Israel, both of whom consider themselves victims of Muslims—which is an extraordinary claim by any stretch of the imagination.

AFTERWORD
AROUND BOSNIA IN A FORD FIESTA
Alina Wolfe Murray

I moved to Bosnia from my country of birth, Romania, in 1996. I was a graduate of journalism. It seemed like the perfect solution: I got to join my Scottish boyfriend, Rupert Wolfe Murray, who was living and working in Tuzla at the time, while also trying my hand at becoming a journalist.

Until the fall of communism, Romanians looked with admiration toward neighbouring Yugoslavia. In Romania, we were struggling with food shortages and power cuts, and could only dream about travelling abroad. We had a megalomaniac dictator—Nicolae Ceauşescu—and lived in fear of the secret police. By comparison, Yugoslavs had a better standard of living and enjoyed more freedom: they could travel and even work abroad. At that time, Yugoslavia seemed to stand tall in the esteem of other nations.

Little did we know that the Yugoslavia we looked up to would soon be engulfed in war and cease to exist; that horrors Europe hadn't experienced since World War II would take place just over the border—the same border many Romanians risked their lives trying to cross to escape Ceauşescu.

While living in Bosnia, I wrote several articles for a Romanian newspaper. I also worked for a Scottish charity—Connect Humanitarian Agency, run by Rupert—which was donating books to destroyed libraries. When Daoud had the idea for this poster book in late 1997, I was keen to help.

At a time when Bosnian number plates followed ethnic lines, and people felt insecure about travelling, my Romanian-registered Ford Fiesta was perfect for driving around the country. And since I was able to converse in Bosnian—although not as correctly as I wished—I could be of great help to the project. When meeting people or speaking over the phone, everyone was very helpful.

I spent time in printing houses, libraries, designers' studios, and cafés. If I got a lead in one place, I followed it, then went to the next place. Sometimes I got several leads, sometimes I got dead ends. This went on for the best part of a year, and in this way, Daoud and I covered most of Bosnia-Herzegovina. I also went to Zagreb, Croatia, looking for posters, and we spent a couple of weeks together in Belgrade, the capital of Serbia, searching for all kinds of visual propaganda.

The Internet was in its infancy at that time, and we relied on fax machines and telephones. I organised notes in a red folder that had one A4 sheet for each encounter: contact details, notes about the discussion—including suggestions of other artists and their work—and a short description of any posters discovered. While I loved the detective work and meeting incredible people, there were times when I felt bad about troubling them. Here was I, a foreigner, looking for *posters,* while Bosnians were dealing with the aftermath of the war, trying to rebuild their shattered lives. Now, more than twenty years later, I would like to thank everyone who gave us their time, support and trust.

When I left Bosnia in late 1998, I was pregnant with our daughter, Lara, and another war was looming, this time in Kosovo. By the following year, Slobodan Milošević—the leader of rump Yugoslavia (at that time, Serbia and Montenegro)—had become an international pariah. Ten years after the fall of communism in Eastern Europe, Tito's dream of Brotherhood and Unity among the South Slavs had been shredded; hundreds of thousands of lives were lost or turned upside down, and the world was repeatedly shocked by horrors that never seemed to end in the Balkans.

Yet recent years have shown us that nationalism and propaganda can wreak havoc anywhere. The scenes of mobs storming the US Capitol in January 2021 proved that no land is free from nationalist fanaticism—no country can claim that such evils will never take hold there.

When the migrant crisis started in 2015, I often thought about a poster produced by the Bosnian Serbs. I'd seen it in a photo book called *Cry Bosnia* (Paul Harris, 1995) that my mother-in-law, Stephanie, published—and I was determined to find that poster during our research. Eventually I did find it, and it is included in this book (see page 141). The poster shows the EU flag turn from blue to green—a colour associated with Islam. The accompanying text is short and blunt: "This is not a paint commercial. This is future."

By the time of the European migrant crisis in 2015, followed by the Brexit vote in 2016, this poster's message would have resonated with many Europeans, capturing commonly perceived fears about Europe losing its Christian identity. The refugees—most of them Muslims from countries ravaged by war, such as Syria, Iraq, and Afghanistan—were seen as potential terrorists. The 9/11 attacks on the Twin Towers, and the subsequent War on Terror, had already fed into the belief that Islam posed an existential threat to the West—and many people started to believe it.

Then, during the Brexit campaign in Great Britain, there appeared the infamous UKIP (United Kingdom Independence Party) poster showing a queue of migrants stretching into the distance, accompanied by the words "Breaking Point—The EU has failed us all." The message was clear: huge numbers of Muslim migrants would come knocking on Britain's door unless she exited the European Union fast.

Bosnian Muslims (or Bosniaks as they are known) are Europeans who converted to Islam centuries ago. They demonstrate that it is perfectly possible to be European and Muslim at the same time. However, when the war started in the former Yugoslavia, their religion set them apart. Once the rhetoric declared they didn't belong, wheels were set in motion for genocide to occur.

BREAKING POINT
UKIP
Great Britain, 2016
This billboard was put up around Britain by the United Kingdom Independence Party (UKIP), led by Nigel Farage, during the Brexit referendum campaign, in support of a vote to leave the European Union. It was likened to Nazi propaganda from the 1930s. The original photograph, of mainly Syrian refugees, was taken by Jeff Mitchell in 2015 on the Croatia-Slovenia border. Mitchell had no say over how UKIP used his image; indeed, the photo was also cropped—with relaxed-looking Slovenian police chaperoning the refugees cut out of the foreground.

ABOVE
NAZI PROPAGANDA
National Socialist German Workers' Party
Germany, 1930s
Two screen grabs from a shameful propaganda film produced by the Nazi party. This archive material was included in a six-part BBC documentary series, called *Auschwitz: The Nazis and "The Final Solution"*. It first aired on BBC Two in January 2005.

In recent years, nationalism has been on the rise in much of Europe; hostility towards Muslims has increased; minorities often become scapegoats during times of crisis, and with the recent pandemic and the prospect of deep recessions I am concerned about what the future might bring.

In moments of a deeper fear, I wonder if what happened in Bosnia and the former Yugoslavia was the prequel to something dark and terrible yet to come. If European ideals disintegrate as Yugoslavia's Brotherhood and Unity did, where do I fit in? I am Romanian; I am also European, and recently became a British citizen. The dominant feature of nationalism, however, is that it demands total loyalty to one country. Coming from the Balkans I see that Byzantine, Turkish, and Austro-Hungarian influences are part of my history and culture. In Bosnia, I learnt how much I love the Balkans, how much I am a product of the Balkans, and also how European I am.

"He had green eyes", a Bosnian mother recalled in a documentary. She was talking about seeing her teenage son for the last time. He was separated from her at Srebrenica and later massacred together with another 8,000 men and boys. This mother looked tormented by the memory of her son's eyes. But it was all she had left. I would like to say to her: "I don't know you, but to me, the colour green will always be the colour of your son's eyes. I'm sorry that we, the rest of the world, failed you. I couldn't help you, but maybe my contribution to this book will show how devastating nationalism was for you, for Bosnia, and the whole of the former Yugoslavia."

Alina Wolfe Murray (née Boboc) is from Piatra Neamț in north-east Romania. She studied journalism in her home country before moving to Bosnia in 1996. She now lives in southwest England, where she works as a project manager.

HOPE RISES; *photograph by Lara Wolfe Murray; Mostar, 2019*
The graffiti appears on a derelict west Mostar high-rise buidling, locally nicknamed Sniper Tower since gunmen targeted Muslim east Mostar from the top floors during the war. Today the building is a graffiti and skateboard park, as well as an unofficial and macabre tourist attraction. Lara took this photo on a visit to Mostar with her mother, Alina Wolfe Murray, who has contributed an Afterword to this book (see page 287).

AFTERWORD
PHOTOGRAPHIC MEMORIES
Steven Gordon

I still struggle to explain why I first went to Bosnia. My life was heading in the wrong direction and things didn't make sense. I needed to break the cycle I was in. One night, in Glasgow, I watched one of Martin Bell's BBC reports on the siege of Sarajevo and it got into my head in a way I couldn't understand. That was my first step in getting to Bosnia.

I'm writing this now in Kabul twenty-eight years later, trying to bring those memories together. My journey began in Croatia in 1993, and from there I went to Bosnia, Kosovo, Iraq, Syria, Yemen, and now Afghanistan. Finally, I can look back on my time in Bosnia and process it, make peace with it, and revisit my memories in a more logical way. It took me over twenty years to come to terms with an experience that changed my life and direction.

At the time I was young and thought I understood things. But I missed the subtle lessons of my Bosnian education. The city of Tuzla wasn't the exciting metropolis an impetuous twenty-something craved. Despite its harsh wartime experience, it was quiet and tolerant and still maintains that outlook. Its values went over my brash head back then. But now I realise what Tuzla taught me: wonderful tolerance and vision.

I suppose I went looking for adventure and to immerse myself in other peoples' problems. If you told twenty-year-old me back then that conflict would be the linking factor in my life for the next 28 years, I'd have been proud to imagine that. Now, all these years later, I know otherwise.

Bosnia. What does it mean to me today? I can be walking along a street and hear a particular song or notice a specific smell, and Bosnia comes to my mind in Technicolor. The summer of 1995 runs in my head like Fujichrome—vivid hues that are as oppressive as they are saturated. Whenever I hear thunder it's never as loud as it was in Bosnia. Whenever I hear an artillery shell explode it never seems to echo the way it did in Bosnia. There was always a perfect silence after a shell landed. Time and space seemed to stop and you existed in that moment, not knowing whether to smile or cry, your mortality all too apparent. Then you heard the birds start to sing again, and you waited for what came next. These are some of the feelings Bosnia left in me. I spent the next years looking for another Bosnia—the people, the places, the landscape, the cause.

Over the years what Bosnia taught me slowly emerged, particularly when in the company of actual evil—a sense of massive injustice carried out by willing participants, usually blinded by national or religious fervour, blinded to the point that the norms of society are overruled in pursuit of a goal so abhorrent that they create a palpable sense of blackness. In Bosnia, I felt this around Mostar and Srebrenica, in Kosovo at Račak, and in Syria very much in Aleppo. True evil is never forgotten when encountered.

Looking at *Bosnian War Posters* now, I see how relevant it is in today's world of the Internet, social media, and fake news. In its own way, the book predicted what would come.

What I experienced in Syria is now denied by many. The barrel bombs, the targeting of medical facilities and civilian infrastructure by the Russian and Syrian regimes. We now see an online war being fought by keyboard warriors with little or no acknowledgement of the actual victims. We see the same denial that happened about Srebrenica. The past is being rewritten. It's churned out in easily digestible lies, and the big lie is the denial of genocide.

There is one poster in the book that seems to have predicted the world we now live in. Three flags are shown: one a pristine European Union flag; then one fading into green; then a totally green flag. The slogan reads, "This is not a paint commercial. This is future."

I remember General Ratko Mladić making the argument that there would be minarets all the way to Paris if the Bosnian Serb Army didn't take a stand against the Bosnian Muslims. Islamophobia, the rise of populism, the fear of refugees—these issues dominated the Bosnian War. Today they are global issues, part of our everyday discourse.

The posters in this book are important. They record the rise of dark forces in the heart of Europe in the early 1990s. For these reasons, travelling around Bosnia in an old Ford Fiesta photographing these posters makes more sense to me now than it did then. Today, sitting in Kabul, I struggle to say how much I owe Bosnia. So let me say it here: Thank you, Bosnia, my love for you will never change.

Steven Gordon currently works for Mercy Corps, an aid agency, and is based in Istanbul.

LEFT
THIS IS NOT A PAINT COMMERCIAL—THIS IS FUTURE
Draško Mikanović et al.
Banja Luka, 1993
Caption on page 140.

BOSNIAN TEXTS

PREDGOVOR
PORUKA IZ SARAJEVA
Bojan Hadžihalilović

Bosanski ratni posteri je, bez sumnje, jedna od najznačajnijih knjiga o ratu u Bosni, posebno kad je u pitanju Sarajevo. Ona odražava sve užase opsade moga grada.

Knjiga osvaja svojom neobičnom i grozničavom energijom, baš kako je to činio Daoud svojom ličnošću i misijom u Bosni i Sarajevu.

Ova knjiga je vjerovatno i posljednji dokument o ratnoj propagandi prošlog stoljeća: vremena kad nije bilo interneta, ni TikToka, niti lažnih vijesti.

Divlji ritam ludila i emocije prožima ovu knjigu, poput odnosa između propagande, umjetnosti, rata, života, i borbe bosanskih civila da prežive.

Tokom rata su dizajneri, ilustratori i umjetnici koristili postere, letke, magazine i novine kako bi se izrazili, borili za istinu i priključili borbi između dobra i zla.

Naš rad u Triju, posvećen Sarajevu, u početku se svodio na rukom slikane postere. Kasnije smo štampali dizajn u manjem formatu razglednice. Koristili smo razglednice s namjerom da ih šaljemo širom svijeta da obznane katastrofu i opsadu Sarajeva, najdužu u modernoj povijesti. Te su razglednice postale neraskidivi dio našeg otpora.

Pokušali smo pokazati dušu Sarajeva u crnohumornoj paleti, paleti gnjeva i nade. Na poleđini razglednica stajala je poruka:

Ovaj dokument je kreiran u ratnim uslovima (bez papira, bez mastila, bez električne energije, bez vode. Samo dobrom voljom).

Bosanski ratni posteri nije romantizirana vizualna biografija bosanskog rata, već gotovo punk knjiga o dobru i zlu, ljubavi i smrti, ulozi medija, i istini.

I konačno, to je knjiga o zlu koje još uvijek stanuje ovdje, i tamo, i posvuda.

Bojan Hadžihalilović je sa svojom suprugom Dadom osnovao Dizajn studio Trio, u Sarajevu 1985. godine. Zajedno sa Lejlom Mulabegović, vodili su Trio tokom cijele opsade Sarajeva, gdje Bojan i Dada još uvijek žive i rade. Ovaj umjetnički trojac zajedno je producirao brojne klasike dizajna.

PREDGOVOR
NA GRAĐASKI NAČIN
Vehid Šehić

Prva stvar koju moram reći je da je Tuzla jedini grad u Bosni i Hercegovini koji nije izabrao nacionalističku partiju od 1990. godine, kad su održani prvi višepartijski izbori. Mi smo slobodni ljudi i nikada nismo slijedili zov nacionalizma. Tradicije Tuzle je zajedništvo, nerazlikovanje ljudi na osnovu njihovog mišljenja ili religije.

Tuzla je stari grad sa rudnicima soli i naši rudari uvijek su se suprotstavljali tiraniji i iskazivali osjećaj solidarnosti među ljudima. Imamo bogatu tradiciju pobune, nezavisnosti, ali i kulture—prvo pozorište u Bosni i Hercegovini osnovano je ovdje. Radnička klasa Tuzle datira iz austrougarskog perioda, kada su mnogi radnici i inženjeri dolazili iz Austrije, Mađarske, čeških zemalja, Italije i Njemačke, da ovdje rade. Brojni narodi živjeli su u Tuzli početkom dvadesetog stoljeća i svaki od njih je donio dio svoje kulture. To je ovdje stvorilo jedan zanimljiv način života.

Tokom 1992, odmah nakon početka rata, jedna grupa muslimanskih intelektualaca u Tuzli se organizirala i svake nedjelje održavala javne skupove. Njihove poruke, među kojima su bile one o prednostima šerijatskog zakona, bile su neprihvatljive jer su protivne našoj filozofiji i načinu života. Oni su davali prioritet muslimanima pred drugim grupama i to je bio jedan oblik ekstremnog nacionalizma. Jedan prijatelj i ja smo shvatili da se moramo suprotstaviti tim idejama i tako, 28. februara 1993. godine, nas sedmorica smo osnovali Forum građana Tuzle na javnom skupu održanom u hotelu Tuzla. Preko 900 ljudi pojavilo se da nam iskažu podršku. Hotel je bio prepun.

Osnivačka deklaracija Foruma obraćala se svima koji su bili zainteresirani za demokratsku budućnost Bosne i Hercegovine, i upozoravala da su religijska ili etnička "rješenja" za našu zemlju veoma opasna. Do dana današnjeg mi ličnim primjerom pokazujemo da je život u slobodi moguć—ako se poštuju prava svih građana, bez obzira na nacionalnost ili religiju.

Oko 13.400 ljudi podržalo je ovu ideju tako što su se pridružili Forumu i, nakon što smo počeli sa radom, ona grupa muslimanskih intelektualaca obustavila je svoje aktivnosti. Nisu imali dovoljno podrške u Tuzli te čak ni danas islamska partija nema nikakvu snagu u Tuzli.

Forum je postao poznat u cijeloj Bosni i Hercegovini. Tokom rata, dobijali smo poruke sa svih strana u kojima su nam govorili da je naš primjer njihova jedina nada. Dobili smo i međunarodno priznanje; Helsinški parlament građana je, naprimjer, uspostavio podružnicu u našem uredu u Tuzli. Verona Forum i neki članovi Evropskog parlamenta pomogli su nam da u ratu organiziramo dvije velike međunarodne konferencije. Na drugoj od ove dvije konferencije, održanoj u oktobru 1994, učestvovali su antiratni aktivisti iz Srbije, Hrvatske, Crne Gore, Slovenije i Makedonije. Gosti su morali prelaziti linije fronta, putovati uskim planinskim putevima, u pratnji oklopnih vozila UNPROFOR-a (Zaštitne snage Ujedinjenih nacija). Sve važne međunarodne TV stanice su bile ovdje i to je bila jedina konferencija te vrste održana na teritoriji bivše Jugoslavije u ratu. Teško je reći kakav su efekat ti događaji imali na konačnu mirovnu konferenciju.

Za nas je najvažnije bilo da se rat okonča, mada nismo zadovoljni sistemom i organizacijom koje sada imamo u Bosni i Hercegovini. Najveća greška učinjena u Daytonu [Mirovni sporazum iz 1995. godine kojim je okončan rat] bila je što nije uspostavljen protektorat nad Bosnom barem na pet godina. Protektorati datiraju još iz Rimskog carstva kada bi carstva u svoje ruke uzimala odluke o vanjskoj politici i odbrani neke teritorije. Najrelevantniji primjer za nas je Njemačka nakon Drugog svjetskog rata, kada su Saveznici uspostavili petogodišnji protektorat, tokom kojeg su sve političke partije bile zabranjene i nisu održavani izbori. Da su u Njemačkoj izbori održani 1946. godine, reorganizirana nacistička partija bi pobijedila.

U Londonu 1995. godine sreo sam Robina Cooka, britanskog ministra vanjskih poslova iz sjene, i preporučio mu da se Bosni i Hercegovini nametne petogodišnji protektorat. Za to vrijeme, sugerirao sam, političke partije i izbori trebaju se zabraniti. Nakon tog petogodišnjeg perioda mogao bi se primijeniti jedan manje čvrsti tip protektorata—poput ovog kojeg sada imamo sa OHR-om [Ured visokog predstavnika]—i tek onda bi bili dozvoljeni slobodni izbori.

Zašto? Zato što nije prirodno da nacionalističke političke partije koje su bile aktivne tokom rata—SDA, HDZ, SDS—budu odgovorne i za provedbu mira. To je potpuno iracionalno. Zato mi još uvijek živimo u ratnom periodu od 1992. do 1995. Robin Cooke mi je rekao da bi protektorat doista bio najbolje rješenje, ali da, po njegovom gledištu, velike sile ne bi bile spremne preuzeti tako veliku odgovornost.

Tokom rata mi nismo imali mnogo medija. Dva dnevna lista (Oslobođenje i Tuzlanski list) bi ponekad bili dostupni, i s prekidima smo mogli slušati Radio Sarajevo. Bile su i dvije lokalne radio stanice u Tuzli (RTV Tuzla i Radio Kameleon), ali električne struje nije bilo pa su ljudi rijetko mogli uključiti radio. Jedan od najefikasnijih sistema komunikacije tokom rata bio je Radio Slobodna Evropa; oni su potpisali ugovore sa lokalnih radio stanicama diljem bivše Jugoslavije i svaka od nih je reemitirala njihov sadržaj na bosanskom jeziku. Imali su i nekoliko emisija o Forumu građana Tuzle i tako smo mi postali poznati u cijeloj bivšoj Jugoslaviji.

Bilo je uistinu teško komunicirati s građanima Tuzle tokom rata i taj problem rezultirao je jednim rješenjem: našom kampanjom posterima. To je bio jedini način na koji smo se mogli obratiti javnosti i političarima, i u tome smo bili jako dobri u tome. Kreiranje tih postera uvijek je bilo timski rad. Pored mene i grafičkog dizajnera—Jasminka Arnautovića, koji je dizajnirao većinu postera—tu su bili jedan ilustrator i još troje ljudi. Kada bi se predložila nova ideja, ja bih okupio tim da radimo na produkciji novog postera.

Ono što je zanimljivo o posteru je da je to način da osoba izrazi nešto—poruku ili ideju. Iznad svega, poster mora biti jasan. Što je jednostavniji, to više navodi ljude na razmišljanje.

Štampali smo najmanje 300 kopija a najveći tiraž jednog postera iznosio je 3.000 primjeraka (stranica 256). Po cijelom gradu su ih raznosili naši volonteri, uvijek noću. U nekim slučajevima, postere su kidali sa zidova, ali većina ih je dugo ostajala. Uspjeli smo naći posebno jako ljepilo koje je zaista otežalo kidanje postera sa zida. Jedino su ga mogli prešarati ili isjeći u komadiće.

Tokom rata, jedan oficir službe za nacionalnu sigurnost Bosne i Hercegovine došao je u ured Foruma. Tražio je primjerak određenog postera i rekao nam da je pokušao da ga skine sa zida, bez uspjeha. Rado sam mu dao primjerak postera koji je želio.

Drugom jednom prilikom, tokom rata, padala je jaka kiša, na ulici sam naišao na jednog starog učitelja. Zahvaljivao mi je što sam mu osvježio dan. Upitao sam ga šta mi želi time reći, jer padala je jaka kiša. Rekao mi je da se uvijek osjeti osvježenim kada vidi naše postere. Zasigurno su naši posteri budili optimizam kod ljudi, ulijevali im nadu da će se nešto promijeniti.

I danas mi na ulici prilaze ljudi da iskažu podršku radu našeg Foruma. Nailazim na pozitivnu reakciju u cijeloj Bosni i Hercegovini gdje me sada prepoznaju zbog TV intervjua koje dajem. Bosanci su veoma dobri ljudi, ali se često boje pokazati tu dobrotu. Međutim, sa mnom se oni otvore i dijele sa mnom svoje strahove, nade i poštovanje. To je ono što mi je davalo snage da preživim rat i daje mi sve do danas. Sada mi je 69 godina i mogao sam davno odustati, mogao sam zaraditi veliki novac, ali obični ljudi su činili da osjećam da ovo što radim vrijedi truda.

Vehid Šehić je rođen u Tuzli 1952. godine. Diplomirao je na Pravnom fakultetu Univerziteta u Sarajevu a potom radio kao tužilac, advokat i sudija. Od 1994. godine do danas (2021) predsjednik je Foruma građana Tuzle. Tekst je uredio Rupert Wolfe Murray, na osnovu intervjua koji je vodio sa Vehidom Šehićem u Tuzli u avgustu 2021.

PREDGOVOR
BOSANSKI RATNI POSTERI: PRIČA KOJA OPOMINJE
Carol A. Wells

Bosanski rat je, dok je trajao (1992–95), mnogima u Sjevernoj Americi izgledao dalek i zbunjujući jer nisu mogli razumjeti kako se rodbina, prijatelji i susjedi mogu iznenada okrenuti jedni protiv drugih. Kad čitam ovu knjigu sada, u svjetlu napada na Capitol početkom 2021. godine, Bosanski rat ima novo značenje i relevantnost. Postao je priča koja najviše opominje.

U današnje vrijeme, diljem SAD-a i velikog dijela svijeta, nacionalizam je u porastu, vjerski fundamentalizam se širi, a zločini iz mržnje postaju sve uobičajeniji. Kako u Sjedinjenim Državama i dalje jačaju društvene podjele, raspad Jugoslavije više nije tako teško razumjeti. Ovi posteri pomažu da razjasnimo prošlost pošto nude upozorenja za budućnost.

Ne iznenađuje što je toliko umjetnika radilo postere tokom Bosanskog rata jer poster je najdostupniji, lako se dijeli i popularna je umjetnička forma za izražavanje sukoba i otpora. Ono što može iznenaditi one koji sada prvi put gledaju ove postere je njihova raznolikost, izobilje i često izuzetan dizajn.

Mada je malo ovih postera šire poznato, mnogi od se mogu učiniti bliskim pošto inkorporiraju prizore iz reklama, umjetnosti i filmskih postera, omota albuma i popularne kulture. Čak i Miki Maus, Supermen i Djeda Mraz, kao i Porodica Kremenko na njima se pojavljuju. Trio Sarajevo, jedna od najpoznatijih umjetničkih grupa predstavljenih u ovoj knjizi, često preuzima slike i svoj naziva rad „redizajnom". Posvuda u svijetu, preuzimanje slika odavno je popularna tehnika. Ona umjetnicima omogućava da privuku pažnju gledalaca time što prikazuju nešto i ugodno poznato i provokativno nepoznato.

Većina preuzetih slika je neskrivena i briljantna—kao što je sad već ikonični plakat grupe Trio Enjoy Sarajevo koji koristi zaštitni znak Coca-Cole (stranica 101), i kreacija Art Publishinga Ovo nije lula mira (stranica 179), koja se poigrava sa slikom *Ceci n'est pas une pipe* (Ovo nije lula) Renea Magrittea. Iako je većina preuzetih prizora očita, neki su tako suptilni da zahtijevaju poznavanje historije regiona kao i historije umjetnosti, ali i historije dizajna političkog postera.

Bosanski posteri u ovoj knjizi inkorporiraju umjetnost od prahistorije do renesanse, od popa do punka. Umjetnost na koju se referiraju uključuje radove Masaccioa, Dürera, Leonarda, Muncha, Picassa, Warhola, Lichtensteina i Fukude. Posteri koji su prvobitno urađeni za Prvi i Drugi svjetski rat, kao i za Španski građanski rat, redizajnirani su za Bosanski rat. Osvaja bliskost ovih zajedničkih kulturnih referenci.

Sjedinjene Države, Evropska unija, Ujedinjene nacije i NATO pojavljuju se na mnogim posterima, prvenstveno kao kritika njihovih neuspješnih, čak patetičnih, pokušaja da taj sukob riješe. Još i sad se raspravlja da li je uključenost mnogih zemalja i međuvladinih agencija poput UN-a, produžila ili skratila rat koji je dokrajčio Jugoslaviju.

Česte vizualne reference na Hitlera i nacizam podsjećaju gledaoce da je tokom Drugog svjetskog rata Hrvatska bila saveznica nacističke Njemačke i da su se diljem tog regiona namnožile mnoge fašističke grupe. One istovremeno upozoravaju da fašističke grupe i dalje cvjetaju. Naprimjer, poster pod nazivom HEEELP Begana Turbića (stranica 92) koristi fotomontažu kako bi pravoslavni krst transformirao u kukasti krst, dodajući mu na krajeve tradicionalne četke kakve prave seljaci. Šezdeset godina ranije, njemački umjetnik John Heartfield (rođen kao Helmut Herzfeld) koristio je ovu tehniku da načini kukasti krst od četiri krvave sjekire.[1]

Heartfield je bio jedan od začetnika fotomontaže i, koristeći ovu tehniku, kreirao je mnogo antifašističkih naslovnica magazina i postera. Turbićevo korištenje fotomontaže da kreira kukasti krst tako povezuje prošlost sa sadašnjošću. Prosječni gledalac možda ne poznaje ovu referencu, ali će je drugi kreatori političkog postera prepoznati, jer Heartfielda mnogi smatraju jednim od prvih dizajnera protestnih postera koji su masovno producirani.

Mnogi se prizori neposredno odnose na bosansku povijest, kako drevnu tako i savremenu, a potpisi nude ključ za njihovo razumijevanje. Crveno-bijeli dizajn šahovske table je drevni heraldički znak Hrvatske, i pojavljuje se na brojnim posterima, bšš kao i bosanski ljiljan. Ponekad se pojavljuju zajedno, ali češće razdvojeno, jer predstavljaju različite strane u ratu.

Poster Adina Šadića (stranica 87), umjetnika koji je bio i bosanski muslimanski borac, iz 1992. godine, predstavlja zapanjujući spoj ta dva nacionalistička simbola.[2] U potpisu stoji objašnjenje da je u ranim danima rata, bilo optimizma—mada kratkotrajnog—da bi ujedinjenim naporima bosanski Hrvati i muslimani mogli zaustaviti srpsku ekspanziju u Bosni. Ovaj poster je posebno važan zato što dokumentira kratki pokušaj uspostave jedinstva da bi se porazio zajednički neprijatelj. Podjela između Hrvata i muslimana uskoro će rezultirati ratom između tri strne, između Srba, Hrvata i bosanskih muslimana.

Iste te godine, Trio Sarajevo je producirao dvije verzije postera Agresija na Bosnu i Hercegovinu (stranica 76). Oba imaju isti naslov i layout, što vizualno naglašava da su i zamišljeni kao par, te time podsjećaju na diptih, na religijski prizor oslikan iza oltara. Na jednom je ratom oštećena munara; na drugom statua sv. Josipa koji drži mladog Isusa, dok stoje ispred zida išaranog artiljerijskim šrapnelima. Posteri iz ovog rata rijetko pokazuju istovremeno suosjećanje za žrtve kršćane i muslimane.

Jedan od vizualno najmoćnijih postera u ovoj knjizi ilustrira nastojanje da se ponovo ispiše historija regiona brisanjem efekata 500-godišnje osmanske muslimanske kulture u Srbiji.

U radu Begana Turbića Istanbul je bitan—ostalo je mit prikazana je knjiga s velikom rupom u sredini (stranica 69). Na knjizi je naslov Srpska historija, kultura i tradicija, a na uklonjenom dijelu je oznaka „Tursko kulturno nasliježe". Predimenzionirani otvarač za boce, koji je korišten da se ukloni taj dio povijesti, stoji uspravno, zaboden u ugravirani mjesec i zvijezdu, simbol Osmanskog carstva.

Na sljedećoj je stranici prikazan drugi izuzetni, bolni poster, nazvan Bratstvo i jedinstvo, Čedomira Kostovića (stranica 71). U bivšoj Jugoslaviji, „Bratstvo i jedinstvo" je bio slogan vlasti kojim se ohrabrivala saradnja među republikama i različitim nacionalnostima. Kostović ga koristi sa strašnom ironijom, pošto je na posteru prikazana krvava testera označena kao „Bosna".[3]

Ova dva postera su usmjerena na primarne karakteristike etničkog čišćenja: masovno ubijanje i brisanje povijesti. Brisanje povijesti se koristilo tokom cijele povijesti s ciljem ponovnog pisanja povijesti. Termin etničko čišćenje je osmišljen tokom Bosanskog rata i on pruža bolni uvid u događaje koje ovi posteri dokumentiraju. Činjenica da je taj termin sada u širokoj upotrebi mnogo govori o stanju današnjeg svijeta.

Posteri su imali suštinski značaj za promociju i suprotstavljanje ratovima, barem od Prvog svjetskog rata, a i sad se koriste diljem svijeta. Produkcijski, oni nisu skupi i kada se zalijepe na zid ili nose na demonstracijama lako su i masovno vidljivi, pogotovo kad televizija i internet prenose te slike. Posteri se koriste i u današnjem svijetu visoke tehnologije zato što su učinkoviti. I zato što su učinkoviti, često ih uništavaju oni koji se protive njihovim porukama. Dodajte ovo namjerno uništenje ratnom razaranju i prirodnim štetama uslijed djelovanja elemenata, zaista je izuzetan pothvata to da su Daoud Sarhandi i Alina Wolfe Murray uspjeli pronaći toliko postera iz Bosanskog rata. Također je izuzetno da ti posteri i dan-danas za nas predstavljaju egzistencijalnu lekciju. Mi im trebamo posvetiti pažnju.

BILJEŠKE

1. Heartfieldov rad iz 1934. godine ironično je naslovljen Krv i željezo *(Blut und Eisen)*, što je bio moto Trećeg rajha.

2. Za ovaj poster, Šadić je zapravo obradio poster Emeterija Melendreras iz Španskog građanskog rata, kreiran 1937. Na Melendrerasovom posteru glava vojnika sa šljemom prekrivena je s osam zastava i simbola onih koji podržavaju cilj španskih Republikanaca, uključujući anarhiste, komuniste, Baskijce i Katalonce. U prijevodu: Sve ove milicije spajaju se u narodnu armiju (stranica 86). Decenijama kasnije, u jednom drugom ratu, Šadić je istu tu glavu vojnika sa šljemom prekrio bosanskom i hrvatskom heraldikom.

3. Slično kako John Heartfield koristi moto Trećeg rajha kao naslov postera (vidjeti bilješku 1), tako i Čedomir Kostović na svom posteru Bratstvo i jedinstvo ponovno koristi slogan jugoslavenskih vlasti da bi pokazao nejedinstvo.

Carol A. Wells je izvršna direktorica Centra za proučavanje političkih grafičkih radova, koji je osnovala 1988. godine u Los Angelesu.

Aktivistica, kuratorica, povjesničarka umjetnosti, profesorica i spisateljica, studirala je Srednji vijek na Univerzitetu Kalifornije, u Los Angelesu, te trinaest godina predavala historiju umjetnosti i arhitekture.

UVOD
SMRT, RAZARANJE, IZDAJA ... I POSTERI
Daoud Sarhandi

Prvi put sam otputovao u Bosnu u oktobru 1995. godine, tri mjeseca nakon masakra civila u Srebrenici. Želio sam nešto učiniti, bilo što, da izrazim svoju zgroženost nad onim što se tamo desilo, da pružim ono malo pomoći koju sam mogao pružiti i da pokažem da nisam dio svijeta koji šutke oprašta ta zlodjela. Tako sam se pridružio humanitarnoj organizaciji Workers' Aid, sa sjedištem u Manchesteru, i na koncu krenuo u Tuzlu, grad na sjeveroistoku Bosne u muslimansko-hrvatskoj federaciji.[1]

Ideja za ovu knjigu javila se u Tuzli nešto više od dvije godine kasnije. Tokom mog četvrtog putovanja u taj grad, u jesen 1997. godine, posjetio sam Jasminka Arnautovića, glavnog dizajnera postera za Forum građana Tuzle, i mog prijatelja. Gledajući Jasminkove antinacionalističke radove, razgovarali smo o informativnom ratu koji se vodio za srca i umove bosanskog naroda. Tada sam shvatio da bi zbirka postera pružila fascinantan uvid u to kako se bosanskom narodu obraćalo, ko mu se obraćao, i sa kojim ciljevima je to činjeno tokom konflikta. Bio sam siguran da bi nam to pokazalo kako su oni reagirali, intelektualno i emocionalno, na sukob koji je njihove živote gurnuo u tamu. Knjiga *Bosanski ratni posteri* usredotočena je na postere nastale između početka Bosanskog rata, u aprilu 1992. i njegovog kraja 1995. godine, nakon mirovnog sporazuma postignutog u zračnoj bazi Wright-Patterson u Daytonu, u državi Ohio, između predsjednika Bosne, Srbije i Hrvatske.

Prikupljanje postera nije bilo lako; trebala mi je kao i mojoj asistentici na istraživanju, Alini Wolfe Murray, cijela jedna godina između kraja 1997. i kraja 1998. Istraživanje je zahtijevalo bezbrojna putovanja diljem ratom rasturene zemlje. Umjetnici su često radili sami, i mnogi su emigrirali tokom rata, odnijevši svoje radove sa sobom; većinu tih umjetnika uspjeli smo pronaći, dok neke nismo mogli. Vrlo malo štamparija je čuvalo primjerke postera koje su producirali, mada su ih često pamtili i upućivali nas u pravom smjeru. Posteri su generalno bili štampani u ograničenom tiražu zbog nestašice materijala, tako da im je još teže bilo ući u trag.[2]

Nakon što je rat završio, posteri su još uvijek igrali vitalnu ulogu u širenju informacija u Bosni, pogotovo u vezi s tako važnim pitanjima kao što su izbjeglice, sloboda kretanja, nagazne mine, obnova, i politika. Ujedinjene nacije, OHR (Ured visokog predstavnika, koji ima odgovornost za civilnu implementaciju Daytonskog sporazuma), SFOR (Stabilizacijske snage u Bosni pod vodstvom NATO-a), OSCE (Organizacija za sigurnost i saradnju u Evropi), i razne nevladine organizacije, svi su oni producirali ogromne količine informacija za javnost. Taj materijal se otimao za pažnju bosanskog naroda, uz postere koje je producirao vrtoglavi broj političkih stranaka. S obzirom na tu realnost, mi smo uključili i bitne postere producirane nakon Daytonskog sporazuma, kao i nekoliko postera iz vremena prije izbijanja rata u Bosni. U ovoj posljednjoj kategoriji su i selekcija postera koje je Alina iskopala u Hrvatskoj. Te moćne slike, kreirane tokom 1991. godine tokom srpsko-hrvatskog rata, izražavaju osjećanja i teme slične onima koje će se kasnije pojaviti u Bosni.

Tokom Bosanskog rata, posteri su postali nevjerovatno važni. Pošto je normalna komunikacija bila onemogućena, većina vijesti išla je od usta do usta. U takvom okruženju, posteri su bili jeftin i učinkovit način širenja informacija. Ne iznenađuje stoga da se u Bosni odvijao „rat" posterima. Suprotstavljene ideološke grupe su cijepale radove jedni drugima i pokušavale zauzeti najbolja mjesta. Jedan grad se mogao probuditi i zateći cijelo područje okićeno s mnoštvom kopija jednog te istog postera da bi se sutra ustanovilo da su nestali, i bili zamijenjeni nekom drugom kreacijom. Posteri su lijepljeni i na bočne strane kamiona i bili voženi okolo. U Sarajevu se ljudima plaćalo da postave postere u najubitačnije ulice, kao što je zloglasna Aleja snajpera.

Dizajneri postera bili su iz svih sektora umjetničke zajednice, a ponekad i izvan nje: profesionalni grafički dizajneri koji su radili u umjetničkim, kulturnim i komercijalnim poljima prije rata; slikari koji su svoje talente prilagodili novoj realnosti; i dizajneri-amateri koji su se počeli baviti dizajnom kao načinom vlastitog izražavanja ili da bi to poslužilo njihovom cilju.

U ekstremnim situacijama, posteri su slikani rukom. Većinom su, međutim, štampani litografski ili u sito-štampi—pri čemu je ovaj drugi metod bio uobičajeniji. Osim umjetničkih vrijednosti sito-štampe, u ratu je vladala i nestašica litografskih ploča, a često nije bilo struje da se pokrenu prese. Sito-štampa je imala i prednost da se mogla ponovo koristiti—jednom kada bi se već postavljena slika oprala, platna su se mogla koristiti za druge radove. Iz tih je razloga je, originalne ploče postera produciranih tokom rata bilo teško pronaći

Od kraja Drugog svjetskog rata, umjetnost postera je igrala značajnu ulogu u srednjeevropskoj i istočnoevropskoj politici, zbog prirode socijalizma i pod utjecajem sovjetskog stila tehnike propagande. Postere su socijalističke države sprva koristile da obilježe godišnjice ili upute jednostavne političke poruke. Sa Staljinovom smrću, umjetnost postera

počela je sazrijevati. Mada su posteri još uvijek bili naručivani u ideološke svrhe, države je više počela interesirati moć televizije. Novi su dizajneri dolazili iz umjetničkih škola i posteri su se počeli razvijati u raznim pravcima. Ali, dok god se nisu otvoreno suprotstavljali vlastima, dizajnere se poprilično ostavljalo na miru.

Mnogi od radova u ovoj knjizi duguju nešto dizajnu poslijeratnog poljskog postera—pogotovo njegovoj vizualnoj zaigranosti i potpunoj jednostavnosti. Također, poput poljskih postera, mnogi od postera iz Bosanskog rata koristili su snažnu simboliku i minimalističku tipografiju.[3]

Raspoloženje na mnogim bosanskim posterima je očaj: rupe od metaka, krv, i srpski slogani postavljeni kraj nacističkog kukastog krsta. Bosanci su nadaleko poznati po svom britkom smislu za humor kojem nije nedodirljivo, i njihove postere često karakterizira i crna komedija. Kada se pregleda ova zbirka, čovjeka zapanji raznolikost radova. Puki umjetnički eklekticizam, u kombinaciji sa emocionalnom posvećenošću, impresionira više od svega drugog.

Za balkansku politiku se misli da je neprobojno kompleksna. Na neke načine to je tačno i to proizlazi iz činjenice da su se u tom regionu stoljećima natjecali strani interesi. Tragično, ta kompleksnost se koristila da se prikriju temeljne činjenice o raspadu bivše Jugoslavije. Problemi su namjerno zamagljivani. Kampanja dezinformacija bila je organizirana u Jugoslaviji nekoliko godina prije no što će izbiti rat. Intenzivirana je tokom vojnih kampanja i opstala je, u nekom obliku, do dana današnjeg. Mada je glavni cilj ove knjige da ispriča vizuelnu priču, potreban je kratki literarni prikaz događaja koji su se desili kako bi se razumio širi kontekst.

Bosanski rat nije izbio spontano zbog nepomirljivih razlika između etničkih i religijskih grupa koje naseljavaju Bosnu i Hercegovinu. Ta činjenica se ne može dovoljno često ponavljati, pogotovo zato što je, tokom većeg dijela rata, popričan broj stranih medija, pogotovo oni koji nikada nisu kročili u taj region, jednostavno propuštali da sagledaju stvarne uzroke rata.

Mada su mnogi dobri novinari radili na terenu u Bosni, ova verzija događaja—koju su promovirali loše informirani (ili dvolični) zapadni političari—toliko je često ponavljana da je vremenom postigla status istine. Uzroci rata su bili uvelike pogrešno shvaćeni i to je išlo direktno na ruku agresoru time što je maskiralo njihovu namjeru i pravu prirodu njihove umiješanosti. Efekat je bio takav da su sve grupe prikazivane kao barbarske, što je cijeloj priči oduzelo legitimni politički kontekst.

Mada su etničke mržnje u Bosni potpaljene tokom rata, konflikt se naprosto ne bi desio bez poticaja srbijanskih i hrvatskih vođa. Predsjednici Slobodan Milošević u Srbiji i Franjo Tuđman u Hrvatskoj—uz grupu nacionalista koju su ih podržavali u objema tim zemljama— zaslužuju da se okrive za ono što se desilo narodu Bosne i Hercegovine i ostatku bivše Jugoslavije.[4]

Nacionalni identitet uvijek je bivao korišten u Jugoslaviji. Redovno su vršene ankete o stvarnoj i percipiranoj nacionalnosti. Prihvatiti da je bilo koja od republika ikada bila potpuno sretna mješavina naroda koji u njima žive predstavlja puko samozavaravanje. Tenzije su postojale. Ali tek sredinom 1980-ih, kada je Jugoslavija počela gubiti svoj strateški hladnoratovski značaj i kada se njena ekonomija počela kruniti, vodeći akademici u Srbiji oživjeli su opasna nacionalistička osjećanja.[5]

Sprva je Milošević—koji je još uvijek bio lojalan komunista—osudio taj srpski nacionalizam. Kasnije, međutim, kada je shvatio da može koristiti njegovu snagu u svoju korist, počeo je i sam promovirati tu ideologiju, igrajući na kartu, ili pojačavajući postojeće tenzije, prvo šireći nepovjerenje, potom strah i, na koncu, mržnju. Neprijatelji

su bili potrebni za ostvarenje težnji za Velikom Srbijom, a Milošević ih je nalazio posvuda.

Kosovo je bilo rani i važan fokus djelovanja na radikalizaciji Srba kako se Milošević penjao na vlast. Većina Srba smatra Kosovo drevnim sjedištem svoje crkve i kulture. Već je 1987. godine Milošević podstrekavao tamošnju srpsku manjinu. Na jednom skupu na Kosovu u aprilu 1987. Pred okupljenom masom je izjavio: „Nikada nije bilo u srbijanskom i crnogorskom karakteru da odustane kad se nađe pred preprekama, da ustukne kada je vrijeme za bitku." I ponovo na Kosovu 1989— slaveći mučenički poraz Srba od Turaka 1389—upozorio je: „Šest vekova kasnije, danas, opet smo u bitkama i pred bitkama. One nisu oružane, mada ni takve još nisu isključene."[6] Prema optužnici Haškog tribunala protiv Miloševića, davanjem takvih izjava on je „raskinuo sa partijskom i vladinom politikom koja je ograničavala nacionalističko osjećanje u [Jugoslaviji] od vremena kada ju je Josip Broz Tito osnovao".[7]

Godine 1989, Milošević je u Skupštini progurao ustavne amandmane kojim je Kosovu oduzeta autonomija. Prema Ustavu iz 1974. godine, autonomne pokrajine Kosovo i Vojvodina su imale svaka po jedan glas u Skupštini i bile izjednačene sa šest jugoslavenskih republika.[8] Srbi su dugo gunđali da na taj način dvije pokrajine, koje su bile dio Srbije, mogu nadglasati Srbiju. Ustavne promjene, usvojene 1989. dale su Miloševiću kontrolu nad Kosovom. U toj su pokrajini izbili protesti i ona je jednostrano proglasila nezavisnost, ali međunarodna zajednica je to ignorirala. Srbija je onda raspustila Vladu Kosova i nametnula direktnu vlast Beograda. U takvoj situaciji kad Srbija počinje prijetiti, Slovenija i Hrvatska počinju strahovati za svoj status unutar Jugoslavije. Ove dvije republike su potom održale referendume (u decembru 1990. i maju 1991. respektivno) i glasale za izlazak iz Jugoslavije. Bosna i Makedonija su to učinile početkom 1992.

Milošević je potom pokušao prigrabiti silom što je više mogao od Jugoslavije koja se raspadala, koristeći pritom Jugoslavensku narodnu armiju (JNA)—tada jednu od najjačih armija u Evropi.[9] Jugoslavenska narodna armija je bila panjugoslavenska armija, ali je do kraja 1980-ih očišćena do te mjere da je efektivno postala srpska vojska, lojalna jedino Miloševiću i ideji jedne dominantne Srbije. Godine 1991. Milošević je naredio JNA da krene na Hrvatsku i time izazvao produženi krvavi sukob. Međutim, koliko god da je ružan bio rat u Hrvatskoj, njegovi užasi su 1992. godine pali u drugi plan, s pokoljem i razaranjem koje je zapljusnulo Bosnu i Hercegovinu.

Rat u Hrvatskoj i Bosni vođen je s plitkim izgovorom da su Srbi koji tamo žive izloženi smrtnoj opasnosti od Hrvata i muslimana. Opsjednutost i mitologiju koja okružuje ideju Velike Srbije koristili su srpski političari redom, sve od drevnih vremena i ishod je uvijek bio fatalan.

Krajem 1980-ih, nacionalizam u Srbiji ohrabrio je nacionalizam u drugim jugoslavenskim republikama. To je stvorilo pogodnu političku klimu da se pojave i budu izabrane druge nacionalističke vođe, kao što je Franjo Tuđman u Hrvatskoj—i u manjoj mjeri, predsjednici Milan Kučan u Sloveniji i Alija Izetbegović u Bosni—na političkoj sceni i preuzmu vlast. Kada su u tim republikama dominantne etničke grupe izabrale nacionaliste, među manjinama se počeo širiti strah. Ti su strahovi potom bili eksploatirani. Bila je to spirala straha i političkog oportunizma koja je započela u Srbiji i kao šumski požar se proširila širom Jugoslavije.

Privlačnost Miloševićevog nacionalizma među Srbima bila je u velikoj mjeri potpomognuta Tuđmanovim nacionalističkim ponašanjem, iako on nije bio u poziciji da započne rat. Situacija u Bosni uvijek je bila nešto drugačija i potencijalno eksplozivnija nego u drugim republikama zbog njenog etničkog sastava. Mada su Bošnjaci (bosanski muslimani) bili najveća pojedinačna grupa u toj zemlji—činili su 44 posto stanovništva—Srbi pravoslavci su činili 33 posto i Hrvati katolici 17 posto, dok su Jevreji, Turci, Romi i druge manjine činili ostatak.

Bosanski predsjednik Izetbegović, koji je došao na vlast na izborima 1990, bio je svjestan razornih posljedica koje bi imao rat u Bosni i sprva je činio sve u svojoj moći da ga spriječi. Početkom 1992. godine jedan mali kontingent UN-ovih mirovnih snaga stigao je u Sarajevo, a Izetbegović je preklinjao UN da pošalje veće, robusnije snage u njegovu zemlju. Rat je već bjesnio u Hrvatskoj, a do političke podjele stanovništva u Bosni na etničkim osnovama već je došlo. Izetbegovićevi apeli međunarodnoj zajednici, međutim, naišli su na gluhe uši.[10]

Komadanje jedne zemlje sa stanovništvom tako etnički pomiješanim kao što je bosansko nije bilo lako. Ali što je bilo više međuetničke brutalnosti, to je više jačala ideja da tri grupe ne mogu zajedno živjeti. Efekat je bila etnička podjela, koja je izgledala kao neizbježno rješenje.

JNA je bila profesionalna armija i nije se na nju moglo osloniti da izvršava onu vrstu brutalnosti kakva je bila potrebna da se izvrši etničko čišćenje. Za to su, tajno finansirane od Miloševića, korištene paravojne snage iz Srbije: Šešeljevi četnici, Draškovićeva Srpska garda, zloglasni Arkanovi Tigrovi (ili Srpska dobrovoljačka garda), i mnogi drugi odredi smrti maltretirali su, silovali i ubijali civile—provodeći etničko čišćenje u Bosni i Hercegovini.[11] Ova tehnika je usavršena u Hrvatskoj i onda s razornim efektom primijenjena u Bosni i na Kosovu. Usto su lokalni srpski civili hranjeni 24-satnom nacionalističkom propagandom iz Beograda. Kad je došlo vrijeme za to, naoružavani su i poticani na vršenje nasilja nad dugogodišnjim susjedima. U Bosni, Radovan Karadžić je pod pokroviteljstvom Srbije postao gospodar rata, a vojska bosanskih Srba (službeno VRS, Vojska Republike

Srpske) stvorena je od civila i jedinica JNA kako bi izvršavala njegove i Miloševićeve naloge.

Frazu „etničko čišćenje" prvobitno su koristili mediji u Srbiji da opišu akte protiv Hrvata u područjima Hrvatske zauzetim tokom srpske ofanzive. Od tada je ušla u rječnike jezika diljem svijeta. Mada nijedna strana u bosanskom ratu nije potpuno nevina kad se radi o činjenju ratnih zločina, eliminacija manjina nikad nije bila službena politika izabrane vlade u Bosni niti je to rutinski prakticirala Armija Bosne i Hercegovine (ABiH).[12] Etničko čišćenje, međutim, vrlo je brzo postalo *raison d'être* srpskih i hrvatskih snaga i njihovih odreda smrti. Teritorijalna dominacija nad Bosnom bila je Miloševićev i Tuđmanov cilj pošto su njih dvojica etničku čistoću smatrali jedinim sredstvom da je postignu. Etničko čišćenja područja koja su prigrabili bilo je njihova središnja strategija, a ne nusprodukt, ratova koje su vodili.[13]

Mada zapadne sile nisu bile uzrok rata, postoji element njihovog dosluha sa onima koji su pokrenuli Bosanski rat. U njihovim nastojanjima da nađu najbrže rješenje problema tog regiona, neki zapadni državnici su davali legitimitet najgorim nacionalistima. Ova situacija degenerirala je od pasivnog saučesništva do tragičnog, aktivnog angažmana kada je Vijeće sigurnosti UN-a, na zahtjev njegovih stalnih članica, insistiralo na nametanju embarga na oružje protiv legitimne države članice UN-a—Bosne i Hercegovine—koja se očito morala braniti od Srbije i u manjoj mjeri od Hrvatske.[14] Pod vodstvom generalnog sekretara Boutros Boutros-Ghalija i njegovog specijalnog predstavnika Yasushi Akashija, UN je stajao i gledao masovno raseljavanje civila i činjenje ratnih zločina u razmjerama koje nisu u Evropi viđena od 1940-ih.[15] Za više od tri godine, posmatrači Evropske unije, UN-ovi vojnici i Sigurne zone postojali su pokraj koncentracionih logora i logora za silovanje, kao i snajpera koji su se otvoreno hvalisali da su hitra sarajevska

djeca bolji test njihove preciznosti od odraslih. Najniža tačka desila se u julu 1995. godine kada su snage bosanskih Srba, pod komandom generala Ratka Mladića, zauzele Srebrenicu, Sigurnu zonu pod zaštitom holandskog bataljona UN-a. Cjelokupno stanovništvo je protjerano a više od 8.000 muškaraca i dječaka hladnokrvno je pobijeno. UN je naredio holandskom bataljonu da stoji i ništa ne čini.

Uveliko zbog onoga što se desilo u Srebrenici, Sjedinjene Države su uzele stvar u svoje ruke. Predvođene SAD-om, NATO snage počele su bombardirati Vojsku bosanskih Srba 30. avgusta 1995, dok je istovremeno Bosanska armija počela postizati uspjehe na cijeloj teritoriji zemlje. To je prisililo Srbe, koje je predstavljao Milošević, da sjednu za pregovarački stol. Mirovni pregovori su održani krajem 1995. godine u zračnoj bazi Wright-Patterson, u Daytonu, država Ohio. Uz goleme teškoće, sklopljen je sporazum koji je okončao borbe, i Milošević, Tuđman i Izetbegović potpisali su ga 21. novembra te godine. Centralni problem Daytonskog sporazuma je da je nagradio srpske agresore sa 49 posto zemlje—efektivno učinivši Bosnu zemljom kojom je nemoguće upravljati.

U Bosni nije bilo pobjednika. Oko 100.000 ljudi je izgubilo život, više od dva miliona je ostalo bez doma ili je raseljeno, ta prekrasna zemlja je posuta nagaznim minama, veliki njen dio sveden na ruševine, a gotovo svi su nosili emocionalne ili fizičke ožiljke. Oni koji su bili dovoljno zavedeni da tvrde da su postigli neku pobjedu, dobili su ništa do prava na život u etnički čistim, ali moralno bankrotiranim getima. Između 1999. i 2020. godine nezaposlenost nikada nije pala ispod 18 posto a znala je porasti čak do 31 posto. U vrijeme kad ovi pišem, procjenjuje se da 640.000 od njenih 3,8 miliona žitelja živi u apsolutnom siromaštvu.

Mir koji se još održava u Bosni je krhak i vještački. Opasne podjele vladaju između njena dva entiteta: Muslimansko-hrvatske federacije i Republike Srpske.[16] Izbjeglice svih nacionalnosti još uvijek se ne mogu vratiti u svoje domove, a oni koji su u ratu počinili zločine i dalje su na slobodi. Mada je situacija mjestimično bolja, čini se da se nacionalizam na svim stranama, a posebno u područjima pod kontrolom Srba i Hrvata, duboko ušančio i da će potrajati u doglednoj budućnosti.

Neposredno nakon što je Daytonski sporazum ratificiran, britanski historičar Noel Malcolm je napisao:

Nova Bosna, koju nagovještava jučerašnje potpisivanje mirovnog sporazuma u Parizu, bit će geopolitički ekvivalent umjetničkom djelu Damiena Hirsta. Hirst uzme kravu, prepila je na pola, i obje polovine potopi u formaldehid. To može biti ingeniozno umjetničko djelo, ali je li to još uvijek krava? Slično je s novom Bosnom. To može biti najpametniji od svih ustava, ali je li to još uvijek zemlja?[17]

Mada je, na mom prvom putovanju u Bosnu u oktobru 1995. godine, konvoju u kojem sam bio trebalo više od dvije sedmice da iz Britanije stigne do Tuzle, mogli smo se tamo zadržati samo tri dana. Želio sam se vratiti u Bosnu: vidjeti ljude koje sam tamo upoznao, i uvjeriti se da je donirana televizijska oprema za koju sam bio odgovoran stigla do konačnog odredišta— do TV Tuzla. Moje sljedeće putovanje u Bosnu bilo je krajem decembra 1995, kada je Daytonski sporazum stupio na snagu. Mada su i vrijeme i ceste bili loši, lakše je bilo voziti kroz Bosnu nego u godinama prije toga. Barikade po cestama koje su bile karakteristika bosanskog rata nestale su. Nestale su i crvene-i-zelene UNPROFOR-ove zastave koje su korištene da upozore na prijetnju od snajperske aktivnosti.

Mada je prijelaz na robustnije Provedbene snage pod vodstvom NATO-a (IFOR) bio u punom zamahu, mi nismo do kraja vjerovali u cestu kroz još uvijek sporni teritorij pod srpskom kontrolom oko Sarajeva pa smo odlučili u Tuzlu uči

poznatim putem putem, preko snijegom prekrivenih planina i blatnjavim putevima. Ovaj put sam u Bosni ostao nekoliko sedmica, željan da vidim više nego što sam to uspio u jesen. Proveo sam nekoliko sedmica u Tuzli a onda posjetio Sarajevo i Mostar.

Po Sarajevu—još uvijek pod opsadom mada su borbe bile prestale—sam zatekao desetine svježih humki s jednostavnim oznakama datuma između 1992. i 1995. Barikade protiv snajpera napravljene od uništenih automobila još su bile ispred zgrada i na mostovima. Upozorenje *PAZI SNAJPER* još je uvijek stajalo ispisano po zidovima i zakucano po stablima. Gomile smeća ležale su posvuda. Ali usred tog razaranja, Sarajlije su se privikavale na ideju da bi ponovo mogli hodati ulicama svoga grada bez straha da će biti pogođeni. Koliko god da su uslovi daytonskog mira bili takvi da su donijeli samo podjele—a demokratski nastrojeni Bosanci su posvuda osjećali da su ti uslovi bili suštinski nepravedni—Sarajlije su se radovale.

Ako postoji mjesto u Bosni i Hercegovini koje ilustrira ono što se ispravno zove „urbicid" onda je to Mostar. Godine 1993, HVO, iza kojeg je stajao Tuđman, pokušao je uništiti cijeli istočni (muslimanski) dio grada.[18] Sudbina Starog mosta je stoga simbolična. Taj delikatni, gracilni most nad Neretvom projektirao je slavni turski arhitekta Mimar Hajrudin 1566. godine; on je gradu dao ime a dao mu je i identitet. Most su srpske snage oštetile 1992. godine, da bi krajem sljedeće godine bio namjerno srušen jednom jedinom granatom ispaljenom sa hrvatskog tenka. U zemlji koja je nekoć bio nebrojeno mnogo mostova, Stari most je simbolizirao odnos između istočne i zapadne tradicije Bosne, njenih različitih nacionalnosti i vjera. Besmisleno rušenje mosta imalo je negativni psihološki utjecaj i na grad i cijelu zemlju.

Iz Mostara sam izašao kroz relativno netaknutu zapadnu (hrvatsku) stranu grada i odvezao se u Zagreb. Put me je proveo kroz Knin, i onda kroz niz sablasnih, spaljenih sela-duhova. Bilo je to područje koje su, 1989. godine, mediji u Srbiji počeli zvati Srpska krajina.[19] Taj siromašni dio Hrvatske bio je naseljen uglavnom Srbima i srpske paravojne snage su ga zauzele 1991. i očistile od svih Hrvata pod izgovorom da su Srbi koji tamo žive—mnogi od njih stoljećima—izloženi smrtnoj opasnosti u Tuđmanovoj nacionalističkoj Hrvatskoj. Kada Miloševiću više nije bilo politički isplativo da podupire tu zločinačku paradržavu—i kad je tražio način da se iščupa iz ratne kaljuže koju je sam pokrenuo—krajinski Srbi su bili prepušteni svojoj sudbini. U julu 1995, ovo područje uz američku podršku hrvatske snage su oslobodile u vojnoj operaciji koja je trajala samo dva dana. Kodno ime te operacije je, ispravno, bilo Oluja. Njen rezultat bio etničko čišćenje cijelog srpskog stanovništva, njih blizu 200.000, koji su formirali očajno tužni konvoj koji će se izvući u Srbiju.

Po povratku u Britaniju, u januaru 1996, otišao sam u prijateljevu kućicu u Lake Districtu. Bila je to strašno hladna zima i u tom kraju je često padao snijeg. Jedno popodne, dok sam se sklonio od hladnoće u jednu starinarnicu u Kendalu, nabasao sam na kutiju sa slagalicom na čijem je poklopcu bila slika. Trebalo mi je nekoliko sekundi da mi se slika i njen identitet povežu u glavi, a onda me je to pogodilo. Gledao sam sliku Mostara: naseljenog, mirnog Mostara; sunčanog Mostara s mostom, kupačima i slikovitim, bršljanom pokrivenim kućama i opranim vešom koji se suši na prozorima. Ukratko, nestali Mostar. Bilo je nečeg zapanjujuće istinitog u toj slici Mostara kao slagalici. Mostar je i dalje podijeljen. Hrvati upravljaju njegovom katoličkom zapadnom stranom, a muslimani istočnom. Djeca idu u zasebne škole, gdje izgovaraju različite riječi (mada u suštini govore isti jezik), i uče po različitim nastavnim planovima.

Doista, metafora slagalice može se prenijeti na cijelu Bosnu. Pogledajte bilo koju mapu nastalu nakon rata i vidjet ćete višebojni kolaž u kojem je gustina naseljenosti iskazana kroz etničku identifikaciju i religiju. Sve su strane sačinile svoje mape na kojima se vidi preklapanje nacionalističkih ambicija, uz prijedloge etničkih podjela i unutarnjih granica. Na terenu su, tokom rata, granice u vidu linija fronta prolazile kroz gradove, gradiće i sela. Voziti se Bosnom u vrijeme borbi—i čak zadugo nakon toga—osjećalo se kao voziti se po nekoj ogromnoj slagalici. I međunarodna zajednica iscrtale svoje linije razdvajanja po toj zemlji. Kako piše novinar Anthony Borden:

Koliko protraćenih sati mora su proveli u UN-ovoj Palais des Nations u Ženevi, nagnuti nad dijagrame trouglastog oblika Bosne, u pokušaju da se mir zamisli pomoću olovaka u boji? Neke su olovke dale više „muslimanima", neke više „Srbima", neke su dale teritoriju određenu za „Hrvate", dok su ih druge povezali s vladom u Sarajevu. Ono što je svima bilo zajedničko je povezivanje etniciteta i teritorije.[20]

Zapanjuje me da vanjski igrači i dan-danas vode proces definiranja balkanskih granica—mada drugi politički igralu vode igru. U aprilu 2021. Godine, takozvani „non-paper" počeo je cirkulirati hodnicima evropske moći s prijedlogom nove podjele Zapadnog Balkana po etničkim šavovima.[21]

U zimu 1995. godine, Tuzla je bila hladna, vlažna, i puna smoga od peći na drva i loženja smeća po kućama. U novogodišnjoj noći mi smo plesali na ulicama usred huke ručnih granata i vatre iz automatskog oružja, slaveći prvu mirnodopsku Novu godinu od 1992. Jedan crno-bijeli poster s prodornim okom blještao je nad prljavim gradom. Bio je to plakat za pozorišni komad *Iza sna*. Kada sam ga pokušao dobiti, ustanovio sam da je pozorište ostalo bez ijednog primjerka. Tri godine kasnije, kada sam započeo ovu knjigu, naći taj poster za mene je postalo nešto nalik na misiju. Jednoga dana sam upoznao dizajnera Adina Šadića. Kada sam mu spomenuo taj zapanjujući, mada donekle zagonetni poster, lice mu je zasjalo: on ga je dizajnirao! Kada sam ga zamolio da mi objasni njegovo značenje, Šadić mi je rekao da se oko odnosi na centralnu temu komada—tezu da je Bosna bila tako zaslijepljena svojom ljubavlju prema Jugoslaviji da je ostala tragično nesvjesna mračnih nacionalističkih snaga koje su se u njoj okupljale.

Bosanski rat je važan. Ne samo za Bosance, već i za građane Sjedinjenih Država, Britanije, i drugih evropskih zemalja čije su vlade u tom sukobu odigrale tako mutnu ulogu. Raspad Jugoslavije—a pogotovo sukob u Bosni—natjerao je te zemlje da shvate ograničenja vlastite vanjske politike. Bosanski rat, i reakcija svijeta na njega, trebali bi biti važni građanima svih zemalja koje su u sukobu uslijed unutarnjih podjela između svojih naroda. Baš kao u Bosni, štaviše, te podjele često produbljuju cinični političari čija je prvenstvena odgovornost briga za sigurnost vlastitih građana, mada oni svjesno čine upravo suprotno.

BILJEŠKE

1. Ime zemlje na bosanskom jeziku je Bosna i Hercegovina. Hercegovina, na engleskom, je južna regija. Ja koristim Bosna i Hercegovina, Bosna-Hercegovina i Bosna naizmjenično u ovoj knjizi. Također, da pojednostavim, koristim ime Jugoslavija, a ne „bivša Jugoslavija", kada govorim o zemlji koja je postojala prije raspada.

2. Iz tog sam razloga izabrao uključiti nekoliko slika koje su dizajnirane kao posteri, mada nikad nisu štampane.

3. Mada ima malo informacija, ima slučajeva direktne veze između bosanskih dizajnerskih radova i slavnih poljskih postera, kao što su oni na stranicama

169 i 189. Hvala profesoru dizajna Janu Nuckowskom iz Krakówa što mi ih je odštampao. Carol Wells je također zapazila zapanjujuće sličnosti između dva postera nastala tokom Bosanskog rata i propagande koju su producirali Republikanci tokom Španskog građanskog rata (vidjeti stranice 14 i 86).

4. Milošević je postao šef Predsjedništva Centralnog komiteta Saveza komunista 1986. godine. Izabran je predsjednika Predsjedništva Srbije 1989. A 1990. je, nakon ustavnih promjena koje su dovele do izbora u svim republikama, Milošević postao predsjednik novoosnovane Socijalističke partije Srbije (SPS), a onda predsjednik Srbije. SPS je bila tek preimenovana komunistička partija. Milošević je bio ponovo izabran 1992. da bi potom bio izabran za predsjednika Savezne Republike Jugoslavije (Srbije i Crne Gore) 1997. Dana 24. septembra 2000, na izborima za koje je mislio da bi ih mogao dobiti, Milošević je poražen od Vojislava Koštunice. Nakon pokušaja da naštima rezultate, smijenjen je 5. oktobra. Od aprila 1992. do 2006. godine, Srbija je bila jedna od dvije preostale republike Savezne Republike Jugoslavije (SRJ)—druga je Crna Gora. U ovom tekstu često koristim riječ Srbija i kada bih tehnički trebao koristiti SRJ. Crna Gora je izašla iz federacije 2006. godine i sada je zasebna zemlja; Srbija, koja obuhvata poluautonomnu regiju Vojvodine, sada se zove Republika Srbija. Predsjednik Tuđman umro je od raka u decembru 1999. Zamijenio ga je relativno umjereni Stjepan Mesić. Hrvatska i Slovenija su sada jedine dvije bivše jugoslavenske republike koje su primljene u Evropsku uniju.

5. Najraniji i najutjecajniji nacionalistički dokument bio je „Memorandum", koji je 1986. godine napisalo 16 vodećih intelektualaca Srpske akademije nauka u Beogradu. Taj dokument je tirada protiv nesrba, koji proročanski upozorava na

prijetnju uništenjem Srba u Jugoslaviji, osim ako se ne preduzmu koraci da se nađe lijeka njihovoj nesreći.

6. Laura Silber and Alan Little, The Death of Yugoslavia (London: Penguin Books/BBC Books, 1995), str. 37–38.

7. Milošević i četiri njegova najbliža saradnika su optuženi na Međunarodnom krivičnom tribunalu za bivšu Jugoslaviju (MKSJ) u Hagu za zločine protiv čovječnosti i ratne zločine počinjene u sukobima u Hrvatskoj, Bosni i na Kosovu. Optužnica je potpisana 22. maja 1999. godine, dok je posljednji od ovih ratova još uvijek bjesnio. Nakon okončanja rata na Kosovu, Miloševićeva moć i utjecaj su brzo slabili, i početkom oktobra 2000. konačno je uklonjen sa vlasti. Pod optužbom za korupciju, zloupotrebu vlasti i pronevjeru, jugoslavenski savezni organi uhapsili su bivšeg predsjednika 31. marta 2001. Krajem juna je predan Hagu radi suđenja. Na žalost njegovih bezbrojnih žrtava, to se suđenje nikada nije okončalo: Milošević je 11. marta 2006. godine doživio srčani udar i nađen je mrtav u svojoj ćeliji.

8. Ove autonomije su dodijeljene 1974. godine, za vrijeme vladavine maršala Tita. Taj akt su nezadovoljni Srbi doživljavali kao izdaju njihovih interesa od strane Tita, koji je bio pola Hrvat/pola Slovenac. Mada Kosovo i Vojvodina nisu postigli potpuni status republika, ostavši ustavno dio Srbije, uživali su važna politička, sudska, obrazovna i kulturna prava na samoopredjeljenje. Vojvodina je ostala dio Srbije. Srbija još uvijek službeno smatra Kosovo dijelom svoje teritorije, mada ga je dosad oko 115 zemalja kao nezavisnu državu.

9. Nakon raspada bivše Jugoslavije, Jugoslavenska narodna armija promijenila je ime u Vojska Jugoslavije (VJ). Danas se zove Vojska Srbije.

10. Radovan Karadžić je bio šef Srpske demokratske stranke (SDS) i takozvani „lider bosanskih Srba". Godine 1995, kratko nakon etničkog čišćenja Srebrenice, Haški tribunal je optužio Karadžića za ratne zločine. Više od decenije je izbjegavao hapšenje, krećući se između Republike Srpske i Srbije. Konačno je uhvaćen u Beogradu 2008, predat i odveden na suđenje te je osuđen za genocid, zločine protiv čovječnosti i ratne zločine. U vrijeme pisanja ovog teksta, još uvijek je u zatvoru i gotovo je izvjesno da će tamo ostati do kraja života.

11. Gospodar rata, gangster i poslovni čovjek, Željko „Arkan" Ražnatović ubijen je u foajeu beogradskog hotela Intercontinetal u januaru 2000. godine. Vojislav Šešelj je još uvijek aktivan u srpskoj politici; predsjednik je ultranacionalističke Srpske radikalne stranke (SRS), koju je osnovao 1991. Između 1998–2000, Šešelj je bio zamjenik premijera Srbije. Međunarodni krivični tribunal za bivšu Jugoslaviju optužio je Šešelja za ratne zločine i on se sam predao. Njegov sudski predmet u Hagu okončao je oslobađajućom presudom 2016. godine. Ta presuda je djelomično poništena dvije godine kasnije kada je proglašen krivim za poticanje na zločine protiv čovječnosti počinjene u Hrvatskoj, ali—začudo, mnogi ljudi će komentirali—ne i u Bosni. Dobio je desetogodišnju zatvorsku kaznu, ali nije vraćen u zatvor jer je već bio odslužio 11 godina u pritvoru. Na izborima održanim u junu 2020, Šešelj i njegova stranka nisu ušli u Parlament Srbije pošto su osvojili manje glasova od potrebnog praga od tri posto. Vuk Drašković je i dalje politička figura u Srbiji, mada je donekle marginaliziran. Po izvještajima, još uvijek je angažiran u promonarhističkoj parlamentarnoj stranci, Srpskom pokretnu obnove (SPO)—koji su zajedno osnovali on i Vojislav Šešelj 1990. godine. Drašković je i pisac, koji se specijalizirao za historijske romane pisane u mračnom nacionalističkom tonu. Drašković je bio jedan od prvih i najžešćih

eksponenata ideje Velike Srbije. Međutim, MKSJ ga nikada nije optužio za njegova gledišta i pisana djela.

12. ABiH je skraćenica za Armija Bosne i Hercegovine a poznata je jednostavno kao Bosanska armija. Tokom rata, ABiH je bila legitimna oružana snaga koja je predstavljala izabranu Bosansku vladu, i činili su je mahom, ali ne isključivo, muslimani. Naprimjer, drugokomandujući, general Jovan Divjak, bio je Srbin, i mnogi Srbi, kao i Hrvati, borili su se sa ABiH da bi sačuvali multietničku Bosnu. Ovu informaciju su tokom rata umanjivali srpski nacionalisti kao i mnogi strani novinari, koji su mislili da bi to moglo zbuniti javnost.

13. Godine 2021, uloga srpske vlade u pomaganju i poticanju odreda smrti odgovornih za ratne zločine počinjene tokom rata u Hrvatskoj i Bosni konačno je dokazana na sudu. Jovica Stanišić (šef zastrašujuće SDB, Službe državne bezbjednosti Srbije, između 1991–98) i Franko Simatović (koji je u istom periodu vodio SDB-ovu Jedinicu za specijalne operacije) osuđeni su pred UN-ovim Tribunalom za ratne zločine u Hagu. Suđenja ovih silno moćnih aparatčika koji su radili direktno za predsjednika Slobodana Miloševića, trajala su od 2003. godine do presuda 30. juna 2021—te tako bila najduža suđenja za ratne zločine u historiji; tokom sudskog postupka, ogromna masa dokaza dobijenih od raznih obavještajnih agencija prezentirana je Tribunalu. Mada se presude Stanišiću i Simatoviću temelje samo na pružanju podrške odredima smrti koji su djelovali 1992. godine u Bosanskom Šamcu, gradiću u sjevernoj Bosni na samoj granici sa Hrvatskom, u stvarnosti je etničko čišćenje srpskih odreda smrti provedeno diljem Bosne i Hrvatske cijelo vrijeme trajanja ratova. Ovo suđenje, međutim—koliko god bilo ograničeno u svom dometu—po prvi put je nekoga iz komandnog lanca predsjednika Miloševića

označilo odgovornim za ulogu koju su imali u pokolju—dokazujući koliko je teško izvesti krupne ratne zločince pred sud. Nataša Kandić, osnivačica Centra za humanitarno pravo u Beogradu, vjeruje, međutim, da ova historijska presuda pokazuje da „Niko ne može očistiti Srbiju i reći da nije učestvovala u izvršavanju zločina". Stanišić i Simatović su osuđeni na po 18 godina, što je smanjeno na 12 godina za vrijeme koje su već proveli u zatvoru.

14. Bosna je priznata kao članica Ujedinjenih nacija 21. maja 1992. Tokom rata, Vlada u Sarajevu je činila velike napore da se ukine embargo na oružje, i indignacija zbog neuspjeha da se to postigne rasla je u cijelom svijetu. Bosna je dobila malo oružja tokom rata i bilo je mnogo glasina u pogledu njegovog porijekla; to oružje, međutim, nije bilo dovoljno da preokrene rat u prilog Bosne.

15. Boutros Boutros-Ghali, šesti generalni sekretar UN-a, i Yasushi Akashi, specijalni izaslanik Boutros-Ghalija za sukobe u Jugoslaviji, nisu uspjeli zaštititi Srebrenici niti Žepu, niti zaustaviti masakre i etničko čišćenje koje se tamo dešavalo u ljeto 1995. Oba ova zvaničnika čini se da su moćnog predsjednika Srbije, Slobodana Miloševića gledali sa krajnjim strahopoštovanjem i bili beskrajno spremni vjerovati mu i stalno mu davati nove šanse. Na međunarodnoj sceni, međutim, Boutros-Ghali i Akashi nipošto nisu bili usamljeni u davanju prednosti podjeli i krvoproliću nad jedinstvom i humanošću. Da ne bismo zaboravili one brojne, uglavnom britanske, američke karijerne političare i diplomate iz UN-a, koji su neprestano putovali između svjetskih prijestolnica i onoga što je ostalo od Jugoslavije, dopustite da ih ovdje imenujem. S jedne strane Atlantika, tu je bio predsjednik Bill Clinton—koji se iskupio i prekasno i premalo—uz kojeg su godinama stajali razni državni sekretari (James Baker, Cyrus Vance i Warren Christopher) i ministri

odbrane (Leslie Aspin i William Perry). S druge strane Atlantika, tu su premijer John Major, ministri vanjskih poslova lord (Peter) Carrington, Douglas Hurd, i Malcolm Rifkind (koji je bio i ministar odbrane između 1992–95). Tu je bio i bivši britanski političar lord (dr. David) Owen, koji je bio UN-ov mirovni pregovarač. Owen je uložio znatan trud da zaraćenim stranama proda koji su značili podjelu Bosne u homogene etnoreligijske kantone. Ti planovi, nasuprot uspostavi mira, ustvari su samo pogoršavali sukob nagrađivanjem agresora. (Doista, toliko su presretni bili separatistički nastrojeni bosanski Hrvati s onim što im je jedan plan ponudio—više Hercegovine nego što su ikad sanjali da su mogli dobiti, da se govorkalo da su zbijali šalu da „HVO" u budućnosti treba da znači „Hvala Vance-Owen.") Kad se osvrne na te mračne godine evropske historije, čovjek ne može a da ne osjeća da je Bosna zaista bila osuđena da bude u tako teškoj situaciji dok god su ti popustljivci dominirali međunarodnom scenom. Nije malo reći, ja vjerujem da je svaka od osoba koju sam ovdje imenovao (plus drugi kojih je previše da bih ih spominjao) na svoj način bio Miloševiću (i Tuđmanu, samo u manjoj mjeri) ono što je britanski premijer Neville Chamberlain bio Adolfu Hitleru 1930-ih godina. Zajedno, ova družina značila je katastrofu za građane Bosne, a posebno—ali ne isključivo—za njene građane, Bošnjake muslimane.

16. Republika Srpska je službeno priznata u Daytonu, Ohio, 1995. godine. Ona predstavlja 49% bosanske teritorije. „Međuetnička linija razdvajanja" odvaja je od muslimansko-hrvatske federacije, koja je uspostavljena nakon zasebnih mirovnih pregovora između Hrvatske i Bosne 1994. godine. Federacija obuhvata preostalih 51% zemlje.

17. Noel Malcolm, "Why the Peace of Paris Will Mean More War in Bosnia", *London Daily Telegraph* (15. decembar 1995).

18. Hrvatsko vijeće obrane (HVO) je hercegovačka hrvatska armija, pod Tuđmanom, koja je bila finansijski i vojno podržana od države Hrvatske. Neki njegovi pripadnici—pogotovo oni u Sarajevu i oko Tuzle—nastavili su se boriti zajedno sa bosanskom armijom (ABiH), i često je među Hrvatima izvan Hercegovine bilo neodobravanja onoga što je HVO činio muslimanima. HVO je sada službeni dio bosanske vojne strukture, kao što je i sada ukinuta Vojska Republike Srpske.

19. Na teritoriji bivše Jugoslavije ima nekoliko *krajina*. U doba Habzburškog Carstva služile su kao odbrana od Osmanlija. U većinu ovih pograničnih, utvrđenih regija naseljavan je srpski živalj koji je bio ohrabrivan da brani evropske, dominantno kršćanske vrijednosti i kulturu.

20. Anthony Borden, "The Lesson Unlearned", *War Report 58* (London: The Institute of War and Peace Reporting, 1998).

21. Za ovaj eksplozivni, anonimno napisani „non-paper" kaže se da potiče iz Ureda slovenačkog premijera Janeza Janše. Glasine sugeriraju da ga predsjednik Borut Pahor podržava i da oni možda djeluju zajednički s drugim nacionalističkim liderima u regionu. Bezazleno naslovljen sa Zapadni Balkan: Put naprijed, ovaj dokument je tako provokativan da, u vrijeme dok ovo pišem, EU još uvijek nije prokomentirala njegov sadržaj, unatoč tome što ga je, prema izvještajima, premijer Janša prezentirao Charlesu Michelu, sadašnjem predsjedniku Evropskog vijeća. Ovaj dokument navodi da još nije završen raspad bivše Jugoslavije (za koji predsjednik Pahor smatra da je suštinski važan da bi se integracija regiona u EU mogla nastaviti) i da ovaj proces treba zaključiti nizom razmjena teritorija između Srbije, Bosne i Hrvatske s jedne strane, i Kosova, Albanije, Sjeverne Makedonije i Srbije, sa druge. Šefik Džaferović, bošnjački član kompleksnog troetničkog

Predsjedništva BiH, vjeruje da je ovaj dokument očiti pokušaj da se destabilizira njegova zemlja: „Dokument [...] je pokazao da secesionističke snage samo čekaju bilo kakav signal iz EU, pa da ponovo pokrenu svoj krvavi pir. Ne mislim da je ovo došlo od zvaničnog Brisela, već od radikalnih krugova, koji pokušavaju prikazati svoje retrogradne ideje kao evropske." Ali da budemo načisto, dodao je on: „ Bilo kakvo prekrajanje granica po etničkom principu, vodilo bi ka destabilizaciji ne samo BiH i regiona, već i ukupne evropske stabilnosti." (Citati preuzeti od *EuroNews*, 20. aprila 2021. Izvor za ovu priču je Slovenačka istraživačka novinska kuća *Necenzurirano,* kojom je non-paper procurio sredinom aprila.) Mi ćemo sačekati da vidimo kakve će efekte imati ovakva vrsta glasnog razmišljanja. Ali činjenica da ideje poput ove mogu biti javno iznesene ne sluti na dobro za budućnost Bosne

OPPOSITE
BOSNIA
Began Turbić
Tuzla, 1992

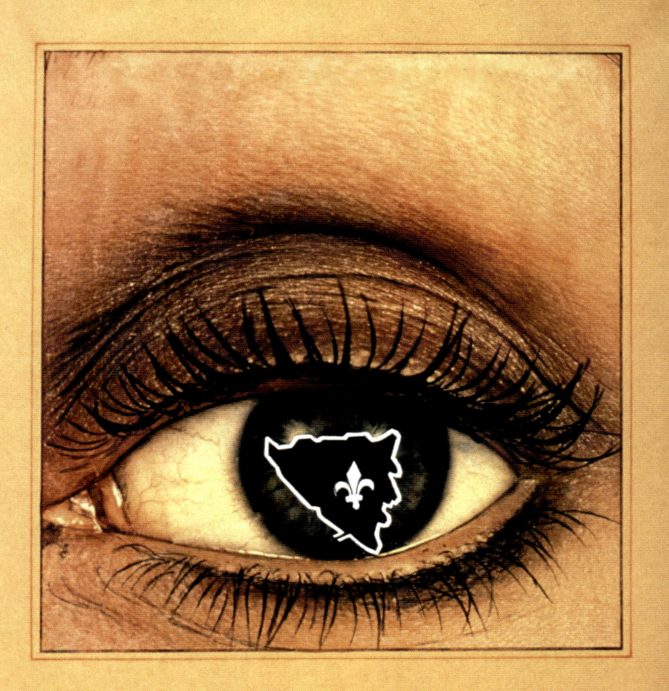

POGOVOR
KAKO JE NASTALA OVA KNJIGA
Rupert Wolfe Murray

Na sljedećim stranicama čut ćete ljude zaslužne što se dogodila knjiga *Bosanski ratni posteri*. Moja uloga u njenoj produkciji ne da se lako objasniti, barem ne kad je u pitanju izdavaštvo. Najbolji opis do kojeg ja mogu doći je producent: kao filmski producent koji nalazi novac kako bi se napravio film.

Ali šta sam ja radio u Bosni netom nakon rata? I kako to sam imao dovoljno novca da finansiram dvoje ljudi kako bi prikupili ratne postere i još jednog da ih snimi?

Činjenica da sam uopće imao novca već je sama skoro čudesna. Stigao sam u Bosnu potpuno švorc, autobusom, na kraju rata. Srećom, moja majka je upoznala jednog inspirativnog bosanskog dizajnera—Jasminka Arnautovića, čije ime se često spominje u ovoj knjizi—i imala je i njegov telefonski broj. Nazvao sam ga, on me pozvao da boravim u njegovom stanu u Tuzli, i ja sam potrošio svoj posljednji novac za autobus od Sarajeva do Tuzle. Jasminko me je hranio, dao mi smještaj i čak mi našao neplaćeni posao pisca-pisama-na-engleskom jeziku za gradonačelnika Tuzle—legendarnog Selima Bešlagića, koji je tokom cijelog rata branio veliki uspjeh Tuzle u borbi za ljudska prava.

Nedaleko od mjesta na kojem sam upijao Jasminkove nevjerovatne ratne priče (i bezobrazne viceve) sletjeli su Amerikanci. Stari tuzlanski aerodrom postao je nova baza za hiljade američkih vojnika. Otvorili su dućan u bazi NATO-ovih snaga za provedbu mira (Implementation Force—IFOR).

Dvije ideje su mi se tada formirale u glavi. Jedna, Amerikanci obično nemaju pojma o bilo kojem mjestu van svoje domovine—oni geografiju svijeta shvataju kao prijetnju. Druga, moja majka (Stephanie Wolfe Murray)—koja se nedavno penzionirala iz izdavaštva—pomogla je jednom ekscentričnom novinaru da objavi knjigu *Cry Bosnia (Plači Bosno):* dobru knjigu fotografija koja se nije dobro prodavala.

„A što ne bi Amerikancima prodavala *Plači Bosno*?", vikao sam se u slušalicu staromodnog telefona u tuzlanskoj Pošti. „Oni vjerovatno nemaju pojma na kojoj su planeti. To bi im moglo pomoći da nauče nešto o tome gdje su i šta se ovdje dešava."

Bosanska pošta jedva da je funkcionirala tih dana, ali majka mi je uspjela poslati kutiju primjeraka *Plači Bosno* preko Edinburgh Direct Aid—prijateljske škotske humanitarne agencije. Pošto je nisam mogao ubijediti da i ona dođe i sama prodaje knjige, ja sam dobio zadatak. Onda sam proveo sedmice pokušavajući da uđem u američku bazu koja je bila tako pretjerano utvrđena da je izmišljena i šala; vojnici su izgledali kao da očekuju napad bosanskih muslimana, mada oni nisu pokazivali ništa do zahvalnosti što su ih spasili od Srba.

Kada sam poslije nekog vremena uspio uspostaviti kontakt sa jednim veselim Amerikancem koji je vodio njihov PX dućan (sleng za Post Exchange) čuo sam od njega da mu se sviđa *Plači Bosno* i odmah je kupio cijelu kutiju. Učinio je i nešto veoma neobično za trgovinu knjigom: platio je gotovinom čim mu je pošiljka isporučena. I ne samo to: na kraju je kupio cijeli tiraž. I nije prošlo mnogo vremena a mi smo imali dovoljno novca da platimo štampanje novog izdanja. U mreži PX dućana u američkim vojnim bazama u regionu, *Plači Bosno* je bila jedina knjiga o ratu, i stajala je uz meku pornografiju i šund.

'A zašto ne uraditi knjigu fotografija o Amerikancima?', predložio sam majci kada sam je nazvao iz pošte. „Mogli bismo njih fotografirati na poslu, saznati šta rade, a upoznati i druge armije koje su ovdje pod NATO-ovom zastavom. Išlo bi k'o halva." Pronaći fotografa bilo je lako jer mi je jedan sjajni fotograf bio prijatelj: Steve Gordon. Steve također nije znao što bi sa sobom u Tuzli. Ali teško je bilo dobiti dozvolu od Amerikanaca jer je njihova utvrda u Tuzli bila sagrađena da drži podalje pisce, novinare i fotografe—kao i potencijalne bombaše-samoubice. Slučajni susret s američkim komandantom, generalom Nashom, međutim, iznenada nam je otvorio vrata.

Par godina kasnije mi smo već imali dvije dokumentarne knjige, bestselere za sobom: *IFOR on IFOR (IFOR o IFOR-u)* i *The Road to Peace (Put ka miru)*. I sjedili smo na brdu love. Tako, kada je Daoud Sarhandi došao na ideju za knjigu o posterima, ja sam ga mogao podržati u početnim troškovima—kupiti vrijeme tako da on i Alina mogu naći građu i da je Steve može snimiti.

Sada sam već bio u poziciji da vodim malu humanitarnu organizaciju sa svojom majkom, a da nisam morao trošiti sve vrijeme razmišljajući kako prikupiti novac i ispunjavati kompleksne birokratske formulare međunarodnih donatora. Nekoliko smo godina finansirali Bosance koji su bili ranjeni u ratu i željeli pokrenuli vlastiti posao. Kupili smo i bijeli kombi i diljem Bosne distribuirali rabljene knjige na engleskom koje je moja majka prikupljala po Britaniji.

U to vrijeme već sam unajmio kuću u Tuzli. Moja djevojka—i buduća žena—Alina Boboc, došla je iz Rumunije u svom starom Fordu Fiesta. Brzo je naučila bosanski i tražila nešto da radi sa svojim novinarskim umijećima. U to smo vrijeme sreli i Daouda—još jednog Britanca koji je bio Jasminkov prijatelj i tražio da nešto radi u Tuzli—i ja sam ga zamolio da nam

pomogne tako što će se vozikati po cijeloj Bosni: dostavljati bibliotekama knjige na engleskom i primjerke mojih knjiga vojnim bazama. Možda je ova suluda rutina stalne vožnje po Bosni učinila da shvatimo, logistički barem, da je moguće objaviti knjigu o ratnim propagandnim posterima.

Sada, više od dvadeset godina kasnije, oduševljen sam da nas je Daoud sve okupio još jednom da napravimo ovu knjigu. Ja se nadam da će ona stići do biblioteka diljem Bosne, do bosanske dijaspore diljem svijeta, i do čitalaca posvuda—i da će biti štampana još mnogo godina. U njoj ima toliko toga što se ne može naći ni u jednoj drugoj knjizi o Bosanskom ratu.

Rupert Wolfe Murray je autor 9 Months in Tibet (*9 mjeseci na Tibetu*). *Mnogo godina vodio je humanitarne projekte u srednjoj i istočnoj Evropi.*

POGOVOR
BOSNA: JEDNO LJUBAVNO PISMO
Daoud Sarhandi

Neki projekti znače veoma mnogo svojim autorima. Ova je knjiga za mene jedan od takvih projekata. Sjećam se gotovo svega o njenom nastanku i stvaranju kao da su se ti događaji desili prije nekoliko sedmica. Zapravo, gotovo 25 godina je prošlo od onog hladnog dana 1997. godine—u Tuzli, u sjeveroistočnoj Bosni—kada sam došao na ideju za ovu knjigu. Bila je to jedna od onih ideja koje te pogode kao munja i od koje ja nisam mogao odustati od trenutka kada mi je došla. Mnogi ljudi su smatrali da je taj projekat nemoguć, ali zahvaljujući tome što je Rupert Wolfe Murray vjerovao u njega i finansirao istraživanje, a njegova vjerenica Alina Wolfe Murray (Boboc, kako se tada prezivala) s impresivnom priljžnošću posvetila jednu godinu svog života radu sa mnom. Bez Aline, istraživanje i prikupljanje postera nikada se ne bi moglo dovršiti. Moram također još jednom zahvaliti svim Bosancima koji su s nama podijelili svoje postere. Bez njihovog povjerenja i velikodušnosti, ništa ne bi proisteklo iz naših nastojanja.

Nakon sveg tog tegobnog i često fizički iscrpljujućeg istraživanja, Steven Gordon je putovao s nama po regionu radeći fotografije postera koje su njihovi autori ili vlasnici sačuvali. To je još uvijek bila era analogne fotografije, i ja sam morao razviti te slajdove u Srbiji pošto je u Bosni to bilo nemoguće. Još uvijek je to bilo preddigitalno doba komunikacija. Staromodni terenski rad, beskonačna vožnja naokolo, i nepouzdani analogni telefonski pozivi, bili su sredstva našeg istraživanja. Treba se sjetiti i da je sva infrastruktura u Bosni bila još uvijek razrušena. Ukratko, ništa u vezi sa ovim projektom nije bilo jednostavno.

Kada danas pogledam knjigu *Bosanski ratni posteri,* ispuni me cijelim nizom emocija. Naravno, tu su lične emocije povezane sa radom na knjizi, i sa svim što se tiče moga života. U to vrijeme ja nisam znao ništa o istraživanju, ili pisanju, i čak manje o grafičkom dizajnu. Ja svakako nisam ovo radio s namjerom da si osiguram nekakav profesionalni početak pošto sam kreativno bio i još uvijek sam pretežno filmski stvaralac.

Angažirao sam se u vezi sa Bosnom na političkom kao i emocionalnom planu. Poput mnogih stranaca koji su tamo odlazili tokom rata, bio sam očaran tom zemljom, užasnut onim što joj se dešavalo, i ubrzo sam postao opsjednut željom da dam svoj mali obol ispravljanju tih ogromnih i zapanjujućih nepravdi. Može zvučati prilično sladunjavo što to ovako kažem, ali kad se osvrnem, jasno mi je da sam se zaljubio u Bosnu. Mislim da i dan-danas pokušavam shvatiti zašto i kako se to desilo. Možda je to povezano s mojom kompleksnom, mješovitom vjerom i porodičnim porijeklom koje uključuje više rasa; možda je to bila bolna želja da se bude na humanoj strani historije. Znam da je bilo trenutaka kad sam bio spreman dati svoj život da pokušam spasiti Bosnu.

Na koncu sam dao i manje i više od svog života: dao sam joj ovu knjigu. To je, ako mogu tako reći, moje ljubavno pismo ovoj kompleksnoj i predivnoj zemlji.

I evo nas u 2021. godini, toliko stariji i mudriji. Ili bismo barem trebali biti pošto nam se toliko toga desilo, i lično i na međunarodnoj sceni, otkako smo sakupili građu. Uzmimo, naprimjer, Sjedinjene Države: Bill Clinton je otišao; George W.

Bush je došao; Blizanci su srušeni; ratovi pokrenuti u Afganistanu, Iraku i Libiji. Izlazi Bush; ulazi i izlazi Obama; zdravo i zbogom Trumpu; Covid-19.

A cijelo to vrijeme Bosna je jako malo napredovala otkad su, 1995. godine, SAD, zajedno sa predsjednicima Bosne, Hrvatske i Srbije, postigle mirovni sporazum u zračnoj bazi Wright Patterson u Daytonu, Ohio. U vezi sa tim događajem, osjećam da vrijedi citirati jedan pasus teksta koji danas zvuči mnogo proročanskije nego onda kada se pojavio u *The Daily Telegraphu,* u decembru 1995. godine. Britanski historičar i zaljubljenik u Bosnu Noel Malcolm je napisao:

Nova Bosna [...] će biti geopolitički ekvivalent umjetničkom djelu Damiena Hirsta. Hirst uzme kravu, prepila je na pola, i obje polovine potopi u formaldehid. To može biti ingeniozno umjetničko djelo, ali je li to još uvijek krava? Slično je s novom Bosnom. To može biti najpametniji od svih ustava, ali je li to još uvijek zemlja?

Za mene, poster koji ovu ideju najbolnije izražava je slika presječene violine Čedomira Kostovića (na suprotnoj strani i na strani 231). Malcolm i Kostović imaju pravo: Bosna je postala jedna od politički najnefunkcionalnijih država na svijetu. Trajni mir još uvijek nije zajamčen. Dobra vijest (ako ih uopće ima) je da do sada nije bilo snajpera i granatiranja; koncentracioni logori i logori za silovanja nisu se vratili. Mada se nije vratila ni većina njenih raseljenih i etnički očišćenih građana.

Ukratko, Bosni još uvijek treba sva pomoć koja joj se može pružiti, i ja se nadam da ova knjiga ima svoj udio u tome.

štampa: Ratna i
PROJECT BY "HELP

BOSNIA

COVINA

Tuzla '92

HERZEGOVINA

POGOVOR
BOSNOM U FORD FIESTI
Alina Wolfe Murray

U Bosnu sam došla iz moje rodne Rumunije 1996. godine. Diplomirala sam žurnalistiku. Činilo mi se to kao savršeno rješenje: pridružila sam se svom momku, Škotu Rupertu Wolfe Murrayu, koji je u to vrijeme živio i radio u Tuzli, dok sam ja istovremeno pokušavala postati novinarka.

Do pada komunizma, Rumuni su s divljenjem gledali susjednu Jugoslaviju. U Rumuniji smo se borili sa nestašicom hrane i struje i mogli smo samo sanjati o putovanju u inostranstvu. Imali smo diktatora megalomana—Nicolaea Ceauşescua—i živjeli u strahu od tajne policije. U poređenju s tim, Jugoslavija je imala bolji životni standard i uživala više slobode: mogli su putovati, čak i raditi u inostranstvu. U to vrijeme se činilo da Jugoslavija uživa ugled drugih nacija.

Mi nismo znali da će Jugoslavija na koju smo gledali s divljenjem uskoro biti zahvaćena ratom i da će prestati da postoji; užasi kakve Evropa nije doživjela od Drugog svjetskog rata dešavat će se odmah tu, preko granice—iste one granice zbog koje su mnogi Rumuni rizikovali život u pokušaju da je pređu, bježeći od Ceauşescua.

Dok sam živjela u Bosni, napisala sam nekoliko članaka za jedan rumunski list. Radila sam i za škotsku humanitarnu organizaciju—Connect Humanitarian Agency, koju je vodio Rupert—koja je donirala knjige uništenim bibliotekama. Kada je Daoud 1997. godine došao na ideju da uradi knjigu o posterima, željela sam mu pomoći.

U vrijeme kada su bosanske registarske tablice slijedile etničke linije, i ljudi se osjećali nesigurnim da putuju, moja Ford Fiesta s rumunskim tablicama bila je savršena za putovanje po zemlji. I pošto sam mogla razgovarati na bosanskom—mada ne onoliko ispravno koliko sam željela—mogla sam biti od velike pomoći za projekat. Kada bih upoznala ljude ili razgovarala preko telefona, svi su bili spremni pomoći.

Vrijeme sam provodila u štamparijama, bibliotekama, dizajn-studijima i kafićima. Ako bi me neko uputio na trag na neko mjesto, slijedila sam ga, i potom odlazila na drugo. Ponekad sam dobivala po nekoliko tragova, ponekad sam završavala u ćorsokaku. To je trajalo skoro cijelu godinu, i tako smo Daoud i ja obuhvatili najveći dio Bosne i Hercegovine. Ja sam odlazila i u Zagreb, u Hrvatsku, u potrazi za posterima, a proveli smo i nekoliko sedmica zajedno u Beogradu, srbijanskoj prijestolnici, u potrazi za raznoraznom vizualnom propagandom.

Internet je tada bio u začetku pa smo se oslanjali na fax i telefon. Organizirala sam bilješke u crvenu fasciklu u kojoj je po jedan list A4 formata bio rezerviran za svaki susret: pojedinosti o kontaktu, zabilješke sa razgovora—kao i sugestije drugih umjetnika i njihov rad—i kratki opis postera koje smo otkrili. Mada sam voljela taj detektivski rad i susrete sa nevjerovatnim ljudima, bilo je dana kada sam se osjećala loše zbog toga što ih uznemiravam. Evo mene tu, strankinje, koja traži postere, dok se Bosanci nose s naslijeđem rata, pokušavajući da ponovo izgrade svoje srušene živote. Sada, više od dvadeset godina kasnije, željela bih se zahvaliti svima koji su nam poklonili svoje vrijeme, podršku i povjerenje.

Kada sam krajem 1998. godine otišla iz Bosne, bila sam trudna sa našom kćerkom Larom, i tad je prijetio drugi rat, ovaj put na Kosovu. Već sljedeće godine, Slobodan

Milošević—vođa krnje Jugoslavije (u to vrijeme, Srbije i Crne Gore)—postao je međunarodni otpadnik. Deset godina nakon pada komunizma u istočnoj Evropi, Titov san o Bratstvu i jedinstvu među južnim Slavenima se raspao; stotine hiljada života je izgubljeno ili su bili preokrenuti naglavačke, svijet su stalno iznova šokirali užasi na Balkanu, kojima kao da se nije nazirao kraj.

Ipak, ove posljednje godine su nam pokazale da nacionalizam i propaganda mogu bilo gdje izazvati haos. Scene horde ljudi koji upadaju u Capitol, SAD, u januaru 2021. godine pokazale su da nema zemlje koja je pošteđena nacionalističkog fanatizma—nijedna zemlja ne može tvrditi da se takva zla ne mogu u njoj dogoditi.

Kada je 2015. godine počela migrantska kriza, često sam razmišljala o jednom posteru koji su uradili bosanski Srbi. Vidjela sam ga u knjizi fotografija pod nazivom *Plači Bosno (Cry Bosnia,* Paul Harris, 1995.) koju je objavila moja svekrva Stephanie—i bila odlučna da nađem taj poster tokom našeg istraživanja. Kasnije sam ga i pronašla i on je uključen u ovu knjigu (stranica 141). Na posteru je zaustava EU koja se iz plave pretvara u zelenu—boju koja se povezuje s islamom. Tekst koji to prati je kratak i uvredljiv: „Ovo nije reklama za boje. Ovo je budućnost."

U vrijeme evropske migrantske krize 2015. godine, nakon koje će uslijediti glasanje za Brexit 2016, poruku tog postera će prihvatiti mnogi Evropljani, jer govori o uobičajenoj percepciji strahova o Evropi koja gubi svoj kršćanski identitet. Izbjeglice—većinom iz zemalja poharanih ratom, poput Sirije, Iraka i Afganistana—doživljavane su kao potencijalni teroristi. Napadi 11. septembra na Blizance, i rat protiv terorizma koji će uslijediti, već su potaknuli uvjerenje da islam predstavlja egzistencijalnu prijetnju Zapadu—i mnogi su počeli u to vjerovati.

Onda se, tokom kampanje za Brexit u Velikoj Britaniji pojavio zloglasni poster Ukip-a (Nezavisna partija Ujedinjenog Kraljevstva) koji pokazuje dugački red migranata, uz riječi „Prijelomna tačka—EU nas je sve izdala." Poruka je bila jasna: ogroman broj muslimanskih migranata će doći i zakucati na vrata Britanije, osim ako ona brzo ne istupi iz Evropske unije.

Bosanski muslimani (ili *Bošnjaci* kako se zapravo zovu) su Evropljani koji su prešli na islam prije mnogo stoljeća. Oni pokazuju da je savršeno moguće biti Evropljanin i musliman istovremeno. Međutim, kad je počeo rat u bivšoj Jugoslaviji, njihova ih je religija izdvojila od ostalih. Kada je retorika proglasila da oni tu ne prijadaju, pokrenut je točak historije ka budućem genocidu.

Posljednjih godina, nacionalizam je u porastu u velikom dijelu Evrope; neprijateljstvo prema muslimanima je u porastu; manjine često postaju žrtveni jarci u vremenima kriza, a s nedavnom pandemijom i perspektivom duboke recesije, brine me šta bi budućnost mogla donijeti.

U trenutcima kad me uhvati dublji strah, pitam se da li je ono što se desilo u Bosni i bivšoj Jugoslaviji bio tek uvod u nešto užasno i mračno što tek treba da dođe. Ako se evropski ideali raspadnu kao što se raspalo jugoslavensko Bratstvo i jedinstvo, gdje ja pripadam? Ja sam Rumunka, ja sam i Evropljanka, a nedavno sam postala britanska državljanka. Dominantna crta nacionalizma, međutim, je da zahtijeva potpunu lojalnost jednoj zemlji. Pošto dolazim sa Balkana ja vidim da su bizantijski, turski i austrougarski utjecaji dio moje povijesti i kulture. U Bosni sam naučila koliko mnogo volim Balkan, koliko mnogo sam produkt Balkana, i koliko sam Evropljanka.

„Imao je zelene oči," jedna bosanska majka sjeća se u dokumentarcu. Govori o tome kako je posljednji put vidjela svog maloljetnog sina. Odvojen je od nje u Srebrenici i kasnije ubijen zajedno sa još 8.000 muškaraca i dječaka. Ova majka djeluje kao da je muči sjećanje na sinovljeve oči. Ali to je sve što joj je od njega ostalo.

Željela bih joj reći: „Ja vas ne poznajem, ali za mene, zelena boja će uvijek biti boja očiju vašeg sina. Žao mi je što smo vas mi, ostatak svijeta, izdali. Ja vam nisam mogla pomoći, ali možda će moj doprinos ovoj knjizi pokazati koliko je nacionalizam bio razoran za vas, za Bosnu, i za cijelu bivšu Jugoslaviju."

Alina Wolfe Murray (djevojački Boboc) je iz Piatra Neamța na sjeveroistoku Rumunije. U domovini je studirala novinarstvo prije nešto što se 1996. godine preselila u Bosnu. Sada živi na jugozapadu Engleske, gdje radi kao menadžerica projekta.

POGOVOR
FOTOGRAFSKA SJEĆANJA
Steven Gordon

Još uvijek se mučim da objasnim zašto sam uopće otišao u Bosnu. Moj život je krenuo u pogrešnom pravcu i stvari nisu imale smisla. Trebalo mi je da prekinem krug u kojem sam se našao. Jedne noći u Glasgowu na BBC-ju sam gledao jedan od izvještaja Martina Bella o opsadi Sarajeva i to mi se uvuklo u glavu na način koji nisam mogao razumjeti. Bio je to moj prvi korak na putu ka Bosni.

Pišem ovo sada u Kabulu dvadeset i osam godina kasnije, pokušavajući da saberem sva ta sjećanja. Moje putovanje počelo je u Hrvatskoj 1993. godine, odakle sam i otišao u Bosnu, Kosovo, Irak, Siriju, Jemen i sada Afganistan. Konačno, mogu se osvrnuti na to vrijeme provedeno u Bosni i obraditi to u sebi, pomiriti se s tim, i prizvati sjećanja na jedan logičniji način. Trebalo mi je više od dvadeset godina da se pomirim s iskustvom koje je promijenilo i moj život i moj smjer u njemu.

U to sam vrijeme bio mlad i mislio da razumijem stvari. Ali nedostajale su mi suptilne lekcije mog bosanskog obrazovanja. Grad Tuzla nije bio uzbudljiva metropola za kojom bi žudio jedan nepromišljeni dvadesetogodišnjak. Unatoč svom gorkom ratnom iskustvu, bio je to miran, tolerantan grad, i on još uvijek čuva taj izgled. Njegove vrijednosti tada, u svojoj nezrelosti, nisam shvatao. Ali sada shvatam čemu me je Tuzla naučila: čudesnoj toleranciji i viziji. Pretpostavljam da sam otišao u potrazi za pustolovinom i da se utopim u probleme drugih ljudi. Da ste rekli onda meni, dvadesetogodišnjaku, da će taj sukob biti onaj faktor koji će uvezati moj život sljedećih 28 godina, bio bih ponosan

da tako nešto i sam zamislim. Sada, poslije svih ovih godina, ja znam nešto drugo.

Bosna. Šta ona za mene danas znači? Mogu hodati ulicom i čuti neku pjesmu ili osjetiti specifični miris i Bosna mi se vrati u misli u tehnikoloru. To ljeto 1995. je u mojoj glavi kao Fujichrome—žarke boje podjednako mučne koliko i zasićene. Kad god čujem grmljavinu, ona nikada nije glasna kao što je bila u Bosni. Kada god čujem artiljerijsku granatu kad eksplodira, ona nikad ne odjekuje kako je odjekivala u Bosni. Uvijek bi nastala savršena tišina nakon što bi granata pala. Činilo se da vrijeme i prostor stanu i da ti postojiš u tom trenutku, ne znajući da li da se smiješ ili plačeš, tvoja smrtnost posve očigledna. Onda čuješ ptice kako počnu ponovo pjevati i čekaš šta je sljedeće. To su neka od osjećanja koja je Bosna ostavila u meni. Sljedeće sam godine proveo tragajući za nekom drugom Bosnom—za ljudima, mjestima, pejzažom, ciljem.

Tokom godina ono čemu me Bosna naučila polako bi se pomaljalo, pogotovo kad sam bivao okružen stvarnim zlom— osjećaj ogromne nepravde koju provode voljni učesnici, obično zaslijepljeni nacionalnim ili religijskim žarom, slijepi do tačke da norme društva odbacuju u težnji za ciljem tako odvratnim da stvara opipljiv osjećaj mraka. U Bosni sam to osjećao oko Mostara i Srebrenice, na Kosovu u Račku, i u Siriji, tako snažno, u Aleppou. Istinsko zlo nikada se ne zaboravlja kad se jednom sretne.

Gledajući sada knjigu *Bosanski ratni posteri,* uviđam koliko je ona relevantna u današnjem svijetu interneta, društvenih medija i lažnih vijesti. Na svoj je vlastiti način ta knjiga je predvidjela ono što će doći.

Ono što sam doživio u Siriji sada mnogi poriču. Ruski i sirijski režimi koji bacaju kasetne bombe, ciljajući na medicinske objekte i civilne infrastrukture. Mi sada gledamo online rat koji vode ratnici za tastaturom s malo ili nimalo svijesti o stvarnim žrtvama. Mi vidimo isto ono poricanje koje se desilo oko Srebrenice. Prošlost se ponovo ispisuje. Ona se iskazuje lako svarljivim lažima, a velika laž je poricanje genocida.

Ima jedan poster u ovoj knjizi koji je izgleda predvidio svijet u kojem sada živimo (stranica 141). Na njemu su tri zastave: jedna besprijekorna zastava Evropske unije; onda jedna koja blijedi u zeleno; i onda potpuno zelena zastava. Slogan glasi, „Ovo nije reklama za boje. Ovo je budućnost."

Sjećam se kako je general Mladić tvrdio da će munare biti sve do Pariza ako vojska bosanskih Srba ne ustane protiv bosanskih muslimana. Islamofobija, rast populizma, strah od izbjeglica—ta pitanja su dominirala bosanskim ratom. Danas su to globalna pitanja, dio našeg svakodnevnog diskursa.

Posteri u ovoj knjizi su važni. Oni bilježe rast mračnih sila u srcu Evrope početkom 1990-ih. Iz tih razloga, putovanje po Bosni u jednoj staroj Ford Fiesti, snimanje ovih postera danas za mene ima više smisla nego onda. Danas, dok sjedim u Kabulu, ja se mučim da iskažem koliko dugujem Bosni. Dozvolite mi da to ovdje kažem: Hvala ti Bosno, moja ljubav prema tebi se nikada neće promijeniti

Steven Gordon sada radi za Mercy Corps, humanitarnu agenciju i sjedište mu je u Istanbulu.

LEFT TO RIGHT
BULLET-RIDDLED WALL; *Photograph by Rupert Wolfe Murray; Sarajevo, 2021*
More than 25 years after the war ended, reminders of the conflict are still visible in Sarajevo and throughout Bosnia-Herzegovina. Scars left behind affect the infrastructure and, more importantly and in a myriad of ways, the people.

LIFE CAN BE BEAUTIFUL; *Mirela Mišković; Sarajevo, 1996*
One of the more optimistic concepts from a series of posters designed for a competition, organised by the Office of the High Representative, imagining the new millennium in Bosnia (see pages 268–269).

LIFE CAN BE BEAUTIFUL

2 0 0 0

BOSNA I HERCEGOVINA

POSTER COMPETITION OHR AND ALU
"BOSNIA & HERZEGOVINA 2000" July 1996.

OHR

ACKNOWLEDGEMENTS

At the top of the list of those who made this book possible during the research period are Rupert Wolfe Murray and Stephanie Wolfe Murray. They believed in and financially backed the hunt for posters in Bosnia, Serbia and Croatia.

Alina Wolfe Murray (née Boboc) made the logistics of collecting many of the posters possible through her organisational and language skills, and her tremendous perseverance. Special thanks also go to Steven Gordon, who photographed the posters in often difficult circumstances.

The many artists and designers whose posters appear throughout this book are credited where appropriate and indexed at the back. It goes without saying that without their generous consent to allow us to reproduce their work, there would be no book.

I wish to express my gratitude to the following individuals and organisations in Bosnia who assisted us with our research:

Tuzla: Dom armije; Sanjin Memišević; the Tuzla Citizens' Forum; Printcom; Ratna štamparija; Sinan Alić at Ogledalo; Fatmir Alispahić at Opštinski Press Centre.

Sarajevo: Amra Zulfikarpašić at the Academy of Fine Arts; Dajana Rešić; Press Centre–Dom armije; Alma Duraković and Snježana Mulić at Dani; Ermin Sarajlija at the Human Rights Centre–University of Sarajevo; Ibrahim Spahić at the International Peace Centre–Sarajevo Winter Festival; Seid Hasanefendić and Ivana Jevđević at the National Gallery; Seada Hadžimehmedagić at the Archive of Bosnia-Herzegovina; Emir Čengić at ULUPUBIH; Edin Numankadić; Kamerni teatar, FAMA; Zlatan Ibrahimpašić.

Travnik: Jasmina Hopić at the Archive of Central Bosnia.

Zenica: Radovan Marušić at the National Theatre.

Mostar: Zlatko Serdarević at RTV Mostar.

Banja Luka: Ljiljana Misirlić at Dom kulture; Saša Grubać; Miloš Šolaja at the Press Club; Verica Stošić and Ljubica Jećimović at the Archive of Republika Srpska; Građanski glas.

Bijeljina: Museum of Bijeljina.

Zagreb, Croatia: Dolores Ivanuša at the Croatian History Museum; Marijam Susovski at the Museum of Contemporary Art.

Serbia: Vesna Manojlović and Nana Manojlović; Đorđe Balmazović and Dragan Protić at Škart; Smiljka Kašić at the National Library of Serbia; Vladan Radosavljević at Radio B92; FIA; Maja Marinković; Women in Black; Goranka Matić at *Vreme;* Milena Dragičević at the Faculty of Dramatic Art; the Centre of Contemporary Art–the Fund for an Open Society; Raša Todosijević; Saša Rakezić; Mihajlo Aćimović; Andrej Tišma; Miroslav Popović at Magnet; Zoran Pantelić at Absolutno. Thanks to Mirko for the flat, and special thanks to Jelena, who showed Alina and me much hospitality and whose friendship made our days in Belgrade so enjoyable.

Additional thanks go to Čedomir Kostović; Steven Heller; Magdalena Szczepaniak-Hill; Mary Sarhandi; Lilijan Sulejmanović; Vesna Marić; Monica Wolfe Murray; Sue Smallwood; Paddy Cramsie; Dino Omerović; Sanda Jelić; Jim Haynes; Jan Nuckowski.

More recently, I would like to thank Rupert Wolfe Murray for his editing skills, his Afterword and photos, and for supporting this book in many other ways; Carol A. Wells and Vehid Šehić for their Forewords; Bojan Hadžihalilović for his Foreword, support and guidance; Alina Wolfe Murray and Steven Gordon for their Afterwords; Asim Đelilović for the cover illustration reworked from his original poster; Gamaliel Pérez Quiché for the maps; Senada Kreso for Bosnian translations of the principal texts, and advice on many topics related to the book.

In Tuzla, Rupert Wolfe Murray and I would like to thank Danijel Stjepanović, Jasminko Arnautović, and Dževad-Džeki Arnautović for their assistance; in Sarajevo, Dado Latinović for working diligently for many months in support of the project; in Bucharest, Claudio Revnic for his marketing skills and help.

I am also very grateful to: Carolina Rivas, for her encouragement and patience; Open Art Association, Catalonia, Spain, for project development support; Michel Moushabeck at Interlink Publishing for believing in, accepting and backing *Bosnian War Posters;* Harrison Williams, also at Interlink, for his help; Damir Uzunović at Buybook, Sarajevo; Emily Sulzer, head archivist at the Center for the Study of Political Graphics, Los Angeles; Roxana Deneb Ruiz in Mexico City for her design tips; Zafirah Sarhandi and Maya Manrique Olortegui for editorial assistance; Andreu Fernández for help with scans of miscellaneous 35 mm material; Ibrahim Spahić and Bojan Bahić for corresponding with me; Vesna Manojlović for short translations and enlightening information about a handful of posters and magazine covers.

And last but not least: Thank you, Zafirah and Hannah, for putting up with your dad's seemingly endless work.

Daoud Sarhandi
Catalonia, Spain
November 2021

Interlink Books

An imprint of Interlink Publishing Group, Inc.
Northampton, Massachusetts